THE SPIRIT SPEAKS
DAILY
SPIRITUAL MOTIVATION
FOR SUCCESSFUL
AFRICAN AMERICANS

Ph.D.

Chicago, Illinois

Front cover design by Tony Quaid
Copyright © 1997 by Rev. Jim Holley, Ph.D.
First Edition, First Printing

Printed in the United States of America

ISBN: 0-913543-51-9

INTRODUCTION

e childhood story of the little train that
go up the hill? The only way it could
climb the hill was to keep saying over
hink I can, I think I can." As children, we
that the philosophy of this beloved story
ughout the Word of God.

we read, "As a man thinketh in his heart,

what we think about all day long.

ur thoughts are the footprints of destiny on
e map of your mind. What you think about
what you become.

l was teaching the Church of God, and what
k is teaching you, the reader, is that as you
our mind, as you begin to concentrate on
hings, you will develop the "right" attitude.
itude directly affects your altitude.

u can develop a "can do" mentality.

o attitude is a mentality. Developing this men-
equires three things:

1. Right thinking.
2. Right believing.
3. Right speaking.

DEDICATION

*To God be the glory and to the
village that raised and made me
the man that I am.*

FORWARD

We all are at sometime or another in search of success. What is it that makes a success? Many of us believe if we only achieve some preset goal for ourselves or those around us then we will be a success. But what happens after we achieve that preset goal?

Are we to be content with our present success? Or, as the nature of human being so often dictates, do we set our eyes on the next goal time after time? This is often the case.

Success is a never ending process, a state of mind, which requires consistency and focus on a daily basis. Consistency on a daily basis is an integral part of the success formula. This begs the question, How do we harness the consistency necessary to make success a part of everyday lives? Where do we get the means to stay on the narrow path of greatness with life's pitfalls destined to stand in our way? This book shows us how to tap into God's infinite power, which abides within all of us, and succeed in spite of the odds.

Undeniably, there is a success formula that has been developing since God created the heavens and earth. The basic formula consists of a vision or idea for success.

A plan then follows to make the vision a reality. Implementation of the plan is the final stage of the success formula. Most will agree that visions and ideas come a dime a dozen. As someone once said "If a person fails to plan, then they plan to fail." We all have visions, ideas, and dreams of success, whether it is to be the best in your chosen field of endeavor or

to raise a strong fa
sistent implementati
decisions, and dream
reality. It is as if the
existed.

We might also look
save the world from si
goal, Jesus knew that he
Mt. calvary so that man
a human perspective, su
humiliation. He must hav
vain. But, just as God was
thirty-three-year ministry
there on Mt. Calvary, motiv
persecution and ridicule to a
the world from sin. His succ
from the grave on Easter mor

Implementation is the m
haps the most difficult phase
The daily motivations presen
help you make your vision a
the sustaining power you'll nee
can not plan for the unforesee
likely stand in the way of achievi
we predict the day when we awa
tivated. In his book, Rev. Holley
sonal spiritual relationship to dig d
nite power to elicit and succinctl
motivations for being successful.

Remember th
was trying to
successfully
and over, "I t
didn't realize
is found thr

In Proverbs
so is he."

We are

Yo
th
is

What Pau
this boo
elevate
higher t
Your att

Y

A can
tality

Gregory J. Reed

Winner of the Americ

You cannot go any higher than you think.

> If you think you are beaten, you are.
> If you think you dare not, you don't.
> If you'd like to win but think you can't, it is
> almost certain that you won't.

Success begins with a person's will to succeed. The
secret to success lies in the state of a person's mind.

> If you think you are out-classed, you are.
> You have got to think high to rise.
> You have to be sure of yourself or you'll never
> win the prize.

Life's battles aren't necessarily won by the stronger
woman or man. Eventually, the one who wins is the
one who says, "I think I can." It doesn't matter where
you're living now. It only matters what you're thinking now. Even in the midst of the most overwhelming
can do atmosphere, you can develop a can do attitude. Once you've developed the attitude, the I'm
doing will take care of itself.

Day 1

> "Either move or be moved."
>
> —Colin Powell

The world is filled with victims. I don't mean victims of crime, abuse, oppression, or any of the many social ills that truly victimize people. I'm talking about victims of that great stumbling block – inertia! The dictionary defines inert as "destitute of inherent power to move." How incompatible this definition is with the very definition of life. Life! It's filled with movement, with passion, with drive, ambition, choices. Immobility defies the life force inherent in all of us and makes a mockery of our common humanity. I contend that remaining alive without remaining in motion is impossible. Either you will choose the direction in which you want to move, or someone else will decide that direction for you. Either you will power yourself toward or away from something, or you will be driven toward or away by someone else's movement. The sheer force of the movements of others will not allow you to remain static. You can either be propelled or be the propeller. Either way, you're going to move. Don't you want to be the one behind the steering wheel?

I can feel the movement. Today I'm taking charge!

DAY 2

Pride is one of those strange words that seem to have two meanings. Throughout the centuries philosophers, teachers, even writers of the Bible have warned against pride. At the same time, we are urged to take pride in our work, take pride in our achievements, be proud of whom we are. The critical difference, I believe, is in pride as opposed to boastfulness. As you grow and achieve, it is right that you should take pride in your achievements. The good feeling of accomplishing something you can be proud of will spur you onto even greater achievements. However, when pride turns to boastfulness, it ceases to be a virtue. Boasting is a way of putting others down. It is a weapon of judgement against those who are progressing more slowly or have chosen different goals and different paths. There's a song I remember whenever I catch my pride sliding close to boastfulness. It goes: "I'm proud to be me, but I also see, you're just as proud to be you. We may look at things a bit differently, but lots of good people do." Take pride in your work, but never boast. Let it speak for itself. Take pride in your success, but don't put others down for making different choices. Remember, whether you're black, brown, white, or green, take pride in the person you are inside; then the person you are on the outside will take care of itself.

I'm proud of whom I am and who I'm becoming.

Day 3

> "Leaning and depending are two different things."
>
> —Grandma Holley

There's no shame in asking for help. There's nothing wrong with accepting help. There's everything wrong with *expecting* help. The journey to success is not a journey away from others. The destination is not independence but *positive interdependence*. None of us, no matter how successful, can live without the help of others. We all rely upon the goods and services others provide. As we buy, sell, and trade time for money, money for products and services, etc., we strengthen the chain of positive interdependence. It is when we break this chain to replace it with the negative chain of *dependence* that we get off course. Suddenly, we're side-tracked. We're getting without giving. We're receiving without earning. We're leaning, and leaning people can't move forward. Does that mean people with can do attitudes never need a helping hand, a shoulder to cry on, a favor to be returned? Certainly not! It means that people with can do attitudes will accept help when they need it but won't be defeated if help isn't offered. Can do people may depend on others, but they have the inner resources to go it alone if others pull away. Can do people may stop and lean for a while, but once they catch their breath, they straighten up and resume their forward movement.

Today I'll check my posture to make sure I'm not leaning.

DAY 4

"We are a Black Gold Mine. And 'The key
that unlocks the door to these vast riches
is the knowledge of who we are.'"

—Tony Brown

Do you remember the first time you stood erect
on your own two feet? Do you remember taking your
first steps? Speaking your first words? Of course not.
Even though these were the most important lessons
you had to learn for self-preservation, you don't even
remember learning them. They were easy. They came
naturally in due time. They were lessons common to
all human beings. Being able to stand, walk, or speak
doesn't make you different; it makes you the same.
Now, do you remember the first time you encountered racial prejudice, sexual bias, or discrimination
based on age, physical appearance, or physical limitations? Those experiences were hard. The lessons we
learn from being different makes us who we are. We
cannot change our different-ness; we can only change
our reactions to it. When we react in positive ways,
we grow. We become better *because* we are different.
It's not easy being black, red, or even green. It's not easy
being short if you want to play basketball. It's not easy
being female if you want to be an astronaut. It's not
easy living with a disability if you want to be an athlete. Yet the people who stand out in the world are
those who achieve their dreams despite their differences. It is your differences that make you exceptional.

I am exceptional because I'm different.

Day 5

> Ethics is about 'oughtness,' especially how we ought to behave.
>
> —Rev. Jim Holley

"You ought to wash your hands before dinner." "You ought to get better grades." "You ought to get along better with your younger brothers and sisters." You can plug in your own personal "oughts." You've surely heard hundreds of them during your lifetime. Some apply to personal ethics, but with equal certainty, most were uttered for the convenience of the speaker. Peacemaking is an ethical way to live your life. Getting along with siblings is required *by* parents to make life easier *for* parents. The difference between personal ethics and the desire to obey and please others lie in the origin of the behavior. "If you go the entire day without one cross word to your sister, I'll treat you to a movie." Ethical behavior is its own reward. Personal ethics affect our concern for both large issues and for our private standards of right and wrong. Your personal code of ethics influences both public and private behavior. The same code of ethics that impels you to publicly speak out against injustice also prevents you from privately participating in destructive behaviors – lying, cheating, pilfering even so much as a doughnut from the corner store. Personal ethics is "oughtness" internalized and transformed into "mustness." A finely honed code of personal Christian ethics is the most powerful tool you can develop for attaining self-esteem and personal success.

Today I will exchange "ought" for "will" in my public and private behavior.

Day 6

"It isn't calamity to die with dreams unfulfilled,
but it is certainly a calamity not to dream."
—Benjamin E. Mays

The quarterback fumbles. The foul shooter misses the shot. The team's best hitter strikes out. Have you ever wondered how superstars maintain their self-assurance when they've just slipped up in front of thousands of people? How are they able to step up to the microphone, cool and controlled, and accept responsibility with dignity? *They appear self-assured because they are self-assured.* They know that they are worthy to be on the team. They know that bad days, mistakes, and outright blunders are parts of life; they do not make a person unworthy. True superstars recognize themselves as blessed with special talents and abilities *just like you.* As long as they hold on to this knowledge, they can succeed. What about you? Have you identified your special talents? Do you know your strengths and weaknesses? If you were related to a superstar you'd boast of your kinship. You are God's child. Would you make a lesser claim on your heavenly parentage?

I am a child of God. I am worthy to be a child of God. I will live this day as a child of God.

"There is no Negro problem. The problem is whether the American people have loyalty enough to live up to their own Constitution."

—Frederick Douglass

The distance between Constitutional rights guaranteed by law, and "people" rights guaranteed by loving, respectful living, can be great. All of us — black and white, rich and poor, male and female, young and old — have at some time faced discrimination. True, some of us have faced it more often and in more serious ways than others. Still, discrimination is simply another word for lack of respect for another. Successful living requires successful conquering of discrimination — our own forms of discrimination. It requires that each of us take a long, hard, honest look at our own prejudices. While speaking out and acting courageously to remove the beam of prejudice in the eyes of society, we must be working equally hard to remove the mote of prejudice from our own eyes. Along the can do journey to success you will encounter many people. Some will be positive encounters; some will be negative. The only certainty is that you will meet no one who is exactly like you. You will have to choose whether to accept the gifts of those who are different, or to reject them for their different-ness. It will be up to you to decide to deal respectfully with all people or to reserve your respect for the chosen few you deem worthy. The choice is yours. So are the limitations or the boundless opportunities of your choice.

Because I hate prejudice, I will guard against it in my own actions.

Day 8

"A man cannot be comfortable without his own approval."

—Mark Twain

Can you remember a time in your childhood when you did something wrong but didn't get caught? Remember how awful you felt inside? Remember how you tossed and turned at night but just couldn't sleep? Nothing made you feel better until you confessed to your parents and were reassured of their love. As an adult, you become, in a way, a parent to yourself. When you've done something that goes against your nature, you just can't get comfortable with yourself. If you're in that position, look yourself in the mirror and confess the deed. Remind yourself that while your behavior was wrong, you are a good person. Do what you can to make things right. Most important, forgive yourself but don't forget. On the road to success we all make an occasional wrong turn. Learn from your mistakes. Get up and keep moving forward.

Today I forgive myself for past deeds. I will remember the lessons I've learned for all my tomorrows.

DAY 9

> "We are the world, we are the children.
> We are the ones to make a better day."
> —Michael Jackson and Lionel Richie

The world is in crisis, people say. That's wonderful, you can reply. It's wonderful because there are two sides to crisis: danger and opportunity. We're already facing many dangers; now we can seize the opportunity to eradicate them. Truly, we are the world. We are children of the God who created the world. We are the ones who have the opportunities and the abilities to make things better, not just for the future, but for today. We are living in a time of instant access. Why shouldn't we instantly access some of the wonderful resources we possess and put them to use in creative problem solving? What resources? you might be saying. I don't possess any resources. Yes, you do. You definitely do! You have the resource of education. It doesn't matter where you're going to school, it matters *that* you're going to school. You have the resource of community. It doesn't matter where you're living, it matters *how* you're living. And you have the greatest resource of all – the unlimited resource of God's can do power. Through faith you know God. Through prayer you tap into God's strength.

Today I'm using my resources to create a better tomorrow.

Day 10

> "Because of the routines we follow, we often forget that life is an ongoing adventure."
> —Maya Angelou

Most of us are creatures of habit. We rise at the same time every day and go to bed about the same time every night. We have a set dinnertime, work schedule, and television agenda. Routine is important; it gives stability and predictability to our lives. But when routine becomes supreme, we become enslaved to the clock. We rob ourselves of the joy of spontaneity. We lose the ability to break out of our individual molds. We exchange comfort for creativity. Stability is strengthening, but stodginess is stifling. Too dearly held routines cause us to cease expecting the unexpected. The sense of adventure that makes life exciting is stolen by that master thief, complacency. We learn to settle rather than seek. Settling for what *is* rather than seeking what *can be* is a roadblock to success for individuals, communities, and nations.

Today I will become a seeker of success rather than a settler for mediocrity.

Day 11

If we kill one another, who will be left for us to
live with? If our communities are turned into battle-
fields, who will be our neighbors? If our streets, our
schools, our playgrounds, our very homes are unsafe,
where shall we go to find security? Each year the rate
of black-on-black crime increases. We blame it on
poverty, yet we kill off our own best resources. We
blame it on lack of education, yet parent involvement
in schools is at an all-time low. We blame it on the
breakdown of the family, yet domestic violence is
commonplace in our homes. We blame it on discrimination, yet we indiscriminately violate our own people;
street bullets are very non-discriminatory. Violence is
not inherent; it is a learned behavior. If it is learned,
there must be teachers. Likewise with nonviolence.
Both begin with thought, which precedes action. By
controlling our thoughts, we control our actions and
thus control our environment.

*Violence has no place in my home or my heart. To-
day I will dwell on peaceful thoughts, solutions, and
actions.*

Day 12

> "I would not change my color for all the
> wealth in the world . . . I might not have
> been able to do all I have done."
>
> —Mary McLeod Bethune

Look in the mirror. What do you see? A perfect face, a beautiful body, flawless skin, lovely hair. You were created by God in God's own image. You can't be less than perfect! Is it hard for you to accept that you are one of the beautiful people? Somewhere along the line have you developed such a poor self-image that you can't even accept compliments? When someone tells you how nice you look, do you immediately point out a flaw? When someone tells you what a good job you're doing, do you remind them of your failures? There's no time like the present to begin raising your self-image. Start by complimenting yourself. Get used to hearing nice things from yourself; it will make it easier to accept compliments from others. Temporarily take your eyes off the end goal and look instead at your many smaller accomplishments. Make a list of obstacles overcome, milestones reached, goals achieved. Celebrate your progress. Have faith in yourself and others will have faith in you also. Keep looking in the mirror until the image of the perfect, successful "you" you already are is implanted in your mind forever.

I'm perfect just the way I am.

Day 13

"I had to make my own living and my opportunity. But I made it . . . don't sit and wait for opportunities . . . get up and make them. . ."
—Madame C. J. Walker

Enthusiasm is not the same as believing in yourself. There are many people who believe in themselves but lack the enthusiasm to put joy into their dreams. Quietly they go about the business of life, keeping their dreams to themselves, sharing with no one, asking nothing of anyone. Enthusiastic people also believe in themselves, but for enthusiastic people, there is joy not only in dreaming, but in the process of working toward the fulfillment of dreams. Enthusiasm turns the travail of toil into the delight of doing – doing whatever it takes to reach a goal. Enthusiasm is never quiet. While it may be personal and private, its ecstasy echoes through every fiber of the individual, making silent organs sing. Such enthusiasm is difficult to conceal. It spills over to bring gladness to every activity. Enthusiasm is contagious; it touches others with its magical power. Enthusiasm imbues success with celebration; it turns setbacks into opportunities. Enthusiasm celebrates successes. Enthusiasm lights the darkest "night thoughts" and precedes the dawn in greeting each new day.

Today I will greet each task with joy and thankfulness that I have been given the opportunity to perform it.

Day 14

> "A person completely wrapped up
> in himself makes a small package."
> —Denzel Washington

Isn't it strange that while we want the time, attention, and love of others, we often fail to give the same in return? In my own church there are people who expect to be visited when they're sick, but would never think to pay a sick call to a fellow parishioner. Somehow, we've come to expect others to respond to our needs even while we ignore the needs of others. A newborn baby is completely self-centered. It screams for food whenever it's hungry, even if it's two a.m. It cries for attention despite how busy its parents may be. It demands cuddling, rocking – all the outward proofs of love – whenever it feels the need for such assurance. We all begin our lives as a selfish, small package known as a baby. Most of us progress beyond that stage to become caring adults responsive to the needs of others. Yet many of us become stuck in the newborn phase. We continue to scream, cry, and demand. We take without giving. We navigate the road of life as if it were a private highway with no other traffic but ourselves. The road to success demands that we get out there on the turnpike. We must learn to watch for the signals of others, to yield to traffic, and to stop when necessary to allow others to proceed. Just try driving with only your own destination in mind. Instead of arriving at your goal, you're sure to wind up in the accident ward – or worse.

I am a child of the universe, an integral part of all that was, is, and will be.

Day 15

"All of us do not have equal talent, but all of us should have an equal opportunity to develop our talents."

—John Fitzgerald Kennedy

Once upon a time there was a village whose inhabitants were all skilled shoemakers. In fact, these villagers made such fine shoes that no one else could compete with their craftsmanship. Soon shoemaking became the only occupation pursued in that village. One day, a child was born who, as she grew, showed no signs of shoemaking talent. In her hands, a needle became a clumsy tool; leather was split and gouged when she attempted to cut it. Instead of practicing to improve her shoemaking skills, the child would take every opportunity to slip away by herself to play her beloved lyre. Because there was no music teacher or printed music available in the village, the child taught herself. Often her music could be heard drifting from the forest where the child took refuge. Instead of thrilling to these beautiful, self-composed strains, the villagers shook their heads in bewilderment. How could an esteemed village such as theirs have produced such a dull, untalented child? As the girl grew, so did the resentment of the villagers. Finally the girl could tolerate their mocking and jabs no longer. In disgrace, she left the village forever, and her glorious music was heard no more.

My talent is my unique gift from God. Today I will take steps to discover it and develop it.

Day 16

> "I have never been contained except I
> made the prison. . ."
>
> —Mari Evans

Wonders are as personal as fingerprints yet as universal as the need for air to breathe. What inspires wonder in one may go unnoticed by another. The common ground of humanity is our ability to wonder. Most will stand awe-struck at a glorious sunset, a star-filled sky, a snow-covered mountain, or some other natural vista. It is the truly perceptive person who finds wonder in common things. Consider the intricacy of an ant hill, the complexity of television reception, the magnitude of talking to someone thousands of miles away via telephone. The ability to wonder, to thrill at a new discovery, to stretch your mind to grasp a new idea – this is what alters life from a monotonous procession of days and makes it an exciting, joy-filled adventure. Wherever you are, whatever your circumstances, there is wonder all around you. Take time to appreciate it. Notice the little things, listen to the silence. Appreciate the greatest wonder of all – your own ability to solve problems, overcome obstacles, think, grow, succeed!

I wonder at God's creative power, around me and within me.

DAY 17

"Can't nothing make your life work if you ain't the architect."

—Terry McMillan

Do you have a child or a relative you love above all others? Would you turn that child over to an authority that would put him or her to death? God did. He sent His only child into the hands of those who would, in the most cruel and painful way, murder him. Why? Because God thought you were worth the sacrifice! God didn't demand that you first become perfect. God didn't require you to first earn this sacrifice. God accepted you the way you are, with all your faults, pettiness, and guilt, and made the supreme sacrifice despite them. How dare we, then, despise ourselves. Self-hate goes against the very nature of God. And it doesn't stop there. When we despise ourselves, we lead others to despise us. This, in turn, leads others into the sin of judging us and failing to love us as a sister or brother. Self-love is the root of God-love. When we value ourselves as the beautiful creatures God created in His own image, we are filled with the wonder of His awesome, infinite love. Don't confuse this with self-absorption, lack of humility, or need for self-improvement. Instead, model your behavior after God's. Love yourself *despite* your shortcomings. While you continue to work on growing into your role as a reflection of God's image, serve as a model for others, who knows she or he is a work in progress.

Today I will let go of negative thoughts and recognize my value as a beloved child of God.

> "You must not fear them, for the Lord
> your God Himself fights for you."
> —Deuteronomy 3:22

There are times when we are dissatisfied, when obstacles come our way, when we wonder if we can do anything to avoid the pitfalls of life. We sincerely believe that most of the bad stuff that baffles us is not of our own doing, that much of it is out of our hands. Never forget, we are spiritual persons living in a spiritual universe. No matter what comes our way, "*we are more than conquerors in Him in whom we have our being.*" Simply put, it's a matter of choice: will you embrace God's spirit, allow it to permeate your family, your work, your entire life, or will you deny God's spiritual power and live without it working for you? The choice is clear. The question comes down to this: Will you let go and let God? Many people have gone further than they thought they could because someone else thought they could. God thinks – God knows – you can go as far as you want. Will you question God's knowledge?

Beginning today, I will embrace the best every day has to offer.

Day 19

"I know nothing more inspiring than that
of making discoveries for one's self."
—George Washington Carver

You cannot reverence God without reverencing His creation. You are the crown of God's creation! You are created in His own image! The oceans are wondrous, but God did not create them in His image. The mountains are majestic, but God did not create them in His image. The entire realm of nature with all its beauty, the vast solar system with all its complexities, are not created in the image of God. Only you were made by the Creator to be an image of Himself. True reverence, then, must begin with reverence for the greatness that is you. Self-respect is God-respect. God is in you. He put himself there. He made you to reflect His wonder and power and perfectness. He made you to be His child and companion, for all eternity. Respect yourself as the greatest of God's creations. Reverence your role as a representative of God himself, made in His own image.

Today I will walk through my world knowing myself to be God's crowning creation.

"There is something about sacrifice that raises one to a new level of spirituality."
—Rev. Jim Holley

Compare: A mother out shopping for a new dress for an upcoming holiday party (she can't be seen in the same one again) stops off at the toy department to buy an additional gift for her youngest child – just to even the piles among the siblings; a mother, after completing her regular waitressing shift, stays on to "work a double." The extra money will guarantee that her child has at least one present under the Christmas tree. The first mother grumbles that the extra stop will make her late for her hair appointment. The second mother whispers a prayer of thanks for the opportunity to earn the extra cash. Which mother do you think experiences true, spirit-lifting joy? Which do you think is the better teacher of success-oriented values? Nothing worthwhile is ever gained without sacrifice. Sometimes the thing sacrificed is time; sometimes it's money; sometimes it's personal comfort or a longing for luxury. Whatever the sacrifice, if made willingly, it blesses the giver much more than the receiver. *Personal sacrifice is the key to success.* Only through generous, private, and selfless sacrifice can the spirit transcend what is and create the full potential of what can be.

Today I will give up all that is standing in my way of succeeding.

DAY 21

> "The attempt to force human beings to
> despise themselves is what I call hell."
> —Andre Malraux

From the slave quarters of America to the prison camps of Nazi Germany, self-loathing has been the weapon of choice for those who would dominate others. God is in all human beings. To foster hatred of self is to foster hatred of God. When we begin to hate ourselves, we begin to hate God. Self-hatred is the greatest sin against both God and humankind. When we despise ourselves, we become our own slave masters. To be enslaved by hatred for ourselves – whether it be hatred of our bodies, our skin color, our minds – is to be chained by the most heinous form of slavery. Self-hatred goes against human nature. It stunts positive growth and denies the God-given potential for achievement that abides in each of us. No one will hold you in greater esteem than you hold yourself. Likewise, when you despise yourself you send out messages to others – messages that signal "I'm not a good person. I'm not worthy of your attention, love, or respect." Success cannot be yours until you eliminate such messages from your mind, your actions, and your speech. Earning the love and respect of others begins with loving and respecting ourselves. Practicing love of God begins with loving the part of God that is in each of us.

God is in me. Today I'll celebrate the wonderful person I am.

DAY 22

> "When you look in the mirror, know who is looking back to you. Know your strength, know your weaknesses, you can create art."
> —Debbie Allen

Life is a mystery waiting to unfold before you. It's an exciting journey into the unknown. No one can predict the future, but everyone can plan for it. One of the great mysteries of life is our ability to think, reason, and plan. It is this ability that separates us from other animals. We alone have been granted the gift of highly developed intelligence. It is our intelligence that gives us the power to unravel some of life's mysteries. It is our intelligence that allows us to recognize that there are mysteries we will never unravel. The mysterious intrigues us; it fascinates us and challenges us. The mysterious should never frighten us. Just because something is unknown or beyond understanding doesn't mean that it is evil or harmful. Just because something is unseen and untouchable doesn't mean that it doesn't exist. It is in the unexplained mysteries of life that we find the greatest beauty. It is in our journey to discover God that we find the greatest fulfillment.

All the mysteries of life are bound up in the human soul.

Day 23

A woman was in a terrible fire; 42 percent of her body was scarred by burns that even plastic surgery could not disguise. For years, she hid herself away from the staring eyes of strangers. She cut herself off from friends and family. Filled with self-loathing and self-pity, she was consumed by anger at God for sparing her life. As a last ditch effort, the woman visited yet another plastic surgeon, a world renowned burn specialist. As she waited for her turn, a young boy emerged from the doctor's office. His face was even more hideously scarred than hers, yet there was about him a sense of peace, acceptance, and victory. As if propelled by forces beyond her control, the woman found that she was engaged in a conversation with the boy. "You seem so serene," she said. "How are you able to live with your disfiguration?" "I'm not disfigured," replied the boy. "I'm just different – different in a way that makes other people appreciate their blessings." What dis-figurations – visible and invisible – do you carry with you from your past? Have they conquered you or have they enabled you to become a conqueror?

My scars are the beauty marks of living.

DAY 24

"Habit is heaven's own redness: it takes
the place of happiness."
—Alexander Pushkin

Every development, every step in humanity's progress has involved a risk. It has been said that necessity is the mother of invention. Risk, then, is the birth process that produces the inventions that alleviate the needs. Every time a woman makes the choice to bear a child, she risks her life, her health, her figure, her future. Every time a farmer plants a field, he risks his time, money, energy, and future to the precariousness of nature, weather, and the economic market. Yet farmers continue to plant, women to bear children. Risks are necessary if the human race is to go on. What things are necessary for you to accomplish your goals? What are you willing to risk to attain them?

Today I will move forward despite my fears.

Day 25

"When you're a Black woman, you seldom get to do what you just want to do; you always do what you have to do."

—Dorothy I. Height

I suspect that if we took away all the excuses for failure – slavery, oppression, racism, poverty, etc. – the result would not be greater success. While all of these factors are real, they are not insurmountable. In fact, it's hard to name a successful person who has not had to struggle with adversity. The difference suffering plays in success and failure seems to rest more in the sufferer than in the cause of the suffering. Suffering can become very comfortable. It gives you something to talk about. It draws people to you. It brings you attention and sympathy. It can give you an excuse for becoming stuck where you are, a convenient reason not to move forward with your life. Attaining a can do attitude requires that you look at all the causes of your suffering, acknowledge their validity, then make a long, hard appraisal of how you're using suffering to impede your progress. Have you let your suffering become an excuse for avoiding positive action? Have you devoted your energy to expounding the raw deal life has dealt you? The time has come to direct your energy to defining and working toward success-oriented goals.

I'm examining my baggage and lightening my load.

> "This is the day that the Lord has made;
> let us rejoice and be glad in it."
>
> —Psalm 118:24

One of the most precious gifts God will ever give you is the gift of today. Today stretches before you with endless possibilities. Today you are alive, and in *living*, you have another chance to choose how you will live! Today you are interacting with others, thus giving you another chance to choose how you will mold your relationships. Today you may be going to work, going to school, parenting your children, or caring for your own parents. This day brings you a new opportunity to decide *if* and *how* you will carry out the tasks of your various roles. Today is yours to use in service to others, in service to yourself, in service to God. If you had trouble sleeping last night because you treated someone badly, today brings an opportunity to set things right. If you were a "gold bricking" employee, a lazy student, an irresponsible parent/child/friend yesterday, today you can do an about face and change your behavior. If yesterday you were mired in a can't do atmosphere, today you can adopt a can do attitude. Today you can rejoice in the gift of a new opportunity to choose success over failure, to make a new start on the road to achievement. Today you can be glad that God has given you this wonderful gift and you can take time to thank Him for it.

I will greet today and its opportunities with excitement and with thanks.

Day 27

"We cannot stand still; we cannot permit ourselves simply to be victims."

—W.E.B. DuBois

Modern life has destroyed the African tradition of strong marriages. Cultural forces have taught black men to become deserters of women and children, to forfeit their role as protector and provider, to resent the achievements of their women, and to use their resentment as an excuse for their own bad behaviors. Black women have become nurturers, providers, and supporters. They did not choose their roles; they were forced upon them. Black men must learn to forgive black women for doing whatever they have had to do for self-survival, the survival of their children, and, ultimately, the survival of the race. The word "sharing" must be restored to our vocabulary. We must reclaim our tradition of expecting success. The strength of black family units can only be achieved by working toward positive expectations, celebrating together each forward step, and supporting one another during times of struggle. Success is the birthright of both men and women.

Today I will both give and accept forgiveness, sharing my innermost thoughts and encouraging my mate to do the same.

Day 28

> "Truth is essential: and the essential is
> to be truthful."
>
> —Nelson Mandela

A lie is a lie is a lie. It isn't a little white lie; it isn't a little black lie; it isn't even a little pink, blue, or green lie. A lie is an untruth; an untruth is the enemy of truth. Lying doesn't twist the truth. It kills it. What's worse, perhaps, is that truth doesn't die alone. Oh no. Truth is inseparable from trust. When truth dies, so does trust. Now, trust is an invader. It lives inside someone else, usually someone very close to you. It is born, grows, and thrives inside of someone else. Nevertheless, it is your actions, words, and behavior that bring it to life and keeps it alive. When you speak the truth, act with integrity, and live morally and respectfully, you bring trust to life inside others. When you speak falsely, act dishonorably, and live immorally without respect for yourself or others, you kill trust. It's a terrible thing to kill someone's trust in you. It's an even worse thing to kill your trust in yourself. Truth and trust, they're inseparable. Truth and success – they're inseparable, too.

Today I will guard against dishonesty in any size or form.

Day 29

"Float like a butterfly, sting like a bee."
—Muhammad Ali

There is nothing wrong with floating through life as long as you are floating toward a positive goal. As they float, butterflies bring a sense of peace and beauty to the world. Butterflies don't know they're doing this; their entire life cycle is directed toward the goal of pollination, of perpetuating the plants and trees that sustain the earth's people. Bees, on the other hand, are engaged in the same kind of work, yet their presence often elicits avoidance and fear. What causes such opposite reactions in people? Butterflies are hard-working but non-threatening; bees also work hard, but they pose a real threat to others – the threat of delivering a painful sting. Which is more productive? Which is more likely to succeed in accomplishing its goal? Perhaps the answer lies in the circumstances. Sometimes it is productive to float peacefully toward your goal, quietly gathering life-sustaining nectar. At other times, a sting is in order. Sometimes only an aggressive reaction to the destructive actions of others will get your message across – a message that, while you may prefer to pursue peaceful progress, you are capable of delivering stinging blows to those who would hamper your personal success.

Today I will pursue peaceful progress, reserving my stings for those who can't understand any other reaction.

"To be young, gifted and black. That's
where it's at."

—Weldon J. Irvine

Every child is both a gift and gifted. For children of
color, this is even more true. Our children are our hope
for the future, and we must pass on our can do attitude to them. While we may not be able to raise them
in fancy houses, provide them with private school edu-
cations, or dress them in designer clothes, we can fill
them with belief in themselves. Our children are also
gifted. They have the ability to carry on the struggle
for success we have begun. They are gifted with the
values and knowledge we've had to work so hard to
acquire. They are bright and beautiful *and* they are
aware of their beauty. They are gifted with the courage to expect and demand the best life has to offer.
They have the gift of mastery, the strength and te-
nacity to transform a can't do atmosphere into a can
do arena for advancement, attainment, and achievement.

*I will take time today to tell a child that she or he is
both gifted and a gift.*

Day 31

"I press *towards* the mark for the *prize*
of the high calling of God in Christ Jesus."
—Philippians 4:14

Now is the time to live each day as if there *was* no tomorrow. Today I challenge you to . . .

- develop the enduring qualities of Booker T. Washington and Madame Walker;

- see the big picture seen by Benjamin Mays;

- study, read, and pay whatever price necessary to secure an education like Yours Truly;

- live like Clara "Mother" Hale, Bill Cosby, and Rosa Parks, by making your home, marriage, and relationship a centerpiece for love and spiritual values;

- step out boldly like Colin Powell and Earl Graves, and, despite the odds, build a profitable enterprise that will make you – and your race – proud;

- emulate Jesse Owens and Al Sharpton by lighting the fires of young, imaginative minds;

- turn a deaf ear to excuses and make your name as inspiring as Ron Brown's;

- write from the heart as did Maya Angelou and Toni Morrison, so that you too may stir the consciousness of people;

- reach deep within and find your personal best, to recognize and praise the good gifts within you, and, like Alex Haley, to share, strongly and vitally, the important truths God imparts.

Today I will accept one of these challenges and begin conquering it.

DAY 32

> "Regardless of what White America does or does not do, the destiny of African Americans is in our hands."
>
> —Robert Woodson

Once there was a goldfish who lived in a small cement pond in a city playground. He had lived there all his life and had grown to be the largest goldfish in the pond. He didn't know his pond was small; it was the only home he had ever known and to him it was his entire universe. The other goldfish were careful to stay out of his way. Then one day the playground closed to make room for a housing project. All the goldfish were swept up in a net and transported to a free-flowing creek. The other goldfish were happy with their new environment. Now they could swim freely, no longer confined by the cement that had imprisoned them. But the big goldfish was miserable. Gone was the regular feeding time; instead he had to search out his own food. Instead of moving out of his way, the big goldfish had to make way for the larger fish. The freedom of the meandering creek frightened him. For him, the move was not liberating but rather terrifying. He could no longer bully the other fish or demand to be first, best, and feared. Instead of being a big fish in a small pond, he had become a small fish in a big pond. He had been forced to recognize his proper place in his world. Are you living like that goldfish?

Today I will lift my eyes heavenward, recognizing that there is a higher power who wants to see me succeed.

Day 33

> *"Do not conform any longer to the pattern of this world, but be transformed by the renewing of your mind."*
>
> —Romans 12:2

Where are you going? What are you going to do? What will you accomplish? Has anyone asked you those questions recently? If not, ask them of yourself.

Some years ago Lawrence Appley, chairperson of the board of The American Management Association, spoke at a large convention. After his presentation, he took questions from the audience. A young student asked him, "What are your ten-year goals?" The speaker looked at him and said, "Do you know how old I am? I'm seventy-five!" The student said, "Yes, I knew that. What are your ten-year goals?" He made his point to the speaker and the audience. We are never too old to dream.

Some men react to this idea of setting goals. They say, "I like my freedom. I'm a spontaneous man. I don't want to be limited." Well, who said setting goals limits you? It's just the opposite. You need to have some thought for the future. We weren't created to drift or to bounce around off the walls of life.

God has a plan for your life, and he wants you to experience the fullness he has for you.

Life is a journey, not a destination.

DAY 34

"For God has not given us a spirit of fear, but of power and of love and of a sound mind."
—II Timothy 1:7

Each day our minds are bombarded by thousands of thoughts, both positive and negative. Some come from the outside, some from within. All create an on-going flow, a stream of consciousness that helps determine our destiny. When God-oriented thoughts fill your heart and mind, you are filled with truthful, positive thoughts. No matter what the day hurls at you, you can live in peace, experiencing all the warmth and beauty life offers, even in the darkest times.

- By seeing the beauty of life, you can reject its gloom and receive its gleam.
- By refusing to limit yourself, you can expand your abilities and form realistic plans to achieve your dreams.
- By staying focused, you can avoid becoming side-tracked.
- By allowing love to be your constant guide, you can make it!

God has good gifts for me. Today I will name them, claim them, receive them.

"I don't know the key to success, but the key to failure is trying to please everybody."

—Bill Cosby

Stick-Ability Versus Quit-Ability

Success, wealth, and growth don't come from fabrication, technology, or even the information highway. Success comes from perseverance and persistence. Achieving your goals comes from never quitting, giving out, or giving up. People who succeed burn with an eternal flame of accomplishment. People who fail lack the eternal flame that ignites their self worth. They fail to recognize – or strive to achieve – their full potential. Which kind of person are you? Ask yourself the question and be very honest with your answer. Name your goals. Evaluate your progress toward them. Take inventory of your positive actions. Regroup if necessary, and NEVER QUIT BELIEVING IN YOURSELF!

Today I will begin living up to my potential.

Day 36

> "Start with what you have and build on
> what you have."
>
> —Kwame Nkrumah

Strength of character, perseverance, integrity –
these form the powerful current that will keep you
going in the right direction. You exist for a purpose, a
purpose that is uniquely and individually your own.
In fact, your purpose is as individual and singular as
the lines and waves of your fingerprints that identify
you as one-of-a-kind. The dynamics that help you
succeed in achieving your purpose are set in motion
when you clearly define your individual purpose. Only
then can you unleash your internal power to pursue
your individual goals. The Bible tells us that "Where
there is no vision, the people perish." (Proverbs 29:18)
It could also be said that without clear vision your
personal purpose will perish. If you don't expect to
find the vision for your personal purpose in life, you
probably won't; without vision, your purpose in life
will be altered and will go unfulfilled. Success requires
seeing the vision, working toward fulfilling it, settling
into the tasks necessary, and aiming for the target of
victory. No matter how hard the tasks, remember that
only if you aim at *no* target, are you certain to hit it!

I have 20/20 vision of my life's purposes.

DAY 37

"Excellence is to do a common thing in
an uncommon way."

—Booker T. Washington

DREAM

Reaching the peak in your life requires that you
Dream — not day-dream but career-dream. Realize
that when you do your very best, you become your
very best at what you do.

If you play basketball, do it to the best of your
ability.
If you run track, do it to the best of your ability.
If you study, do it to the best of your ability.

Gleam!

Everyone has a God-given gift. Determine it and
polish it to a gleam.

Scheme!

Success depends on planning, praying and preparing.

Team!

Find a support team of parents, relatives, friends, and
associates and tap into the resources of your team.

Beam!

Be proud of your progress but don't let pride get
in the way of your success. Always reach for the
Superior Being — God!

*Today I will identify my dream, learn to scheme, start
to beam, and form a team.*

"Some people change jobs, spouses, and friends –
but never think of changing themselves."

—Paula Giddings

"If I had the wings of a bird, I would fly away and
be at rest," says David, the Old Testament Psalm
writer. But we have no wings, we can't fly away, and,
most importantly, there is no place on earth called "at
rest." Sure, we can go running off, change our names,
and start over somewhere else. But first we must consider the common denominator of our problems. Usually we'll find that they have more to do with *us* than
they do with *other people*. When we search inward
for areas in need of change, we begin to see everything in a different light. Suddenly, what we thought
was vital becomes trivial. We learn the wonderful truth
that *we have the power to change from victim to vic-
tor*. We don't have to spend our lives hoping circumstances will change. We can change our circumstances
by changing ourselves! Things change when we
change. As a wise person once said, "Unless you
change what you think, you will always get what you
got." The fastest runner on earth can't run far enough
or fast enough to escape from himself. When the problem is within us, we take it with us wherever we go.
Most of what hurts us is self inflicted. Resolving negative issues means changing something(s) within us.
Fortunately, when a problem is within us, the solution
is within us as well. All we have to do is commit to
finding the solution and implementing it.

*Today I will look within, rather than without, for life-
changing solutions.*

DAY 39

"Self-help is the best help."

—Aesop

Please don't think or feel today that someone else has your best interest at heart. Please don't think or feel today that someone else is more concerned about your success than you are yourself. Please don't think or feel today that someone owes you something because of slavery, Jim Crowism, or racism. **Don't say, think, or feel these things today or ever!** Sitting back and expecting others to fix your problems is unrealistic. Believing others will unselfishly create opportunities for you is absurd. Giving others power over your life is foolish. *True help is self-help*. We are each actively involved in our own destinies. By learning to help yourself you gain the capacity for life-long learning. You'll be able to get yourself into or out of any situation. Most importantly, you'll be able to distinguish between good and bad situations and use each to your best advantage.

I am my own best influence on me.

Day 40

> "Trust in the Lord with all your heart and lean
> not on your own understanding."
>
> —Proverbs 3:5-6

Success is a state of mind that allows you to obtain the desires of your heart. Success resembles human survival. Both depend on a vision of your future – of seeing yourself healthy and thriving in specific life situations. Following major surgery, a young person found herself out of a job with no way to pay her doctor bills or her college tuition. Undaunted, she took a job as a waitress. Eventually, she was able to pay off her bills and return to college. On graduation day she was asked how she had managed to endure. What powers did she possess that others lacked? How had she stayed focused throughout all her hardships? She gave some clues to those who inquired. "I never thought that I wouldn't make it," she said. "I refused to entertain the thought or idea of failure." The young woman had leaned on the Lord. She had exercised her faith. When her faith faltered, she decided that although she did not understand His plan, she would trust Him to direct her path. There really is enough faith to go around, enough to sustain all of us, but we have to work, and work hard, to get our share of it.

Today I will lean on the Lord, trusting Him to direct my path even when my own faith falters.

DAY 41

"No one else can retrieve our values and
salvage our people better than we can.."
—Dorothy I. Height

Fifty years ago the mushroom cloud of the first
nuclear bomb became a symbol of death and devasta-
tion for the entire world. For decades this symbol
haunted us, filled us with fear, and fanned the flames
of the superpower race known as the Cold War. Today, the global Cold War has ended, yet we are continually plagued by another kind of cold war. This one,
too, carries its own devastating symbols. Consider:
black skin symbolizes poverty, lack of education,
danger; living in the "good" neighborhood symbolizes
safety and success; wearing the right clothes and the
power tie symbolizes having "made it" in the corporate world. Lest people of color boast, Beware! *Judgements based on outward symbols are not confined to
the white race.* Many people of color hold beliefs just
as strong and just as prejudicial about other racial and
ethnic groups. The cold war of negative symbols continues to stunt our ability to grow. But we can win this
cold war. Knowledge is the great overcomer. By taking the time and effort necessary to really get to know
those different from us, we can dispel the power of
symbolism. Meanwhile, we can replace negative symbols with the positive symbol of our own behavior --
behavior that shows knowledge, growth, and success.

*Today I will test the truth of one symbol I use to form
judgements.*

DAY 42

"When the people lead, the leaders will
have to follow."

—Ben Harper

One of the most important things you can do to promote personal success is to register and vote. "My one vote won't make a difference," you may say. Then why did our people fight so hard for the right of each person to cast one individual vote? And what about the power of many votes? Can this power be denied? Political activism doesn't mean hammering on others until they agree to see things your way. Rather, it means being one of those rare thinkers who examines the candidates, becomes familiar with their platforms, and studies the effects a victory would bring to your neighborhood, your beliefs, your journey toward success. Strong opinions can be shared. Sharing your strong, informed opinion about a particular candidate will help turn your one vote into many votes. Many votes will help achieve victory. Voting is a vital "can do" step toward success.

*Today I will begin to educate myself about those who
ask to be my public leaders.*

Day 43

"Equal makes the best friend."

—Aesop

Nothing stands in the way of success so much as "no" people. Practically from the day we're born, we hear the word *no*. Is it any wonder that *no* is one of the first words a child learns? Just observe any two-year-old: No, I won't eat my vegetables. No, I won't take a bath. No, I won't let Grandma give me a hug. The child may be fond of vegetables, love the bath tub, and long for a hug from Grandma. It doesn't make any difference. No means no (even when the child really means yes). As we grow older, we hear *no* more often: No you can't continue working (even though you're quite capable). No, you can't drive, manage your bank book, handle your household — whatever. *No* is a powerful word. It has powerful ramifications. So why deal with it? Yes, you can succeed! Yes, you can overcome! Yes, you can be anything you choose! The first step to success is eliminating all the *no's* that you've been taught throughout your lifetime. Replace them with *yes*. Cultivate friends with positive attitudes. Surround yourself with *yes* thinking people. Refuse to allow negative self-images to enter your thoughts. Adopt a new, positive "yes I can" lifestyle, and live it in every area of your life.

No "no" people will dominate my life today!

"Men are disturbed not by things, but
by the view they take of them."

—Epictetus

A child walking down the street encounters a stray dog and is delighted. Another child walking down the street encounters a stray dog and is terrified. Although both dogs have behaved in the same way – playful, friendly, and outgoing – the first child has seen in the dog a new and faithful companion. The second child has perceived a threatening, inescapable, dangerous enemy. The difference is not in the behavior of the dogs but in the views of the children. Every confrontation in life can be compared to these childlike encounters. Reactions are based upon learned behaviors. Remember, nothing that comes your way can disturb you unless you let it. Your views of situations defeat you, not the situations themselves. Short of causing you physical harm, people and events cannot hurt you. Only your own negative thoughts about the people and events that make up your life have that power. If your views hold negative power, conversely they also can hold positive power. Destructive, self-defeating viewpoints will unleash negative power. Positive viewpoints will unleash positive power.

Only I can make myself feel inferior.

Day 45

"It is Afrikan that woman and man join
in smiles, tears, future."

—Haki R. Madhubuti

Strong, enduring bonds between men and women
are part of our African heritage. Why, then, do marriages between blacks in America result in some of
the weakest unions? Why are husbands and fathers
absent from our homes? Why are women left alone
to fend for themselves and their children? How can
this picture be changed, this plague that is destroying our people be stopped? The end can begin with
you. Forget what you've been taught about possess-
ing women, dominating men, begetting children to
fill the void left when marriage fails. Remember that
you are capable of making wise decisions. You are
capable of waiting for the right person, the right time,
the right circumstances. You are capable of restoring
your heritage of forming a strong, life-long alliance
built on mutual respect, empowerment, and love. You
are capable of succeeding in anything you try, including marriage.

*I have the inherent wisdom to recognize my God-
ordained life-mate.*

Day 46

> "Guilt is the mafia of the mind."
> —Bob Mandel

I never knew I had a problem with undeserved guilt until a few years ago. It was a rainy day, a day of torrential downpour. I was meeting a friend for lunch. "This rain is terrible," he remarked, shaking off his drenched overcoat. "I'm sorry," I replied, not missing a beat. "Oh," my perceptive friend replied. "I didn't know you were responsible for the rain, too." Assuming guilt for events way beyond my control had become a regular element of my psyche. Guilt can rob us of the pleasure everyday living has to offer. It can make us assume personal blame for things that are not our fault. It can make us assume that we are bad and unworthy of the gifts God has given us. Guilt can destroy our ability to overcome by convincing us that we are undeserving of success. When we allow this mental mafia to dominate our actions, we become enslaved to a "can't do" atmosphere.

Today I'm pleading "not guilty!"

DAY 47

"If there is no struggle, there is no progress . . . crops without plowing up the grounds is not an option."

—Frederick Douglass

Life will always have moments of pain. This pain will differ in intensity. A third-grader hurts, and hurts a lot, when she fails a test. A teenager feels real pain when rejected by a first love. As adults, we know the child will probably forget that test, the teenager will find a new love. Yet at the moment of disappointment, the pain is real and intense. As life proceeds and we get older, we experience the pain of permanently broken relationships, unemployment, death of a loved one. Whatever our age, the pain that comes to us is real and devastating. In short, pain hurts. Suffering, on the other hand, is optional. Suffering is our choice. We have the ability to decide to put a time limit on the suffering pain causes. We can acknowledge that while the hurt may never go away, we will move away from its effects. We can choose to move forward with our own lives despite the pain of living and make a success of ourselves. Achieving a can do attitude means overcoming the can't do atmosphere created by pain, an inevitable part of life.

Today I acknowledge my pain and let go of my suffering.

DAY 48

"You are the thinker that thinks the thoughts,
that make the thing. If you don't like it, change
your thoughts.."

—Johnnie Coleman

The alarm clock sounds. You wake, stretch, and turn your eyes to the window. "What a beautiful day," you think to yourself. Suddenly the day stretches before you, full of promise, laden with possibilities. Same scenario. This time, you turn your eyes to the window and let negative thoughts take over. "What a dismal day," you think. "If only I could stay in bed. Nothing good could happen on a day like this." Nothing is closer to us than our thoughts. Just try not thinking about anything at all for even a few seconds. Can't do it, can you? A blank mind defies nature. We spend all of our waking hours, and perhaps our sleeping hours too, engaged in the thought process. No parents, friends, job, or activity is with us as much as our thoughts. Thoughts can be your best friends or your worse enemies. Choose wisely!

Today I will spend my time with my best friends--my thoughts.

Day 49

"Courage is one step ahead of fear."
—Coleman Young

Learning that you can do – can succeed – can achieve – while everyone and everything around you are proclaiming that you can't, is tough. You won't learn it in a day, a month, or even a year of reading the messages covered in this book. Success comes by conquering thousands of stuck moments *one at a time.* This takes real courage, the kind of courage that doesn't allow you to rest on your laurels or to quit when the going gets tough. In fact, this kind of courage gets you unstuck for the moment and helps you face the fact that the next stuck moment is just around the corner. You already have this moment-by-moment courage inside you. It's there to help you make the long uphill climb, but first you must decide to dig it out and use it.

Today I will triumph over one thing, rejoice that I am momentarily unstuck, and acknowledge that another negative moment will need conquering tomorrow.

Day 50

> "Opportunity follow struggles. It follows
> effort. It follows hard work. It doesn't
> come before."
>
> —Shelby Steele

Success – we want it and we want it now! How like little kids we are! "I want the toy, the candy, the ice cream cone" – whatever the current demand. Children are born wanting – and needing – instant gratification. As children grow older, learning to wait is a hard but important lesson. Learning to work for what we want is even harder, yet it is a lesson vital for adults. Developing a can do attitude is not an instant process. Progress is often slow and results are often hard to see. Yet results will come, no matter how strong the can't do atmosphere that surrounds you, *if you don't give up.* Ultimate gratification may not be instant, but gratification itself can be found in the daily process of becoming who and what you want to be. Perhaps the accent should be placed not on "instant," but on "gratification."

*"Overcoming obstacles does not happen in an instant.
I will take my time."*

Day 51

> Spend a moment with yourself, the true
> person inside you.
>
> —Rev. Jim Holley

It is imperative that you spend some time alone each day, not with the public you, but with the very private you – the self who exists deep within. There is no one better to spend an hour with, or an hour on, for that matter. Successful people find that a few minutes of solitude enhance their effectiveness and productivity for the rest of the day. Such self-reflection affects every decision, every relationship.

S Sacrifice momentary desires for what really counts.
E Energize yourself.
L Love unconditionally.
F Faithfully follow your plan for today.

I can do it by my self.

> "Each of us has the right and the responsibility
> to assess the roads which lie ahead."
> —Maya Angelou

There was once a far eastern Zen master, who had a great serenity and peace about him no matter the surroundings. "How do you maintain that serenity and peace?" someone asked him. He replied, "I never leave my place of meditation." Each of us is blessed with an internal sanctuary. The name of that sanctuary is Self. It is where you have your deepest roots, your wisest thoughts, your most treasured moments. Only when you let someone evict *you* from *you* do you become vulnerable and unfocused. Don't allow that to happen. Whatever is going on around you, remain focused. Hold fast to your inner sanctuary. Visit this sanctuary regularly and often. A renewed and deepened concept of self will build both physical and spiritual strength to enable you to handle the challenges of life. Remember, while you cannot entirely protect your "self," you can connect with and cooperate with Him who can.

I have a special place reserved just for me. I visit there often.

DAY 53

"The greatest power of sin is its power to blind us to itself."

—Rev. Scott Lawson

People never cease to amaze me. They either don't believe in sin at all, or if they do, they believe that sin is something someone else does. You ask them point blank, "Is lying a sin?" "Of course it is," they answer. "Is stealing?" Same answer. "Is covetousness, disrespect, laziness, violence?" The answer is always the same: "Yes, those things are sins." Yet these same people think nothing of calling in sick when they're not or wasting time wishing for things others have. I've even known them to brag when a cashier accidentally gives them more change than due! (Today, those few honest people who return incorrect change keep their deed a secret. They don't want others to think they're weird!) What's worse, people are teaching their children to sin, too. "Just say you're twelve so you can get in at the child's price." (Stealing) "Tell them I'm not home." (Lying) "If I had nice clothes like that I could get a job instead of being stuck here." (Wasteful, lazy living, covetous living) They have been so blinded by sin that they no longer see it in themselves. We all know that it's impossible for a blind person to see. Isn't it amazing how weak our eyesight becomes when we look too closely at ourselves?

I will use my keen eyesight to scrutinize my behavior.

DAY 54

> "She does not know her beauty, she thinks
> her brown body has no glory."
>
> —Waring Cuney

Once elephants freely roamed the plains of Africa. Then the hunters came. They slaughtered the elephants for their ivory tusks. Soon all the tusked elephants learned to fear the hunters. They no longer roamed free and proud but hid themselves in the darkest, deepest parts of the jungle. Gradually they recognized that it was their tusks the hunters wanted. It was their tusks that put them at risk. They came to hate their tusks, the very part of them that made them beautiful and valuable. But they couldn't eliminate their tusks. The tusked elephants could not breed tusk-less offspring. Their frustration at not being able to change the essence of whom they were caused them much anger and pain. Their self-hatred grew; their pride diminished. Elephants are incapable of thinking and reasoning and problem-solving beyond the most elemental level. Thankfully, we are not elephants.

I am bright! I am beautiful! I love who I am!

DAY 55

"When I look at my 'want-to-be-like' and
my 'don't-want-to-be-like,' the difference
I see is a respect for work and time."
—Rev. Jim Holley

There are some people who interpret "ambition"
to mean being pushy, aggressive, or insensitive. That
isn't the case. Truly ambitious people are value-driven.
They "read" reality and they know how important time
has become in modern-day life. They set personal goals
and personal time-lines for achieving them. And, they
don't allow other people or other things to deter them
or get them off course. I have found that goals come
in phases. There are long term goals and short term
goals. Goals need periodic updating and, often, alter-
ation. Most important, achievement requires measure-
ment. Ask yourself where you want to be three, five,
seven, ten years from now. Then evaluate your
progress monthly. You cannot invert the process of
achievement anymore than you can harvest a crop
before you plant it. The buck in life does not stop
with you but it starts with you!

*Today is the first day of the rest of my life. I'll make
it a productive one.*

DAY 56

"Liberty without learning is always in peril
and learning without liberty is always in vain."
—John Fitzgerald Kennedy

A baby resents the confines of the playpen. It wants the freedom to explore its environment. But the environment is filled with steep stairs, small objects, electric sockets – all kinds of dangers that the baby hasn't learned to recognize and avoid. Many a convict spends countless days in the prison library amassing a great wealth of knowledge. They learn about business, professions, all sorts of wonderful things that can make a positive difference in the world. But the convict isn't at liberty to put this learning to use. Both convicts and babies have the ability to learn but lack individual freedom to put their learning to use. For both, though in different ways, unbridled freedom would be dangerous. For babies, learning will eventually be used for successful growth. For many convicts, learning will remain unused and therefore will be in vain. What have you learned about yourself and your world on your journey toward achievement? Are you using what you've learned to further your progress? Are you like the prisoner who has gained knowledge but isn't using it? Or are you like the baby who would ramble freely without purpose, destination, or recognition of the dangers that wait to overtake it?

Today I'll exercise my freedom to put what I've learned to use for myself and my world.

DAY 57

> "He who starts behind in the great race
> of life must forever remain behind or run
> faster than the man in front"
>
> —Benjamin E. Mays

All of us are striving for something. How far you reach is up to you. Success is a matter of setting goals, making plans, and getting yourself into action. In today's high-tech world, it's easy for the average person to feel insignificant. Yet it is the contributions of individuals, most no more talented or gifted than you or I, that have made the biggest differences in our world. There is no one formula for success. Every one of us must find his or her own way. But there are some common elements to our individual search. One is accepting personal responsibility. Only you can create a fulfilling life for yourself. Personal responsibility begins with using your personal talents to make your life the very best it can be. God has given you many talents. Ultimately, you will be asked to account for how you have used them. Have you squandered them or wasted them? Have you stored them away, left them buried and undeveloped?

I'm a talented person. I'm responsible for living a talented life.

DAY 58

On this day let me be reminded.
—Rev. Jim Holley

The **6** most important words:
I admit I made a mistake.

The **5** most important words:
You did a good job.

The **4** most important words:
What is your opinion?

The **3** most important words:
If you please . . .

The **2** most important words:
Thank you.

The 1 most important word:
We

It is in thinking of others that I am thought of!

DAY 59

"A bitter person is a person in the process
of destroying himself."

—Dempsey Travis

On your path to success there will be times when
you feel that the whole world is against you. This can
range from mere "bad hair" type days to real, enduring times of struggles with health, employment, relationships. Times like these tests your faith and your
fortitude. More difficult to bear, though, are the times
when you get down on yourself. This leaves you without the resource of your own good company. It is
right and good for you to get down on yourself when
you've been mean-spirited, inconsiderate, lazy, or dishonest. We all need a good talking to once in awhile,
especially when it's a heart-to-heart with ourselves.
What is wrong is getting down on yourself and *staying* down on yourself. You become mired in regret
and remorse; you lose the ability to move forward. If
you don't get unstuck, you risk losing the gains you've
made. Your growing can do attitude can quickly drag
you back to your can't do atmosphere. Being stuck in
self-despair puts you out of touch with God. You are
a child of the King. Never forget it! You're not perfect. You've made mistakes in the past and will make
mistakes in the future. Your success lies in learning
and growing with each mistake – growing closer to
the successful person God created you to be.

If God is with me, who can be against me!

Day 60

> What makes you so strong?
> —Rev. Jim Holley

You are strong and getting stronger. Tell yourself and others the source of your strength:

Not the color of my skin
Not the color of my eyes
Not the color of my hair
Not my ability or availability
Not punctuality
Not height, nor depth, nor width
Not my family pedigree
Not my social organizations or political affiliations
Not my support system, my mentor, or my teacher
Not my creative ingenuity
Not my own independence or my high regard of others

What makes you so strong? It's the strength within!
Find it. Develop it. Cherish it. Exercise it!

Today I will tap into my own source of inner strength.

DAY 61

> "Life is a series of moments. To live each one is to succeed."
>
> —Kathe Kichula

This is one of my favorite quotations and one I keep with me every day. It reminds me that each new day, each new hour, each new moment is a gift from God. Someday I will have to account for what I did with these gifts of time. Once, when I was a kid, my favorite aunt gave me a pair of the ugliest pajamas I'd ever seen. I hated them and somehow managed to lose them, even though they were the only pair of pajamas I had. A few weeks later my aunt phoned and invited me to spend the weekend at her house. Weekends at my aunt's were always fun-filled times I looked forward to with great excitement. This time, her invitation filled me with apprehension and overwhelming regret for my hasty action. How could I show up without any pajamas? How could I tell her I had wasted her gift? I couldn't seize the moment and accept her wonderful invitation; I had to stay behind. God's gifts are too precious to waste. Success lies in planning and preparing; it also lies in recognizing the wonderful opportunities each moment holds. Even when we can't see the immediate benefit, we must learn to see the potential for wonderful opportunities in the future. Each moment brings a gift. Seize each moment!

This moment is precious. I will live it to the fullest!

DAY 62

"All that you touch you change. All that
you change, changes you."
—Octavia E. Butler

Each of us has unlimited power and potential.
Anything that cripples that potential is evil. Likewise,
when we try to cripple the potential of another, we
are doing evil. The power and potential you have
inside you have been given to you for a purpose.
Whether or not you accomplish that purpose is entirely up to you. You are the captain of your own ship.
You control your own fate. The same is true for
everyone else in the world. Most times, working to
fulfill your potential can best be done in coopera-
tion with others. When we recognize that our sisters
and brothers have their own goals – goals that may
be similar but are never exactly the same as our own
– we learn to work together in friendship. We are not
threatened by their successes. We can be happy for
them without being sorry for ourselves. Sometimes,
though, we must go it alone. It is during these times
that we must truly hold the reins of our own destinies. At other times, the accomplishment of individual goals is dependent upon the achievement of
universal goals. It is then that we must work in unity
and in harmony for the common good. It is only in an
environment of freedom for all that individual freedom thrives, that individual success is facilitated.

*My power is great; my goals are worthy. The same is
true for those around me.*

DAY 63

> "I can do all things through Him that strengthens me!"
>
> —Philippians 4:13

I saw this cartoon about a chicken:

Frame 1: an egg
Frame 2: a cracked egg
Frame 3: a chicken trying to escape the shell
Frame 4: the chicken sticking his head out of the shell
Frame 5: the chicken looking to the left
Frame 6: the chicken looking to the right
Frame 7: the chicken putting his head back into the shell as if refusing to be born

What did he see that made him want to go back and refuse to be born? Drugs? Crime? AIDS? Racism? Lack of opportunity? Don't be a chicken! Be born and come alive! Oh, chicken, you looked to the left and you looked to the right, but you didn't look up!

Today I will lift my eyes upward knowing I have endless strength available to me.

"The nation begins in the family."
—Haki R. Madhubuti

The "founding fathers" – all wise and all white. From our very first history lessons, the superiority of these wise, white men is pounded into our minds. We learn to accept – even unquestioningly believe – that nations are founded by the actions of such "national heroes." Missing from history lessons are the roles played by other heroes – heroes whose names are unknown, whose actions are unpublished and unsung. These are the men and women who build nations from the ground up, family by family. When families are strong, nations flourish; when they are weak, the very foundations of a nation crumble. People of color can decry the historical backgrounds that have led to weakened family structure. As valid as these claims may be, the past is the past; it can't be changed. Only the future is held malleable in our hands. What kind of molders will we be? The birth of a nation begins with the birth of a child into a strong, loving, value-oriented family – a family where both mother and father are dedicated to founding a new nation based on liberty and justice for all.

Today I will take up a new profession; I will become a builder of nations by building strong foundations for my family unit.

DAY 65

"If your home is unbearable, maybe you're the bear."

—Sign on a Church Lawn

What does your family see when you come in the door? What words do they hear from your lips? What body language do you express with your movements? Do they see the same smile your boss sees? Do they hear the same polite and courteous speech patterns your coworkers hear? Do they find you open and warm, receptive, interested and caring -- you know, the kind of person you are with your friends? I hope your answer to all these questions is "NO." No, because I hope the person you are at home is *better* than the person you are at work, school, the shopping mall, a neighbor's house, etc. Success begins with interpersonal relationships. Being the best you can be *with* and *for* those closest to you is vital to both your growth and theirs. Being a true, life-forming example of success for those closest to you helps to guarantee that the successful person you're becoming will help others become can do people, too. What greater success could you ask for than to be a positive force for those you love?

Today I will save my best for the best -- those I love.

DAY 66

> The greatest battles of life are fought out everyday in the silent chambers of our own heart.
> —Rev. Jim Holley

If you want to change a situation, you first have to change yourself. Before you can effectively change yourself, you have to change your perceptions. The lens through which you see the world shapes your interpretations. We must look at the lens as well as the world itself. Each of us has many, many maps inside our heads. They can be divided into two main categories: maps of the way things are – realities – and maps of the way things should be – values. Is-ness vs. ought-ness. Rewriting your personal maps requires discipline. Change is frightening. It is also hard work. If you're committed to success, you must be committed to the hard work of change. Successfully and continuously undergoing the hard work of change is necessary if you are going to achieve your goals.

Today I will evaluate my perceptions, decide what changes I must make, and commit to the hard work of transformation.

DAY 67

"First we make our habits; then our habits
begin to make us."

—Anonymous

Where did it begin? Sometimes it's hard to remember. We do something, usually something we know at the time is wrong or dangerous or irresponsible, and we get away with it. Next time, it becomes a little easier to do. We don't feel quite so guilty or bad afterward. Soon it becomes an automatic way of behaving; we don't give it a second thought. We've developed a habit. Next, without our knowing it, *our habit begins to develop us.* We are what we do! What we do is the sum of our conscious and our unconscious actions. Habits are conscious actions repeated so often they become unconscious actions. How can we "see" what no longer is visible to us? Through introspection, reflection, meditation, and prayer! Only God's help, and strenuous efforts on our part, can reveal the habits that may be standing in the way of progress.

God, today please open my eyes to any "can't do" habits that are impeding my success. Help me to deal with them.

DAY 68

> The alternative to failure is to believe
> in success.
>
> —Rev. Jim Holley

I would like to think that what has kept me going is the fear of being poor again. I don't speak of poverty as finance only; it encompasses attitude. There are times when I have failed. Instead of dwelling on the failure, I knew that success existed somewhere. I just had to go and find it. If the sun is down in New York, it must be rising somewhere else. I could either wait or go and find it. Success is the same way. Never allow the negative to drown you. Find the hope, find the safety net, find the raft, and hold for a while. Likewise, when success comes, don't get too caught up in it; remember, success is a life-long unfolding of challenges conquered and battles still to be won. Learn from each success. Enjoy the rewards of each victory. Take pleasure in the moment knowing the moment won't last; failures come regularly on the upward road to success. Never become complacent; someone is looking for a job, position, relationship, business, etc.; make sure they don't get yours. Remain vital; keep growing; never stop trying.

I believe in myself. I can succeed. Today I can make a new start.

DAY 69

> "Sin's greatest power is its ability to cause blindness – especially when looking in the mirror."
>
> —Dorothy Rose-Brennan

Ask any eye doctor. Our eyesight worsens as we age. Somewhere around age forty most people begin to need corrective lenses for certain activities. When I got my first pair of contact lenses, I sure had a hard time putting them in and out. I remember buying a magnifying mirror with a high intensity light attached. It made the job much easier. Sin-blindness is more insidious than normal age-induced eyesight impairment. It can't be corrected with glasses or contact lenses. It doesn't stand out in a bright light, and it is virtually invisible in the mirror. On my journey toward success, I wouldn't go on a job interview or try to take a test without my corrective lenses; I wouldn't be able to see and would fail for sure. Isn't sin-blindness a greater deterrent to success?

Lord, today please grant me 20/20 mirror vision.

Day 70

To live is to change. We ourselves, and the people
and places we love are changing every day. Nothing
holds back the changing process. No, you can't stop
change, but you can direct the way changes are made.
And, even more importantly, *you can control the results of change*. Only YOU can form your own future.
Only YOU can decide how you will respond to change.
Only YOU can direct the impact of your constantly
changing environment. Graduation, marriage, births,
and deaths – all signal times of change. The very aging process itself is an evolution of second-by-second
change going on in every part of your body. Change
makes life an exciting, challenging adventure. Accept
the changes in your life as the inevitable results of
growth. Even while you're suffering the growing pains
of change, remember to ask yourself, "What am I
learning from this experience?" Carry that knowledge
with you and apply it to the ever-changing circumstances that form your life.

*I'm different today than I was yesterday; I'm differ-
ent today from what I'll be tomorrow.*

DAY 71

"Riches are not from an abundance of worldly goods, but from a contented mind."

—Mohammed

What happens when you lie down at night? Do you drift peacefully off to uninterrupted sleep? Or does your mind mistake your bedroom ceiling for an empty screen on which to replay every encounter, every action, every decision you've made that day? Perhaps your "night thoughts" go back to experiences, relationships, judgements you've made over your entire lifetime? If your mind is not content, maybe it's time to face yourself squarely in the mirror. What are you doing that you know you shouldn't be doing? What have you gained from underhanded or immoral dealings? Are you putting wealth above integrity? Are you breaking a promise, letting someone down? Are you being false to your own ideals? Developing a can do attitude includes developing skills and resources that will lead to success in all phases of life, including financial security. Relying on yourself as an honest, capable, trustworthy person of integrity is the only way you'll enjoy your success and sleep well at night.

I'm not ashamed to face myself.

DAY 72

"To love is to make of one's heart a swinging door."

—Howard Thurman

When counseling engaged couples I always ask the question: "Why do you want to marry her/him?" Invariably, I get the answer, "When I'm with her/him, I feel complete." Does that mean that before you met you were only half a woman? If something happens to her, will you be an incomplete man? Never marry, or bring to a marriage, an incomplete person! First, get yourself together. Know who you are, where you're going, and how you're going to get there. Make sure the mate you choose is a together person, too. Be sure you know one another's goals and that your goals are compatible. Understand one another's aspirations; be sure you want to move in similar directions. Weak people make weak partners. Without resources within themselves, they whine for your attention, make unreasonable demands on your time, express jealousy where no cause exists. Only strong, complete, positive people can love strongly, completely, in positive ways. Only when the sense of "me" is strong, can a relationship be strong enough to form a lasting, successful "us."

Today I celebrate my wholeness.

DAY 73

"If you cannot find peace within yourself,
you will never find it anywhere else."
— Marvin Gaye

In Liberia, an army of dope-controlled children wreak terror on civilians. In Bosnia, Muslims and Serbs vow unending hatred. In South America, covert strikes are carried out by blood-thirsty mercenaries. In our own communities, stray bullets from gang warfare indiscriminately kill young and old, innocent and guilty. What are we fighting over? If we "win," will that be the end of it? Will we be satisfied with our victory? Peace begins in the heart and soul of each of us. It spreads throughout our bodies, calming and strengthening. It permeates our minds with the voice of reason. Inner peace is the most strengthening force on earth. It stills raging thoughts, muzzles smoking guns, and halts violent actions. Inner peace must be achieved before we can hope for outward peace. How can you find inner peace? Turn to yourself for answers; you're the best authority on what's good or bad for you. Take time for reflection. Dig deep into your hidden self. Take time for prayer. Reach high for Him from whom nothing is hidden.

I'm not too busy to spend time with myself and my God.

DAY 74

> "If you know what you want, you will recognize it when you see it."
>
> —Bill Cosby

In researching this book, I used many resources. One was a large volume borrowed from the public library. Several weeks later, I received an overdue notice. Sure that there was a mistake, I went to see the librarian. "Why don't you look again," she told me. So I looked again and again but still no book. In desperation, I was just about to pay for the book and be done with it when the librarian said, "Wait a minute," delving into her computer. Up came a screen with a complete description of the book – it's size, number of pages, etc. Armed with the description, I went back to my office and, after a cursory look, found the book. It was simply a matter of knowing what I was looking for. Once I knew what I wanted, I was able to recognize it when I came upon it. Do you know what you want? Are you sure of what you're looking for? Will you recognize it when you see it?

Today I will identify three things I want out of life.

DAY 75

"Mental violence . . . injures only the person whose thoughts are violent. . . . Mental non-violence . . . has potency which the world does not yet know."
—Mohandas K. Ghandi

Individual energy is a limited resource. Each of us has only so much energy to expend each day on the business of living. Thought requires energy. When thought-energy is burned on violent thinking, there is less energy available for nonviolent thinking. The same is true for nonviolent thought. The big difference is in the results. Violent thoughts eat away at our being, slowly eroding all that is good in us and propelling us to actions that hurt us and others. Nonviolent thoughts stimulate creativity. Our thought-energy is turned to finding and implementing productive solutions that benefit ourselves, those around us, and eventually our global community. You wouldn't turn on the faucet and allow the precious, limited, life-sustaining resource of fresh water to run until the well is dry. Thought-energy is just as precious and limited a resource. Why waste it on violent thinking that can only bring destruction to yourself and others?

Today I'll practice energy conservation by using my thought-energy for positive, empowering thinking.

> "I'm no martyr. I just had a hard day at
> work. My feet were hurting and I was
> too tired to give up my seat."
>
> — Rosa Parks

Rosa Parks saw a problem, applied a simple solution, and became a hero of the civil rights era. She didn't set out to be a hero; she didn't set out to defy "the system" or to cause the unrest that followed her action. She wasn't making a statement. In fact, she was neither loud nor obvious. She was simply too tired to move her aching feet to the back of the bus. Yet, the dignity of her simple act sent shockwaves across the South and launched a movement that changed a nation. Success is like that. The successful person is neither boisterous nor boastful, conceited nor arrogant. Heroes and heroines are created when sensitivity and insight are translated into simple actions and applied to situations to solve problems and bring about change. Do your actions reflect sensitivity and insight? Are you right now, today, becoming someone's hero?

Today I will think before I act and act in ways that preserve the dignity of myself and others.

DAY 77

"Let's get busy!"

— Arsenio Hall

Getting busy is the first step to success! Nothing good, nothing fruitful, nothing of great benefit comes without work. In America today we see a widespread deterioration of the work ethic. More people do less, leaving fewer people to do more. Developing a can do attitude takes hard work. It means getting off your duff and getting out your resume. It means working over, around, and through obstacles to achieve your goals. It means getting to work on your relationships, your education, your job skills – on all areas of your life. On your journey to success, you'll be kept busy. You won't have time to complain about others or to cry over failures. You won't have time to worry about what others are saying or doing. You'll be so caught up in your progress that work will become joy, improvements will become blessings, relationships will be healed, and talents will be developed. Income, self-respect, and dignity will grow in direct proportion to the energy you exert. As you travel the road to success, you'll be gathering blessings for yourself and others.

Today is one of the busiest days of my life – I'm working on myself!

"Nothing will ever be attempted if all possible obstacles must first be overcome."
—Samuel Johnson

"I would, except . . ." "I could, but . . ." "I was going to, only . . ." How many times a day do you hear phrases like these? How many times a day do you say similar things yourself? Nothing stands in your way of succeeding so much as you yourself. That's right, *you are your own biggest obstacle.* Sure, in a perfect world you'd have enough time, money, education, help, support – whatever – to help you soar to success. But then, in a perfect world you wouldn't have to strive for success, you'd already have it! List the obstacles you believe are keeping you from your goal. List only true roadblocks – things that are absolutely, unequivocally, 100% impossible to overcome. Chances are, your list will be a lot shorter than you expected.

Today I will get out of my own way to success!

DAY 79

"Your mind is what makes everything else work."

—Kareem Abdul-Jabbar

Without warning, a drunk driver careened around the corner, jumped the curb, and struck the young mother as she stood with her child waiting for the bus. She was left paralyzed from the neck down. Never again would she walk, feed herself, hug her child, or even take care of her own personal hygiene needs. Yet within months of the accident, the young woman was learning to compensate with her brain for the things she could no longer do with her body. While she couldn't hold a book, she could still read to her child. Although she couldn't feed herself, by having a table moved into her room, she could share mealtime with her family. With the help of a written inventory, she could dictate the weekly shopping list, the clothes her child would need for school, the spring house cleaning schedule. In short, she was using her mind to make her world work. The mind controls every action in life. We think, decide, and plan in our minds before we take physical action. It follows, therefore, that the way we think will influence the way we live. By envisioning yourself in the job you strive for, the relationship you long for, and the place you desire to be, you put your inner thoughts to work in making positive changes in your outer world.

Today I will see myself as the successful person I'm working on becoming.

DAY 80

> "The only justification for looking down
> on others is to pick them up."
>
> —Jesse Jackson

Remember the story of Cinderella? Her family cruelly abused her, relegating her to the most menial position and then looking down on her for the lowly tasks she was forced to perform. It took a total stranger, the prince, to see beyond the dirt and grime to the beautiful, innocent person she was. The prince looked down at Cinderella for the sole purpose of picking her up. It's not much of stretch to compare the prince in the Cinderella story to God in our lives. God looks down on us amid our sin and failure and stretches out His hand to pick us up. He goes so far as to send His own Son as the supreme sacrifice necessary for our uplifting. How dare we do less for our fellow sisters and brothers? None of us knows the potential that lies beneath the dirty exterior of a street person. None of us knows the wisdom the old, the poor, the lowliest among us possesses. In many of our communities and churches, people volunteer to feed the hungry, visit the shut-in, and give to the homeless out of a sense of superiority. It makes them feel good to see how much above others they are. All the charitable acts in the world are done in vain unless they are rendered in a sincere effort to uplift others. No one can know true success until she or he has recognized the equality of the lowest and has unselfishly worked to help them succeed too.

My success occurs in direct proportion to my efforts to help someone else achieve today.

DAY 81

> "It was clear as day. I saw myself beating
> the odds and coming back to play again."
> —Bo Jackson

"They don't hire/admit/promote etc. people of color. The odds are against me. There's no point in knocking myself out trying. They'll never let me succeed." How often do we hear statements such as these? Ironic, isn't it, that usually they're uttered by those who have failed because they haven't tried! Sure, we all know that the odds for winning are often stacked against people of color. But then, so are the odds in the lottery, the casinos of Atlantic City and Las Vegas, and games at local carnivals. Yet we see people of color flocking to the casinos and standing in long lines to purchase lottery tickets. Blaming the odds is a cop out. It is an excuse, and a poor one at that, for not trying. Look around. Take stock of the thousands of successful people of color. They succeeded because they refused to accept failure. They set goals, made plans to achieve them, and worked without ceasing to beat the odds. So can you! Too long we've whined that the world isn't fair, that the system is stacked against us, that we just can't get a break. We must make our own breaks. How? Through hard work. By believing in ourselves. By holding in our minds a vision of the person we want to be and refusing to accept anything less.

Today I will stop blaming others and start holding myself accountable for my own success.

"It's not the load that breaks you down, it's
the way you carry it."

—Lena Horne

In Jack London's immortal story, "The Call of the
Wild," the inexperienced owners of Buck, a sled dog
in the Yukon, demanded that the team pull an im-
properly loaded sled. Despite repeated beatings and
abuse, Buck refused. The rest of the ill-fated team,
along with their owners, perished in the effort. It wasn't
that the load was too heavy. Buck went on to pull
even heavier loads for a subsequent beloved master.
The difference was the way the cargo was loaded.
The burdens of life are like that cargo. Our success in
bearing our loads depends upon the way we choose
to carry them. If we undertake our journey to success
with a negative attitude, we soon find that we are
"overloaded." Conversely, as successful people we can
recognize that while it may not be possible to lighten
our loads, we can find positive ways to carry them.
We can prioritize rather than tackling the entire burden at once. We can break our loads down into man-
ageable pieces. We can "work smart" by applying our
resources to the tasks at hand. Most of all, we can
recruit help -- the divine help of God who promises
that He will never lay upon us burdens too heavy for
us to bear.

*Today I will lighten my burden by sharing its weight
with God.*

DAY 83

"It's okay to color outside the lines."
—Jimi Hendrix

The teacher was perplexed. Little Bobby was a bright, successful student, yet his artwork displayed an astonishing assortment of blue dogs, purple moons, and a variety of "inappropriate" renditions of commonplace objects randomly adorning the entire page. After repeated attempts to get Bobby to complete his projects "correctly," the exasperated teacher finally asked the reason for his unorthodox technique. "The other kids color things the way they really are," Bobby explained. "I like to color things the way I wish they could be." Success comes with seeing things not only as they are, but also as they can be. This is the difference between sight and vision. You can look around you and see nothing but the facts: the stack of unpaid bills, the worn carpet, the X-ed out Help Wanted ads. However, you can choose to see all these things but add the extra dimension of "vision." With vision you see the rewards of your new career, elimination of debt, a move to a new home, upward mobility in the work place. You are coloring outside the lines of current reality and glimpsing the reality of your vision. That's what vision does. It lifts us above the ordinary and shows us the extraordinary. Why settle for the ordinary when you have the extraordinary? All you need is the vision to create it!

I have extraordinary vision! I see extraordinary sights!

DAY 84

"In spite of everything that was done to
me and my race, in spite of the adversity
and the bitter moments, again we rise!"
—Maya Angelou

Across our nation, black faces are appearing in advertisements, text books, and all sorts of printed materials. Many of our brothers and sisters are busily engaged in rewriting the history that for too long has been presented from the white perspective in books primarily written by white historians. The accomplishments of people of color are at last receiving the recognition they deserve. This advancement of the black experience is an important and worthy endeavor. However, it is worthy only as a means to an end. We must guard against our new-found status becoming an end unto itself. It is not enough for our children to learn of the isolated successes of their foreparents. These lessons must be used as a launching pad for ever greater achievements. Our past as both individuals and as a race must serve to motivate us to work for a higher standard of living. Knowledge of what our foreparents accomplished in spite of adversity must serve to spur us to rise above our backgrounds and to create a new history of success for ourselves and our children.

I will apply the lessons of those who went before me to the journey I am embarked upon today.

DAY 85

> "The best way to prepare for tomorrow
> is to do your best today."
>
> —Lou Gossett, Jr.

"Please, Reverend, will you talk to my boy?" "All I'm asking, Pastor, is that you speak to my daughter. I know she'll listen to you." In my role as a minister in a predominantly black urban area, I am often called upon to counsel the children, spouses, and significant others of those in my congregation. Time and again in counseling sessions I hear, "I've tried but I can't . . . get a good job . . . get good grades . . . do what it takes to earn a promotion . . . fulfill the requirements for graduation." Invariably, these statements are accompanied by a host of excuses for the "can'ts." I've learned to ask one simple question: What have you done to try? The answer is almost always the same: The person has not tried! Success requires 110% effort. If you want a good job later, you must stay in school today. If you want a promotion at work, you must bring your best attitude and effort to your current assignments. If you want to succeed as a spouse, parent, friend, you must take steps now to learn the techniques to accomplish your goals. Don't wait until its time to look for a job to learn job skills. Don't wait until after the wedding to find out what it takes to make a marriage succeed. Don't wait until the baby is born (or even conceived) to acquire positive parenting skills. Success tomorrow comes from preparation today.

I will make no more life decisions without being prepared for their outcomes.

"The essence of optimism is that it takes no account of the present, but it is a source of inspiration, of vitality and hope where others have resigned."
—Dietrich Bonhoeffer

A child, knowing there is no money for Christmas toys, still believes that somehow Santa will come. A family, told there is little chance a loved one will live through the night, continues to believe that a miracle can happen. Optimism is not the denial of reality. Rather, optimism is recognition of what is and belief in what can be. What happens when beliefs fail? Optimistic people reach down inside themselves and find some good in the worst situations. Sometimes, despite steadfast belief in that possible miracle, the loved one dies. While optimistic people grieve the loss just as deeply as others, they are able to turn a negative to a positive: the death is grievous, but the family discovers ways to strengthen their ties. Optimism is a strong motivator, both to the person who possesses it and to those who witness it. Optimistic people conquer failure. Rather than say, "I'm beaten," they ask themselves, "What can I learn from this disappointment? How can I, despite the odds, achieve success?"

There is a positive side to every disappointment. Today I will repeat this phrase until it becomes part of my outlook on life.

> "Kindness is the language that the deaf
> can hear and the dumb can understand."
> —Desmond Tutu

In the rock opera *Tommy*, The Who tells the story of a deaf, dumb, and blind boy who was brutalized by his uncle. Despite his multiple handicaps, Tommy finds fulfillment in being the very best pinball player around. He can't hear the ping of the pins, the crack of the flippers, or the bells of the score as it increases. But he can sense the kindness, however false and self-serving, of the gang that pits him against all contenders. The same phenomena can be seen in the elderly who, though unable to walk, talk, or even control their bodily functions, respond to the gentle touch of a kind caretaker. When we learn the language of kindness we learn an important lesson shared by all successful people. Certainly we can point to millionaires who are known for their self-centeredness and contempt for others. But despite their money, I contend that they never achieve true success. The very fact that we know them by their nefarious reputations is proof of their failure in the most important area – the regard in which they're held by others. God dwells in each human being. Would we treat God cruelly? How then can we hope to be successful unless we practice kindness toward our sisters and brothers?

I recognize the face of God in the faces of those around me and will treat them accordingly.

DAY 88

"Don't face the day until you've faced God."
—Maya Angelou

When I think back to my childhood, I remember how ashamed I felt when I'd done something that would disappoint my grandmother who raised me. Sometimes I felt so awful that I wanted to be caught so that I could accept the consequences and begin again. Facing God is like that. When we begin each day by facing up to our shortcomings, we receive the comforting assurance that we are still loved. We have the wonderful opportunity to begin again. Facing God doesn't mean that we'll escape the consequences of our actions. God never promises that our fellow humans will be as forgiving as He is. Yet facing God gives us the strength to accept the earthly consequences of our actions. By forming the habit of facing God at the beginning of each new day, we can often escape trouble before it happens. Knowing how ashamed we'll feel in the presence of the One who loves us so much is our best guard against behaviors and actions that cause us to fail in our quest to become the successful people God calls us to be.

I may never achieve perfection but I can begin working toward perfection by facing God today.

DAY 89

"Sooner or later we've got to polish ourselves
up, we've got to let the shine come through."
—Lou Rawls

You baby boomers will remember the fantastic
song "Let The Sun Shine In" from the marvelous hit
show *Aquarius*. To be successful in overcoming a can't
do environment, all of us must come to the point
where we let the sun shine. This sun can be the recognition of how far we've come toward achieving our
goals. It can be the acknowledgment of the obstacles
we've overcome, the negative behaviors we've conquered, the personal victories we've achieved. Periodic "time outs" to reward ourselves with well-earned
praise are important milestones on our journey to success. There's nothing wrong with being good to yourself. This isn't self-indulgence. It isn't a false assumption that you've reached the end of your journey and
have no more road left to travel. Rather, letting the
sunshine of personal satisfaction illuminate the person you're becoming lights the roadway ahead, keeps
us motivated. It rejuvenates the soul, allows us to appreciate our progress, and rekindles our zest for developing our can do attitude.

*I've come a long way. Today I will pause to congratu-
late myself on my progress.*

DAY 90

> "It's better to look ahead and prepare than
> to look back and regret."
> —Jackie Joyner Kersee

Do you know the two saddest words in the English language? "If only!" Those two little words hold a world of regret, remorse, missed opportunities, and damaged dreams. If only I had stayed in school . . . If only I had chosen my mate more wisely . . . If only I had delayed getting pregnant, paid more attention to my child, been kinder to my parents. How different our lives would be if we could replace the "if onlys" of our past with "I'm glad I did." Is it really possible to live life with no regrets? Probably not, but there is a way to greatly reduce regrets and the agony they cause, and that is to look ahead and prepare. By looking ahead and preparing, we equip ourselves to meet the future unhampered by inadequacies. Choosing to prepare is especially difficult when we can't or won't see the future opportunities for which we're preparing. The effort necessary to pass a course for which you see no future application appears pointless. None of us knows what the future holds. Preparing now to face many options is the best way to succeed in the exciting, unknown future.

Today I will look ahead and prepare so that tomorrow I won't look back and despair.

DAY 91

> "There's more power in the open hand
> than in the clenched fist."
>
> —Dr. Martin Luther King, Jr.

Rosa Parks rests her weary body in the only available seat and quietly refuses to move to the back of the bus. A lone little girl braves jeering crowds to begin her first day of classes at an elementary school in the South. In an isolated Missouri laboratory, George Washington Carver plugs away at his experiments with peanuts. A continent away, Desmond Tutu offers no resistance as he's led off to prison. On country roads and city thoroughfares, Martin Luther King leads thousands in a movement based on peace, unity, and non-violence. The examples they set are so power-ful that, though years may pass and generations may grow old and die, their force will never fade. Each of them, and countless more, made their mark not with bullets, but with bravery – the sort of bravery that gives credence to their beliefs. If we are to succeed as a people and as individuals, we must adopt the concept of non-violence and apply it to every area of our lives. Success never comes by overpowering the weak. Domestic violence, child abuse, violence in our homes, schools, and communities only serve to enslave us. The power to succeed is the power to rise above violence. Brutality toward persons or property dehumanizes the perpetrator, diminishes progress, and destroys the achievements of those who have gone before.

I have within me the power to change myself and my world.

DAY 92

"God speaks wherever He finds a humble, listening ear."

—Lena Horne

Even by backwoods West Virginia standards, my grandmother was poor. Yet my grandmother was rich in faith and the spiritual gifts that made her life abundant with blessings. When family circumstances deposited me on her doorstep, she welcomed me with open arms. She never paused to consider the costs involved in taking a six-year-old into her two room home. She trusted God to provide for my material needs while she provided the loving guidance necessary to raise a growing boy. Years later, she gave me a wonderful gift. That gift was her Bible. But this wasn't any ordinary Bible. Throughout the volume, my grandmother had marked countless passages with the cryptic notation, TAP. "TAP?" I asked myself. What could this possibly mean. Driven to know, I put the question to my beloved grandmother. "Why Jimmy," she replied, "I thought you knew. TAP stands for 'Tried and Proven.' I've written it beside each of God's promises that I've tested in my life. As you'll see, He's never let me down." Grandma wasn't an educated person. She was neither sophisticated nor trained in religious philosophies. Hers was the simple faith of a humble believer that transforms the lives of others.

Today I will listen for the voice of God, knowing that all answers come from Him.

DAY 93

> "If a man hasn't discovered something that he will die for, he isn't fit to live."
> —Dr. Martin Luther King, Jr.

There are those who say the assassination of Dr. Martin Luther King, Jr. caused his great work to be left unfinished. Perhaps this is true. How many people have been inspired to continue the work so well begun by this great hero of the civil rights movement! It's a sad commentary on the human condition that disaster is the greatest motivator. Yet history has proven the motivational power of martyrs. Perhaps only through tragedy are we able to glimpse victory. If this is true, would we not be better off forsaking our quest for victory? The tragedy suffered by Dr. King, Robert and John Kennedy, Abraham Lincoln, the freedom riders whose deeds are remembered even if their names are forgotten, and countless other victims of racism, are certainly an inspiration to us all. Tragedy is not a requirement for success. What one thinks gives meaning to life. The single-minded pursuit of that one overriding goal must be at the heart and core of every action. While the successful person may not be *called upon* to die for that one thing, he or she must be *willing* to die for it. Only then will sacrifice become joy, hardship become blessing, and life become the meaningful experience God intended it to be.

Today I forsake scattered pursuits, trivial goals, and focus instead on the purposes that will bring personal fulfillment to my life.

Day 94

"I would just like to get on with my life."
—Anita Hill

Why is it that those who are first to tout the lessons to be learned from adversity seem to have such little hardship in their own lives? Why does the rain seem to fall only in others' backyard? If good things come to those who wait, why do some people move from success to success without pausing to appreciate each victory? In the face of such unfairness, platitudes ring hollow. If you're looking for explanations, justifications, or reassurances that someday "they" will "get theirs," you've come to the wrong person. I simply have no answers. What I do know, though, is that dwelling on the inequities of life is unproductive and self-defeating. Success comes to those who are able to take adversity in stride and move on. If you're one of those privileged people who sail through life with only mountain top experiences, congratulations. My hope for you is that you appreciate your good fortune and remember to give thanks for it. But if you're like most of us (all of us, I suspect), my prayer is that you will find the strength to believe in yourself and your abilities no matter what curves life throws your way. Success comes in varying degrees. Overcomers will achieve a higher level of success than those who have never faced – and conquered – the test of adversity.

I'm moving my life onward and upward.

DAY 95

"You don't always have to have something
to say."

—Sammy Davis, Jr.

A young boy signed on as a live-in hand on a large
cattle farm. He did his work well and the farmer was
well pleased. One night a fierce tornado struck the
area. Awakened by the storm, the farmer ran to the
boy's attic room. Despite his frantic efforts, the farmer
was unable to rouse the sleeping boy. Not wanting to
waste time, the farmer rushed out to check on the
animals. He found the barn door securely bolted, the
sturdy pasture gate in place, the next day's feed carefully stored in the rain-proof bins. In fact, the farmer
could find nothing left undone. Still, the farmer was
angry. Certainly the boy should have gotten up and
accompanied him on his midnight rounds rather than
remaining peacefully asleep in his warm, dry bed. The
next morning the farmer confronted the boy. "Didn't
you hear the storm last night?" he asked. "I had to run
around by myself in the wind and rain checking on
the animals." Surprised at his anger, the astonished
boy looked the farmer straight in the eyes. "I can sleep
on stormy nights," came his meek reply. How wonderful it would be if we would carry out our tasks
with such thoroughness that when the storms of life
come, we could rest peacefully, secure in the knowledge that we are prepared.

*Today I will replace my weak excuses with positive
actions.*

DAY 96

"I figured that if I said it often enough, I would convince the world that I was the greatest."
—Muhammad Ali

Our thoughts are like a tape recorder. They play their messages over and over until they are assimilated into our very beings. We become the people we tell ourselves we are. If our internal messages are positive, we become positive people. Conversely, if our internal messages are negative, we begin to believe the negative thoughts we repeat to ourselves. We act in accordance with our negative messages. We become inept, unreliable, incompetent people doomed to fail at whatever we try. With our failure a foregone conclusion, we soon decide there is no reason to try at all. We adopt the "can't do" beliefs of our negative environment. Once we form this image of ourselves as a failure, we begin living up to it. Successful people are positive people. This doesn't mean that they are blind to their shortcomings and weaknesses. Rather, they face their deficiencies head-on and develop strategies to overcome or compensate for them. God does not give us all equal talents. The piano virtuoso may be horrible in science; the writer may never conquer the mysteries of balancing a checkbook. Successful people acknowledge that they will never be great at everything.

I will cultivate the positive and weed out the negative.

"Opportunity will not only knock on your door,
if you're not careful, it will knock you down."
—Wally "Famous" Amos

Believing that God wants you to succeed and that God has a plan for your success leaves you open to all kinds of bumps, bruises, and hard knocks. You see, God doesn't give up on us, even when we give up on ourselves. He constantly opens opportunities to us. When we fail to recognize an opportunity or close the door on a chance for God-ordained success, He confronts us with yet another possibility. So many fathers and mothers gladly work hard all their lives to give their children the best possible chances in life. They dream of providing opportunities that they themselves never had. They make sacrifices so that they can put a little aside each month for their child's education. Then the day comes when all their sacrifices will be acknowledged, all their dreams fulfilled. And what happens? The child rejects the opportunity to go to college, choosing instead to "do it my own way." The parents are crushed. They know from experience the value of education. Yet do they turn their backs on the child? No, the parents never give up hope. Like the father in the story of the prodigal son, parents wait in the wings, ready to rescue their child from folly and help him/her find the path to success.

Today I will listen for God's knock and respond to the opportunities He brings to my life.

Day 98

Above the shimmering beauty of Washington's illustrious structures stands the Washington Monument. Its graceful image is mirrored in the serene surface of the Reflecting Pool. Its majestic shadow falls on young and old, rich and poor, touching all with a rare sense of noble tribute. Each year thousands of tourists visit the monument and marvel at its loftiness. Standing at its base, they are dwarfed not only by its height but by the noble ideals it symbolizes. Glimpsing the Washington Monument for the first time is an unforgettable experience; revisiting it again and again does not diminish its inspiring effect. Yet for those with the stamina to climb the steps and view our nation's capital from the top, the Monument offers a different perspective. From that high vantage point, visitors are treated to a vast panorama of the city known worldwide as the heart of democracy. The view from the base is impressive, but the view from the top is expressive of the ongoing "noble experiment" that is America. The true thrill of victory is a mountain top experience. Gaining that victory requires an uphill run. The road to success has always run uphill. Perhaps it is only by putting forth the effort to make the climb that we can come to appreciate the view from the top.

Today I'll scale the mountain and experience the view.

DAY 99

> "The secret to happiness is not getting what
> you want but wanting what you get."
> —George Pleasant

When I received my dream car for my 21st birthday, I was ecstatic. It didn't matter that the tires were bald, the engine wouldn't turn over, replacement parts were impossible to come by, and the wooden floorboards were rotted through. I was confident that these "minor" problems could be taken care of by a mechanically-inclined friend. After many months of watching my car grow dusty in the driveway and many more dollars spent in making it minimally roadworthy, I was at last able to drive my dream car. My first trip was to the supermarket. This proved to be more than a simple first spin. Because the passenger seat didn't lock in place, I couldn't use a car seat. This necessitated hiring a babysitter for my infant daughter. The electrical system was a little fluky – either the lights went off or the windshield wipers came on with each bump. The trunk key had been lost over the years and without a back seat, the grocery bags had to be unloaded and the food placed on, under, and behind the front seats. The gas gauge didn't work, and on the return trip from the supermarket the engine sputtered once, then died. My dream car quickly became more of a nightmare. Soon I longed to trade my spiffy little sports car for a dull but reliable station wagon. I learned an expensive but important lesson: Happiness was more easily found in wanting what I had than in having what I wanted.

Today I will take stock of the things I already have and appreciate them for the happiness they bring to my life.

Day 100

"Our vision will equal the promise."
—Haki R. Madhubuti

Many black women have a vision of black men – lazy, abusive, irresponsible, no good. Whether this vision was born from actions that occurred yesterday, last week, last year, or so long ago we can't remember its origin, it is real. It colors our actions and reactions, our relationships or our avoidance of relationships. Whatever our vision is, it equals the promise – the promise we make to ourselves of how our futures will be. Yes, black men have committed all sorts of "crimes" against black women for all sorts of reasons. But how much of a woman's vision creates, even encourages, the actions of black men? Today both sexes are standing on the brink of change. Our vision of that change can and will equal the promised outcome of that change. Black women must forgive black men for past transgressions, *and* they must adopt a new vision of what can be. Black men must adopt a new vision of marriage, commitment, responsibility, and equality. The positive vision of new behaviors by both sexes *will* fulfill the promise of couples of color living in harmony with equal respect and authority, striving together for relational success.

Today I will adopt a new, positive vision of my mate. I believe in the promise of a stronger relationship.

DAY 101

"In search of my mother's garden, I found my own."

—Alice Walker

Food, clothing, shelter — these are the basic needs of life. It's not hard to understand why these needs must be met. But what about the other needs that are so basic to humanity? The need for human contact; the need to communicate and be understood; the need to be loved — surely these can't be denied. Understanding these needs begins with understanding yourself. Know that as a child of God, you need the love and understanding of your fellow brothers and sisters. Know, too, that getting your needs met begins with you. Take time to get to know yourself. Communicate with your inner spirit. Learn to understand your deepest feelings, the things you fear the most, the things that please you most. Take care of yourself — true, nurturing care. Love your own body, your fine mind, your unique spirit. Understanding and meeting your own needs is the starting point for becoming the kind of person who both reaches out and is reached out to by others. Human contact, understanding, communication, and love will come *to you* from others only after it first comes *from you*.

Today I will take time to understand and meet my own needs.

> "You never know which key unlocks the safe."
>
> —Bryant Gumbel

An early 1960s television show featured a large treasure chest. Contestants got to choose from a rack of keys. If their key fit the chest, they received all the prizes inside. Of course, there were only a few contestants per show and many, many keys from which to choose. People would stand in line for hours just hoping to get tickets to be in the TV audience. Once inside, their chances of being picked as a contestant were slim. Yet their hopes were undaunted. Everyone was sure she or he could find the key to unlock the chest if just given the chance. Those same people who were willing to go to such great lengths on the TV show, were often the very people who were ignoring the chances to find the right keys to open the treasure chest of prizes in their lives. Are you struggling in a relationship? Have you tried the many keys that will unlock the feelings, hopes, and dreams of your partner? Are you struggling in your career? Have you tried to find the right key to advancement? Maybe your struggles are in school or in your community. Perhaps you're locked in a spiritual struggle? Explore the many avenues open to you. Try each key until you find the right one. Remember, you'll never know which key unlocks the safe until you've tried them all.

I hold the key to my own success. Today I will use my inner keys to open a locked door in my life.

Day 103

"There's no goal too far, no mountain too high."

—Wilma Rudolph

So often people tell me that the reason they're not pursuing anything is that they don't know what they want to pursue. I always ask, "What are you doing to find out?" This is usually answered by an embarrassed pause, muttering, and finally an admission that they're not doing anything. You can't let time keep passing you by while you wait for inspiration. Remember, *inspiration comes most often through perspiration*. Define your goals, then GO FOR IT! Keep trying. If one plan fails, formulate another. Never stop seeking. It's okay to change directions; it's *not okay* to have no direction. Remember the words from the hit song: "Ain't no mountain high enough."

Today I'll experience a "runner's high" as I race toward a goal.

"Every new idea is an impossibility until it is born."

—Secretary Ron Brown

Erich Segal's best selling book *Prizes* tells the story of several scientists locked in a battle to make new breakthroughs in genetics — breakthroughs that will cure diseases and halt the aging process by manipulating human genes. Their ultimate goal is the Nobel Prize. The pathways they take to reach the prize are uncharted waters. Each idea, no matter how bizarre or unorthodox, is viewed as a possibility until it is proved to be an impossibility. The scientists who finally stand before the King of Sweden on the great stage in Stockholm are the ones who went to the greatest lengths to prove possibility before admitting impossibility. Think of the potential for success if we would only learn to apply the techniques of the science world to our own lives! Instead of assuming anything is impossible until proven possible, the assumption would be reversed. Everything would be assumed possible until all avenues had been explored. The potential for future possibility would be open ended. That's really how it is, you know. Nothing is impossible if you want it badly enough to fight for the highest prize — success.

With God, all things are possible. With me and God together, nothing is impossible.

Day 105

> "This is a tough game. There are times when you've got to play hurt, when you've got to block out the pain."
>
> —Shaquille O'Neal

We all have times when life deals us painful blows. A relationship fails despite your best efforts. A well-deserved promotion is given to someone else. The financial aid you need for tuition doesn't come through in time for registration. A loved one dies, moves, or separates from you in some way. A child is arrested. An accident occurs or an illness hits that changes your life in a split second. None of us is immune to the pain of life. It's how you handle the pain that makes a difference in your ultimate "game plan." The Bible tells us that "there's a time for every purpose under heaven." There's a time to mourn — to allow yourself to grieve over your losses, to pause awhile and let the pain begin to heal. But there's also a time to begin again, to go back out onto the playing field, to acknowledge that while you may be damaged, you're not dead. Life is a tough game. Succeeding at your life goals means that sometimes you have to "play hurt." But healing does come, and it comes most quickly to those who get back out there, put themselves back on track, block out the pain, and simply get on with life.

Today I will acknowledge my pain then put it aside and get back to pursuing my goals.

DAY 106

"Honey, it's so easy to talk a good game. What we need are folks who will do something."
—Congresswoman Maxine Waters

There's a saying in the well-known twelve step recovery program: "You might be talking the talk, but are you walking the walk?" We all know people who can talk a good story. But when it comes to action, they fall by the wayside. Talk really is cheap. It's the walk that's expensive. It costs dearly. It requires us to sacrifice, to work when we're tired, to try when we're weary, to move on, over or through every obstacle. It costs us our spare time. There's a time to sit down and think, plan, even talk over your goals with appropriate people. Then there's a time to stop talking and start acting. Ask yourself: Am I a talker or an actor? Am I walking the walk or just talking the talk? Be completely honest with yourself. Then act according to your answer. If you're walking the walk and acting on your plans, good for you! You're doing something beneficial for yourself that will have positive ramifications for everyone around you. If you're still stuck at the talk stage, revamp your plans. Make a definite timeline for positive actions. Set a deadline for talking and a launch time for walking. Stick to your schedule. Periodically review your progress. Be sure your next review is a great one.

Today I will set a definite time for taking a new step on my walk toward success.

Day 107

"We can finally say that we're in love."
—Whitney Houston & Bobby Brown

As a pastor, I do a lot of pre-marriage counseling. I always ask the couples two questions. First, I ask, "Why do you want to get married?" The ready reply is, "Because we're in love." Then I ask, "Tell me what it is you love about him/her." Here the couples pause. I can see the internal struggle as they consider their answers. I know they're thinking, "I can't say I love him because he has a good job. I can't say I love her because she's educated, beautiful, or has a great body." It's amazing that such a simple question can cause such a dilemma for two people who are about to join their lives together forever. What does it mean to be "in love"? I'm not sure I know myself. I don't think of love as something you can be in. Being in implies that you could also be *out*. If you could run out of love for the other person, you have no business getting married. Love is a constant; it may change but it never diminishes. Love must cover you from within, without, backward, forward, around, and through. Love means acting out of love even when you're tired, busy, or distracted. Love means being willing to put everything second to the other person, yet knowing that the other person will never ask you to do this. Love bears all things, believes all things, hopes all things, endures all things. *Love* never ends.

Today I will practice the art of loving in a pure, unselfish way.

DAY 108

"Man, nothing happens until somebody
cuts on the juice."

—Louis Armstrong

Have you ever had the embarrassing experience
of calling in a repair person only to find that the appliance wasn't plugged in? I have, and believe me, I
felt foolish. No matter how intricately made a thing is,
in the end, making it work comes down to the simple
act of cutting on the juice. What are the sources of
juice in your life? What energizes you, gets you moving in the morning and keeps you moving throughout
the day? Maybe it's the loving greeting you receive
from your spouse, or the sweet face of your child
reaching up to kiss you before you leave. Maybe it's
sunshine or a brisk breeze, the sound of birds chirping or of rain on the roof. Whatever your particular
source of power, it stems from the one eternal source,
God. However you conceive of God, God is the one
divine power source. God is love, therefore God is in
each loving relationship. God is nature, therefore God
is in the sun and the rain, the wind and the river. If
you feel that you're not energized, that your life is
going nowhere, perhaps you simply haven't cut on
the juice.

*Today I will plug in to God before plugging into the
world.*

DAY 109

"Sometimes I just feel so good all over."
—Stephanie Mills

You wake up in the morning, yawn, stretch, rub yourself all over. You jump into the shower and feel yourself come alive. Your outfit matches, you're having a great hair day, everything is going fine. You just feel so good all over; you know nothing can wreck this day. What replenishing miracles are days like this! Thank God, and I mean really stop and thank God, for these wonderful days of respite from problems. Each one is a treasure. These days give us the strength to get through the not-so-good days. When you find one of these little unexpected pearls of joy along your pathway, value it and remember it. Let it be a source of sustenance on the long stretches between such moments. Realize, too, that you've earned your feel good days. They're your reward for hard work and dedication. The harder you work to implement your plans and to reach your goals, the more frequently these wonderful feel good days will appear. Why? Because you'll be feeling better about yourself, your life, and your world.

I'm really moving. I feel good about my progress. I like me!

DAY 110

"Wait means never!"
—Dr. Martin Luther King, Jr.

"Instant gratification" is a 1980s term. It implies that some people are unable or unwilling to wait for what they want. They have to have it *now*! Of course, we can't have everything we want instantly. But too often, waiting is just a disguise for withholding. It's a ruse that has been practiced against people of color, women, minorities of any type, for far too long. However, when we practice the deceit of waiting against ourselves, it is the worse kind of dishonesty. Maybe you can't have what you want today, but you can begin working for it right now. Maybe all your wishes won't be granted, all your dreams won't come true, but waiting to pursue your goals is the surest way to guarantee that you'll never reach them. If you're stuck playing the waiting game, stop kidding yourself. You've become your own biggest obstacle. Stop making excuses! Stop lying to yourself. If you can do something tomorrow, you can begin to do it today. Get started — before waiting becomes never — before tomorrow becomes forever.

There's no better time to begin than today!

DAY 111

"Stretch your mind and fly."
—Rodney King

Desperate times prompt desperate actions. It is no accident that racism is breaking out in new, or newly-recognized places. We live in a time that has seen people of color reach new heights of achievement. Despite oppression, repression, and depression, we are there — in the board rooms, the operating rooms, the computer rooms, the penthouse rooms. Our presence, our force, our abilities and capabilities are outshining the sun. They can no longer be denied, ignored, or unappreciated. Unfortunately, this causes a great deal of fear among those "establishment" people who just don't understand. We're not trying to hurt anyone else, we're just trying to stay alive ourselves. Really alive! Alive to all the goodness and the goodies the good life brings. There's abundance in this world. It just takes a little redistribution to get things in proper balance. Who should be the new distributor? You! You must take charge of your own life. You must create and not escape. You must prepare now so that when you're compared later, you won't be found lacking. You must do more than just try to stay alive. You must work toward bringing the very fullness of life to yourself, while being sure not to deny it to others.

Today, I'll reach for the stars! No one is more deserving.

DAY 112

"I've got my faith, and that's all I need."
—Nelson Mandela

Jesus said that if you have faith as big as a mustard seed, you can move mountains. Have you ever seen a mustard seed? Well, unless your vision is perfect, you may never see one. Mustard seeds are among the smallest seeds in the world! Yet with faith only as big as that tiny speck, Jesus promises that you can do anything. Of course, Jesus was speaking of having faith in God. But Jesus also tells us that God dwells inside each of us. Does it not follow, then, that if you have faith in yourself you have faith in God who is within you? When you combine faith in God with faith in yourself, you don't need anything else. You can do it all, have it all, become it all! Nelson Mandela had faith in God and faith in himself. It's what kept him going through those long years of imprisonment. His faith took him from prisoner to president. He moved the mountain of apartheid. He moved the mountains of captivity, oppression, repression, regulation, and servitude. With faith, even faith so small as a mustard seed, you too can move the mountains in your life.

I'm a mover and a shaker. I believe in God and in myself.

> "Mountain, get out of my way!"
> —Montel Williams

"I was the kind of nerdy kid who always got sand kicked in his face," writes a renowned psychologist in a recent study on bullies. The study goes on to explain that bullies are often the most frightened people around. In fact, they're so afraid that they offer an intimidating offense as their greatest defense. Well, you sure could have fooled me! Still, I've come up against some pretty tough odds in my life — bullies bigger and meaner than I, barriers higher and wider than I, obstacles taller and greater than I. One thing I've learned: You can't run away! You have to face up to the bullies, the barriers, the mountains, and the obstacles. You have to be willing to create, educate, negotiate, and navigate. And sometimes you just plain have to say, "Get out of my way!" It's amazing how effective those five direct words can be in getting where you want to go. This is especially true when you're dealing with yourself — often your own biggest obstacle. How much time we waste arguing with ourselves, fooling ourselves, kidding ourselves, making excuses to and for ourselves. How often is that mountain that's in our way put there by us?

Today I'm a mountain mover and remover. I'm unstoppable!

Day 114

"When you face a crisis, you know who
your true friends are."

—Earvin "Magic" Johnson

A crisis hits — a sudden illness, accident, death.
The friends and family gather 'round. You hear from
and see so many people you haven't been in touch
with for years. It's amazing how a crisis draws folks
together. But it's in the weeks and months that follow
a crisis that you really discover your true friends.
They're the ones who were there at the bedside or
the graveside and are still there by *your* side after all
the others have gone. When all the flowers have
wilted, all the cakes have been devoured, all the cas-
seroles frozen, your true friends will still be there for
you. Why? Because true friendship blossoms in the
good times but puts down roots in the bad times. It
gives without counting the days or the ways. It's not
just there for you when you're on top — so that it can
share your limelight. It's not just there for you when
you're on the bottom — so it can share in your drama.
It's there for you all the time. And if no one is there
for you? Maybe you need to examine your own responses to others. True friendship is always a recipro-
cal relationship.

*I won't wait for a crisis. I'll spend time with a friend
today.*

DAY 115

"We must turn *toward* each other and not
on each other."

—Rev. Jesse Jackson

There's nothing sadder than a person who's forgotten where she or he has come from. To deny your roots is to deny the very soil where you were born, were nurtured, and grew. Yet throughout the thousands of years of recorded history, humanity's story has been one of people turning their backs on their roots. Success seems to be the driving force of natal amnesia. The higher one climbs socially, financially, intellectually, the greater the temptation to forget one's roots. How this has hurt us as a people! How it continues to hurt us! We struggle, we work, we succeed, and then we forget. We've become our own worse enemy! We don't have to worry about what others might do to us; we're doing the worse possible things to ourselves. We must turn GOT toward one another, not on one another! Those who are "there," what are you doing to help others arrive? Those who have made it, what are you doing to help others complete the journey? Those who are still in route, what are you doing to help others set out?

*Today I will remember my roots; never will I forget
my beginning.*

"There's nothing behind me except faith
and belief that the walls will come down."
—Rev. Leon Sullivan

Remember Joshua, that gallant prophet you learned about during your Sunday School days? Joshua was a mighty man of God. He was mighty in faith. He was mighty in belief. He was mighty in courage. Still, when God told him to go march around the city and the walls of Jerico would come tumbling down, it must have been Joshua's greatest test of faith. You know what happened, don't you? What always happens — *God does what God says He'll do*! How many times does God have to prove this? I sometimes think that if I were God I'd be pretty much out of patience, even with my beloved children. God doesn't want whiners and cryers. God doesn't want grumblers and complainers. God doesn't want people who demand that He prove Himself over and over again. *God's already proven everything*! Now all you have to do is take Him at His word! You don't need anything behind you except faith. You don't need anything inside you except belief. You don't need anything beneath, atop, around, under, through or out of you but God. Believe in God. Believe in yourself. The walls will come tumbling down!

There's nothing that can happen to me today that God and I together can't handle.

> "What you see is what you get."
> —Flip Wilson

One of my pet peeves is false advertising. Nothing makes me feel more ripped off than finding out I've been buying something I didn't know I was buying, or not buying something I thought I was paying for. For example, if I buy candy, I know I'm buying a sweet, sugary treat that tastes great but isn't too great for me. But if I buy cereal, I want to believe I'm buying a safe, healthy breakfast food. I don't want to have to read the label to find out if I'm getting candy or cereal. I want to believe that what I see is what I get! How wonderful life would be if we could all be up front with one another. What a world it would be if everyone knew exactly what they were getting when they entered a marriage, had a child, took a job, chose a college, etc. None of us can change the world, but all of us can change that small part of the world in which we're personally involved. We can make a difference.

Today I'll search out any dishonesties I'm committing and set the record straight.

DAY 118

"I'm ready to close this chapter of my life."
—Billie Holiday

Moving from a can't do atmosphere and developing a can do attitude doesn't always carry you in a straight line. The geometry of the human make-up is too complicated for that. Sometimes we make false starts. Sometimes we discover that what seemed like a good decision at the time doesn't turn out to be good in the long run. Sometimes the simple act of growing older and growing wiser requires that we re-evaluate our current position, our future plans, and our ultimate goals. It's okay to change direction. It's okay to make mistakes. It's okay to change course, change places, change attitudes. Sometimes it's okay, no, even beneficial, to close a chapter on your life and begin anew. Change, even dramatic change, is okay — as long as it's well thought out positive change. Change doesn't mean failure, it means growth. Change can be one of the most thrilling experiences in your life journey. The only time change is truly irreparably bad is when it causes you to stop moving, to halt the game plan without formulating another, to give up without picking up, to stop and not restart. Change is an active verb. Life is an active process.

Today I'll reevaluate my plans and decide if I'm on the right track.

"Let poverty be a stranger in my household."
—Dahomey

There's no shame in being poor. The shame lies in staying poor. Poverty robs the human spirit of dignity as surely as it robs the physical body of longevity. Poverty steals away childhood, diminishes adulthood, decreases potential, and dashes hopes for the future. No matter how poor you are — in body, mind, spirit, or in worldly goods — *you don't have to remain impoverished!* The opportunities are there. The resources are there. The vast wealth of wisdom, knowledge, and experience are there. Where? Right in your own community! If about now you're saying, "Jim, you can't be talking about *my* community," you're wrong. I am talking about your community, wherever or whatever that community is. Think of the sports heroes, the movie heroes, the heroes of history, religion, medicine, science, poetry, literature, business. How many of them rose above poverty to become successes? The list is too long to count. Now think about your unsung heroes — your parents, grandparents, foreparents, neighbors, teachers, preachers. They shared your background and your community. They are your best role models. They are your best resources. They are shining examples of hope.

I'll take time today to list my heroes and research their backgrounds.

"The antidote to what is fundamentally wrong is
the cultivation of what is fundamentally right."
—Marianne Williamson

Once a farmer in New Jersey decided to plant artichokes. Each year he would till the fields, plant the crop, and wait for it to grow. Each year the new plants would straggle up through the sandy soil, get blasted by the dry summer sun, shrivel and die. New Jersey is just not the right climate in which to grow artichokes. After years of trying, the farmer finally switched to tomatoes. The crop sprung up sturdy and strong. The harvest was abundant and the farmer made a great deal of money. The farmer's success came when he stopped planting what was fundamentally wrong and began cultivating what was fundamentally right. When we plant the seeds of fundamentally right crops — values, honesty, ambition, nonviolence, respect — we leave little room for the weeds of fundamentally wrong crops to grow.

Today is a great day for planting the right seeds in my life.

DAY 121

"Most of us measure our success by what others haven't done."

—Tina Turner

Why does it always seem easier to look down rather than to look up? Because looking down doesn't require us to do anything! When we measure our success by looking down on others, we feel so superior. We adopt the "I have" philosophy. "I have a job and you don't. Therefore, I'm more successful." Or, "I have an education and you don't. Therefore, I'm smarter." The "I have" philosophy allows us to stay right where we are, smug and haughty and going exactly nowhere! As long as we keep measuring our own success by the failures of others, we remain stuck at our own current level. There is no progress, no striving, no forward or upward movement. It is only when we look up that we move up. Look up to your heroes and role models for inspiration. Look up to God for strength and guidance. Look up to your own individual potential. You have come a long way!

Today I will look up and see my own personal mountain top.

DAY 122

"Today, I'll reach up to the reaching down
hand and reach down to help the one that's
reaching up."

—Whitney Young

How will you know when you've succeeded? What
will be the signs of your success? That depends on
the goals you set. Flashy cars? Fancy clothes? Invitations to the best parties? If that's what you're going
for, good luck! You're in a race without a finish line.
You'll just keep running and running, buying and buying, proving and proving to the world how successful
you are. When the cars get dented, the clothes fade,
the parties become boring, how will you feel then?
True success requires that we not only achieve ourselves but that we help others achieve also. Those
who get have an obligation to give something back.
Why? Because none of us gets anywhere alone. We
are both independent and interdependent. Sure, you
can have your share of the "good things" in life. You
will have earned them! But material success can ring
very hollow. A penthouse can be awfully lonely. Someday you'll want to just take off your shoes, kick back,
and chill out. And you won't want to do it alone. Make
sure, on your journey, you've brought some friends
along.

*Today, I'll reach up for a helping hand and down with
a helping hand.*

Day 123

"It's better to look where you are going than to see where you have been."
—Florence Griffith-Joyner

There's a rule in racing: Never look back! Looking back takes time; even the split second spent turning your head can make the difference in a close race. Looking back takes energy; that backward glance could eat up the reserve you'll need at the finish line. By focusing on the goal, you retain all your energy and concentration for the competition at hand. Looking forward gives the inspiration that justifies the perspiration. Knowing where you are going, seeing your goal clearly, marking your forward progress, opens new vistas of success. See yourself doing exactly what it is you want most to do. Hear yourself being offered the job, receiving the diploma, taking the vows. Never lose sight of your dream.

I am a champion. I can see myself achieving my goals.

DAY 124

"It takes twenty-one years to be twenty-one."
—Reggie Jackson

In our family we love iced tea. We drink it all year long. We have a special way of making it that makes our iced tea pretty famous. First, you have to get the water to a full, rolling boil. Then you pour it over the tea bags. Next comes the hard part; you let it brew overnight. One time, when we were expecting some company, the unthinkable happened; we ran out of iced tea. Now I knew these folks particularly enjoyed our iced tea and would be expecting to have some, so I sort of rushed things. I didn't let the water come to a full boil. I used lemon juice instead of squeezing real lemons. Worst of all, I didn't let that tea brew long enough. The result: I served inferior iced tea. Our guests were disappointed and went away wondering if my tea had ever been so outstanding after all. Some things just can't be rushed. Rushing some things will only result in creating an inferior product. Wisdom, experience, and maturity, like iced tea, take time to perfect.

Today and everyday I'm learning as I go.

Day 125

"Success always leaves footprints."
—Booker T. Washington

We start today at a point others struggled to reach. We'll end our journey at the next generation's starting point. In between, we'll leave our footprints in the halls of colleges and universities, in the board rooms of great corporations, in the neighborhoods of "safe, nice" houses, in the families headed by women *and* men dedicated to rearing moral, successful children. Each stride we make leaves a footprint for someone else to follow. Each trail we blaze marks the pathway for coming travelers. Each gain we achieve lifts a burden from the next generation. Travel your own personal road to success with energy and rigor. But travel it wisely. Your footprints will show others where you have trod. Be sure you're proud of the road you've traveled.

Today I will proceed with wisdom and courtesy, knowing my success will leave my footprints for tomorrow.

Day 126

"It's better to be prepared for an opportunity and not have one than to have an opportunity and not be prepared."
—Whitney Young

In my boyhood home in West Virginia, there was a creek that ran behind the house. Sometimes during the summer, my friends and I would build a raft and launch it on that creek. There wasn't much water, and we'd just drift along under the summer sun. But in the fall, during the rainy season, that creek would rise until it became a full-flowing stream. Then we'd have to paddle our raft with all our might to keep from being swept along on the swift current. We felt so alive as we battled the water! Careening off rocks, ducking under fallen branches, straining every muscle, we'd lean our backs into the task of steering our course and keeping upright. Drifting along in the summer was a time of relaxation and reflection. But rowing fiercely as we set our course was the real challenge. Whatever you do in life, remember — the greater the challenge the greater the fulfillment.

Today I'll set my course and row toward my destination.

DAY 127

> "If Rosa Parks had taken a poll before she
> sat down on the bus in Montgomery, she'd
> still be standing."
>
> —Mary Frances Berry

If there's anything certain in life, it's that at times it's going to be tough. No one gets through this life without encountering heartaches and troubles. For some people, life seems more troubled-filled than for others. Yet no matter how bad things are for you, there is someone nearby who would gladly trade your troubles for theirs. Knowing that somebody else has it worse may not make your own troubles easier to bear, but watching how others handle troubles can teach you how to handle your own. Next time you encounter a friend, neighbor, co-worker, or loved one who is confronting great hardship with great courage, pause to observe them. Talk to them about how they manage to deal with their pain. Listen closely to their answers. Don't be surprised when they tell you that God is their sustaining force. These are people who have learned the most important lesson. It's true that the only thing certain in life is that at times it's tough. It's equally true that the only certainty in life is God's promise of a safe landing to those who trust in Him.

Today I'll ask one brave person to share the secret of her courage.

DAY 128

"To get to heaven, turn right and keep straight."
—Anonymous

Have you seen the TV commercial for Jeep? First a carload of guys, lost on a back road, stop and ask for help. The gas station attendant looks at their sleek car then proceeds to give them complicated directions involving a network of super highways. Next a pretty young woman pulls up in a Jeep and asks for the same directions. The attendant looks at her vehicle, smiles broadly and says, pointing to a dirt road running up and over a mountain, "Just turn here and keep straight." Ah, the directions are so simple if we just have the proper vehicle! With the proper vehicle we can travel dirt roads, climb mountains, and cross rivers. With the proper vehicle we can overcome all obstacles and safely reach our destination. When our destination is heaven, there is only one proper vehicle. That vehicle is faith in Jesus Christ. Faith can carry us up, over, around, and through any obstacle. Faith can forge new roads and repave worn ones. Faith will give us the strength to turn right and keep straight.

Today I'll check my vehicle, make any needed repairs, and set out on the straight road to heaven.

DAY 129

"Blessings hemmed with praise won't unravel."
—Blurb in a church bulletin

A crisis strikes. Suddenly we are on our knees praying for help. We beg God for deliverance. In our very human and very futile attempts to make a deal with God, we promise Him anything. Then deliverance comes. The crisis passes. Where are we now? Out celebrating with our friends! How quickly we forget who it was that delivered us from the crisis. How often do we forget the promises we made during our darkest hours. God fills our lives with blessings both during crisis days and everyday. When we take time to praise Him for His goodness, our memories improve; we are less apt to call on God for crisis intervention only. Make it a point to set aside time everyday to spend in praise to God for His blessings in your life. You'll quickly find more and more blessings for which to give praise. The fabric of your life will be strengthened. The material of your soul won't tear. When trouble comes, your world won't unravel.

Today I will make and keep a daily appointment with God.

Day 130

> "The past is all that makes the present
> coherent, the past will remain so long
> as we refuse to assess it honestly."
> —James Baldwin

This quote is one of the mainstays of my life. It has kept me going more times than I'd like to remember. Sometimes, when things are so bad that I can't find my way out, I hang onto this promise. In those darkest hours when I have to reach up just to touch bottom, when even God seems far away and my prayers get lost in the silence of infinity, I hold tight to these words. I give them to you now as my gift. Try them out for yourself. Use them when needed most. Cling to them. Let them sustain you. Let them be your lifeboat when there's no going around and the only way is going through. Go through, and know that all you're going through will someday be behind you. You may carry some scars, but wear them proudly. They are badges of your courage. And when the high times come, remember that they too will pass. Life is never level. Growth is never steady. Good times and bad times, all shall someday pass.

Today will pass. Tomorrow will come. I will go on.

"If you run, you might lose. If you don't run, you're guaranteed to lose."

—Jesse Jackson

As hurricane survivor Kevin Dunmont knows, when crises come in our lives, they leave behind some very important lessons. Sometimes they teach us how strong we really are; sometimes they point out our weaknesses. Crises give us new insights into ourselves and our relationships. A crisis is always a test of faith. When there's nowhere to go, no place to turn, and no one to turn to, we are left to face ourselves. I've known many brave people, many strong people, many people who are superb leaders under stress. Everyone of these brave, strong leaders acknowledges that in their darkest hours, they clung to their faith. I've never understood why anyone would choose to go through any day, let alone dark days, all alone when the strongest force in the world is waiting to be called upon to see them through. Ask the survivors, the ones who have really come through life's storms. They'll tell you that they were never alone.

I can face today and everyday because God is by my side.

DAY 132

"To see over a million black men disciplined, nonviolent . . . full of positive feelings and spirituality; I think that's a wonderful thing."
—Roger Wilkins

The Million Man March has come and gone. Some say it was the black man's finest hour. Others are critical of the leadership behind the march. All are asking, "Where do we go from here?" The march is symbolic of every person's journey through life. "Discipline," "nonviolence," "positive feelings," "spirituality" — these are the things that will make or break our individual *and* our collective futures. The world is watching, and not just the "white" world, but the whole world of people of color. We are looking around at one another to see what will unfold. Instead, we should be looking inside and asking, "Where will I go from here?" The answer will be different for each of us; we are a diverse people with vast potential. The way we will get "there" is the same: through discipline, nonviolence, positive feelings, and spirituality.

Today is a new beginning for me and for my people.

Day 133

"The student of truth keeps an open mind,
an open heart, and an open Bible."

—Anonymous

Does your family have a family Bible? Many families do. They are so proud of these books. They keep them on a special shelf, or put them out on the coffee table when the preacher comes to visit. They keep the cover carefully dusted. The pages lay smooth and unwrinkled. In fact, the Bible is often the newest book in the house. And it stays brand new no matter how old it is, *because nobody ever reads it*! I challenge you today to set aside time, even just ten minutes, every day to read your Bible. Read it with an open mind. Don't look up just your favorite verses or passages, those that prove your point. Approach it as a true seeker of truth. Let the words sink in. Mull them over during the day. Look for new meanings that may have escaped you before. Read it with your heart as well as your mind. It is a history of all histories — the history of God's interaction with the human race. It the story of all stories — your story, the story of your creation, your progression, and your destination. The Bible is the ultimate source of truth for now and eternity.

Today I'll make, and keep, a daily appointment with my Bible.

DAY 134

"A world without dreams and hopes is no world at all."

—Aretha Franklin

"Once upon a time. . ." How many wonderful stories begin this way! "And they lived happily ever after." How many wonderful stories end this way! In between lie the stories of hope and dreams, the stories of courage and bravery, the stories of make believe and make it happen. Our world survives because of hope and dreams. In all the centuries of human mistakes and failures, human cruelty and oppression, human brutality and carelessness, we would have given up long ago were it not for hope and dreams. Spend time with your dreams; they are the gifts that make life rich. Spend time with your hopes; they will give you the power to make your dreams come true. Spend time in good company; family and friends are life's truest rewards. Spend time with your true self; you'll be near the heart of God.

Today I'll plan my week, leaving time to hope, time to dream, time for companionship, time for solitude, time for God.

DAY 135

"It is through the practice of goal setting that one can compensate for life's short comings. . ."
—Dennis Kimbro

The commercial reminds us to "Capture the Kodak moment." Our scrap books are filled with mementoes of the important occasions of our past. Between all the highlights — the proms and graduations, the births and birthdays — life is happening. Somehow we forget that each day is a special gift. Each day holds a special promise. We get so busy making plans for tomorrow that we miss living today. Yet tomorrow never really belongs to us; it is a possibility but not a reality. Planning for the future is vitally important. Setting goals is the way to achieve. Yet let us never get so caught up in tomorrow that we miss today. Let us never be like many tourists who get so busy snapping pictures that they miss the trip. Let's never get so busy making plans that we fail to enjoy what's happening now.

Today is a "time out" day. I'll pause to notice and enjoy what's happening now.

Day 136

"To walk in the light while darkness invades, envelops, and surrounds is to wait on the Lord."

—Howard Thurman

It was the tying game of the baseball world series. The league's leading batter was up. The tension was high. The crowd was on its feet. The pitcher wound up — and pitched the ball just inches from the batter's head. Both teams erupted onto the field. A massive fist fight ensued. The teams had become so caught up in getting even that they lost sight of trying to get ahead. None of them were playing like the superstar sportsmen they were. They had diminished themselves in the eyes of the fans, the league, and the country. Getting ahead takes enormous amounts of energy and ingenuity. None of us have enough reserves to waste them in quest of getting even.

"Even" isn't good enough to waste time on. Today I'll work to get ahead.

"Prayer is the path God has given us whereby
our lives can be taken over by love, praise,
thankfulness."

—Rev. Scott Lawson

Atheists say they do not believe in God. How sad
for them. Imagine what it must be like to see a beautiful sunset, hold a newborn baby, walk the beach, or
view the world from a mountain top, and have no
creator to thank! When our lives are touched by the
deepest experiences, we most deeply experience
God. When we experience God, we want to reach
out to Him. The way we reach out to Him is through
prayer. Prayer is a two-way channel. God's love flows
to us as we spend time in prayer. Our love flows to
God in the form of praise and thankfulness. Transformation occurs. Our lives are filled by love, thankfulness, praise, and appreciation in direct proportion to
the time we spend in prayer. When prayer becomes
an undercurrent constantly running through our stream
of consciousness, we become conscious of God's love
constantly streaming through our lives with blessings,
beauty, and strength.

*My life is rich in blessings. My day is filled with
thanks.*

DAY 138

"Our prayers are our ladders to God."
—Anonymous

There are so many excuses for not praying. Too busy. Forgot. Fell asleep. Got interrupted. Prayer needs to have a sacred, set, permanent time in every life. However, prayer does not have to be limited to a certain set, permanent time. When awareness of God wraps itself around you, you know that you are in His presence wherever you are, whatever you're doing. Your day is filled with constant little prayers sent up to God as fleeting thoughts, unformed words. The mind and heart take over and hold you in His presence even while you're in the presence of other people, other things. Developing this kind of prayer life begins with building solid ladders to God through set prayer times. As you discipline yourself to spend this designated time with God each day, you'll find God filling the un-set times of your days. Your awareness of God will grow as our ladders of prayer grow. Each step will take you closer to His presence, closer to the heart of God.

God enternally holds me in His presence. Through prayer, I hold Him in my present.

DAY 139

"Faith expresses itself in fervent, persistent prayer."

—Marianne Williamson

Prayer presents us with a baffling decision: Do we take something to God in prayer once, then in faith turn it over to Him, believing that He'll take care of it? Or do we keep praying over and over about the same thing? The Bible gives us examples of both. Remember the story Jesus told in Luke 18 about the woman who kept pleading to the judge to grant her justice? At last the judge gave her what she wanted just so she'd stop bothering him. Anyone who has kids knows how their whining and crying and nagging can wear down your resistance. We don't want to "bother" God, yet Luke says Jesus told this story to show the need for persistence in prayer. On the other hand, the Bible is filled with stories about people who asked just once and got what they wanted. Luke himself tells of the centurion (chapter 7), Jarius' daughter (chapter 8), the boy with the demon (chapter 9), and on and on. In my prayer life I've learned that I do both. Of course, turning it over to God isn't the end of prayer until the next request pops up. Sometimes God grants exactly what we ask; sometimes God answers prayer in unexpected but wonderful ways. But always, God answers prayer.

Today my prayers will include time for listening for the voice of God.

> "The cross is a sign that in 2,000 years,
> not a heck of a lot has changed."
>
> —Anonymous

In Jesus' time they crucified dissenters. Today, we shoot them! No, not a heck of a lot has changed. John Kennedy was shot in 1963; a few years later his brother Bobby and Dr. Martin Luther King, Jr. were both assassinated. More recently, Gerald Ford, Ronald Reagan, and Bill Clinton all were shot at, with Reagan receiving a serious wound. In 1995, Israeli Prime Minister Yashak Rabin was assassinated. Dissent, when approached positively, can lead to assent or at least a win/win compromise. Peaceful dissent is the way intelligent, moral people approach their ideological differences. Violence is the tool of maniacs, fanatics, people who are easily led, and people who have impaired internal controls. In the 2,000-year recorded history of humanity, only one leader was perfect. He is the one who was able to heal people sick in body, mind, and spirit. He was the one who could feed the hungry from meager earthly rations and abundant heavenly rations. He was the one and only one to raise some from the dead and, ultimately be raised from the dead himself. But even that wasn't good enough. They killed Him, too.

Lord, keep my mind open to new ideas and closed to evil ideas.

Day 141

"We cannot stand still; we cannot permit ourselves simply to be victims."

—W.E.B. DuBois

Relationships are like "The Little Engine That Could." With just a little more effort, many of them would succeed. "Sure, honey, I'm tired but I'll be happy to get you some coffee anyhow." "I'm sorry, dear, I forgot the milk, but I'll go back and get some." "I put the next load in the washer while I was in the basement, dear, so you don't have to worry about it." Such little things, but when done between spouses, they are so very, very important. All of the successful relationships we see around us are models of two people who lovingly put out just a little more effort. Success can't possibly come to any relationship without effort. A little more effort yields a lot more success. This doesn't mean you are to be a love slave or a doormat; respect and self-respect prohibit both. But putting out just a little more effort to be courteous, polite, and kind to those we love can save more relationships than all the counseling in the world. Remember, "Love is patient. Love is kind. Love is never rude." (I Cor. 13)

Today I'll show my love for those I love by putting forth just a little more effort.

Day 142

"Next time you say, somebody should do something about that change your phrase to, I can do something about the situation."
—Benjamin Hooks

   With your busy, hectic lives mae busier, though hopefully less hectic, by your new "can do" model for pursuing personal success, you might think you don't have time to get involved with other people and issues. Think again. People of color always have been people of community. What hurts one hurts us all. What holds back one holds back all. You never can know true personal success until you're engaged in doing something that promotes communal success. No, you can't help everybody, but you can help somebody. No, you can't change everything, but you can change something. If each of us will pick up a little piece of the burden, it will become light. If each of us will work together for communal progress, we'll experience personal progress as well. In so doing you *can* make a difference in your life and in your personal sphere of influence. Think of the difference-making potential that can be ours when all of us commit to making a difference *right where we are.*

Today I'll join hands with a brother or sister in working for our mutual good.

DAY 143

"If you can't make a mistake, you can't make anything."

—Marva Collins

Perfectionism goes against nature. The human condition is simply not perfect. While you can — and should — strive for perfection, you must remain aware that you'll never achieve it in this earthly lifetime. Once you accept this fact, you can accept yourself with all your very human frailties and foibles. You'll be liberated from the frustration and heartache that comes with demanding the impossible of yourself and, perhaps, from those around you. You'll be free to pursue your goals without fear of making a mistake. Do your best to minimize your mistakes by thinking things through. Internalize the fact that some of the world's finest creations have come about by mistake. Bring the knowledge you've gained from past mistakes to new endeavors. Never let the fear of making a mistake paralyze you. Don't get stuck in the limbo of your fear. Fear of failure, fear of embarrassment, fear of making the wrong decision — these are the most crippling fears of all. Get out of your mental braces. Walk forward with confidence, knowing that you can handle your mistakes as well as your successes. Embrace the opportunity to be a creator. Remember, you can't make anything until you can accept making a mistake.

I'm not perfect, but I'm getting better. Today I'll learn from my mistakes.

> "The truth will set you free."
> —Bible paraphrase

Remember the story of the ugly duckling? No matter how hard that little duckling tried to be like the rest of the ducklings, he just couldn't succeed. He always felt like a failure and a misfit. One day the little duckling grew up and turned into the beautiful swan he was always meant to be. Are you living like that little duckling? You will never know your true beauty of body, mind, and spirit as long as you're trying to fit someone else's mold. You'll never fulfill your own potential if you're pursuing the dreams of others. You will never know true satisfaction, that elusive thing known as "self-satisfaction," until you learn to be true to yourself. Stop trying to be someone you're not. Start loving the wonderful person you are. This is one of the most success-promoting lessons — one that practically guarantees happiness. Parents, teach it to your children. Help them pursue things that truly interest them, not just things that interest and please you. Spouses, remember that your mate needs space to follow her/his own dreams. Never ask someone you love to act in any way that is contrary to his/her own God-given nature. "To thine own self be true." Whoever said William Shakespeare is outdated?

Why would I want to fit someone else's mold when my own is so beautiful!

Day 145

"The heart is ever restless until it finds
rest in thee, oh Lord."

—St. Augustine

As a pastor, I spend a great deal of time with griev-
ing families. Inevitably they ask me, "Pastor Holley,
what do you think it's like to die?" At times like these,
worn out platitudes, glib banalities, even the "party line"
fall like empty words on blank paper. None of us knows
what it's like to die. We really do have to rely on the
party line — the Christian party line. We have to take
it on faith that what Christ promises, Christ fulfills. Jesus
said He was going to prepare a place for us in His
Father's house, a house that has many mansions. What
a beautiful picture! It speaks to us in our human state
in words we can feel, words with which we can identify, words that hold meaning and comfort and peace. I
believe death is like those times when, as a child, I
would fall asleep in the chair or the car. While I was
sleeping, strong arms always picked me up and carried
me to my own bed. When I awoke, there I would be,
exactly where I should be, in the special place that
belonged just to me. The special place that is heaven
represents security, safety, comfort, and love. When
we wake in God's presence we might not know how
we got there, but we'll sure be glad we did! All of our
life's troubles and fatigue will be gone. We'll be re-
freshed. Our restless hearts will be at peace. We'll at
last be home.

*Today I'll face my fear of death and reflect on my
personal vision of heaven.*

DAY 146

> "God is always capable of making something out of nothing."
>
> —Minister Louis Farrakhan

Growing up in my grandmother's house in the hills of West Virginia, we didn't have much. For years there was no inside plumbing. We heated water on a wood stove for our baths. Meals were plain, often meatless, usually made of things we'd grown in the garden and put up for winter. Just looking at that house, at our town, at the little one-room school for "coloreds," you'd say nothing good could ever come out of that place. But that little house was filled with love — my grandmother's for me, mine for her, and ours for God. Grandmother taught me to love God with all my heart, strength, and mind. She taught me to look on the inside of myself and others to find true quality. She taught me to believe in myself, to set goals, and to go after them. Probably the people who lived there didn't look like much either. But I believe, and I know that grandma would agree, God took our nothingness and made it into something pretty special — my life. We need to remember this when we walk through ghetto neighborhoods past broken down churches and broken-into houses. God *is* capable of making something out of nothing. Our neighborhoods *do* have potential. Our cities *are* worth the effort of revitalization. *We must stop judging and start joining* in causes that can redeem our people.

Today where I see nothingness I will replace my view with a vision of what God can bring about.

Day 147

"There are three kinds of people in the world: those who make things happen, those who watch things happen, and those who wonder what happened."
—Anonymous

Life is tough and full of obstacles. Prepare yourself now for the pitfalls and hurdles that will come along. Don't just float, row! Don't be a spectator, participate! Don't sit and wonder, work! Remember, you're not the only one who can change the world around you. You share that space with lots of others. Your world will change and will continue to change. Who's in charge of those changes is up to you! You can make things happen. This gives you an awesome amount of control. That's right. You can take control if, and it's a big if, you're also willing to take responsibility. Control and responsibility — they go hand-in-hand. Sounds scary? Well, you could opt to be one of the people who never makes anything happen, who is never in control. If you don't accept responsibility you'll never be in line for blame. You may think that's playing it safe, but of course, there's really not much safety in that. You'll simply be trading personal control of your world and accepting someone else's control of your world. Be responsible only for your decision to give up responsibility. But if you believe in yourself, then act for yourself. Be someone who makes things happen, good things, for yourself and your world.

I control my own destiny by controlling the actions I take today.

DAY 148

"Most people think they know the answer.
I'm willing to admit I don't even know the
question."

—Arsenio Hall

A group of high school students nervously filed into
the classroom to take the final exam. Prior to handing
out the tests, the teacher told the students to read
the entire exam before answering any questions. She
repeated her instructions twice. For the next two hours
students struggled over impossible questions. This
wasn't what they had studied! This stuff wasn't even
in the textbook, they silently moaned. As the clock
ticked steadily toward the cut-off time, one student
burst into tears, another wadded up the test, threw it
in the trash can, and stormed from the room. After
class, there was much weeping and gnashing of teeth.
All were sure they had failed, and they had. You see,
the very last line of the instruction sheet said, "Ignore
all of the questions, sign your name, and hand in your
test. Have a good day." The students had simply failed
to listen, really listen to the teacher's words. She had
given them the only answer they needed before the
test even started. Perhaps it was because her words
had become too familiar; the kids had heard the same
directions a hundred times before. They had tuned
out and flunked out. Listening is the key ingredient to
communication. Listening to your own voice is the key
to success.

*Today I'll tune out the world and really tune in to
myself and others.*

DAY 149

> "I wasn't looking for appreciation, recognition, or acknowledgment. I just did what I knew was the right thing."
>
> —Joseph Lowery

No one thought he could do it. No one believed that a man could care for three young children, maintain a house, see to their school work, and still hold down a good job. They were amazed when the children appeared on time for school everyday. Their clothes were always clean and neatly pressed. Their grades didn't slip. They were in church every Sunday. The house was tidy, the lawn cut, the pantry stocked. The meals were hot, nourishing, and varied. The children grew up secure and happy, knowing they were loved. Years later when the last child graduated, the school principal remarked to this single father, "I certainly hope your children appreciate what you did for them. I hope they give you the recognition and acknowledgment you deserve." Replied the father, "You don't understand. I didn't do it for appreciation, recognition, or acknowledgment. I just did what I knew was right." Are there special situations in your life? How are you handling them? Are you working for the praise and admiration of others, or you are doing what you know is right? Praise and admiration are wonderful. They feel great when they come. But lasting satisfaction comes with doing things simply because they're the right thing to do, regardless of whether anyone else ever notices.

Today I'll examine my motives. I'll measure my performance by my own standards.

DAY 150

"There is an eagle in all of us. Just soar, soar!"
—Jeremiah Wright

Some of us have struggled for so long that we've come to believe that unless we're fighting an uphill battle we're really not moving. Such people diligently creep along, moving inch by careful inch. With noses to the grindstone, they barely lift their heads to see the sky. People like this never give in to the impulse to soar. Soaring is the highest form of movement. Surprisingly, it also is the epitome of rest. Soarers aren't flapping their wings, they're riding the currents. Soarers aren't fighting against the wind, they're gliding along, letting the wind carry them. Now it's true that it takes effort to get high enough to soar. It takes strength to take off from the ground and reach that altitude where soaring is possible. Some people never get poised for take-off. Others are already high enough to soar but never seem to realize it. What is success if not the achievement of the ability to take time to soar? There will always be higher skies to conquer, new winds to battle. When the opportunities present themselves, take time to soar. It's the justification for the journey, the purpose of the pursuit, the prize for perseverance.

Today I'll test my wings. I'll soar serenely above my struggles.

Day 151

"It is my solemn responsibility to stand against
a budget plan that is bad for America."
—President William Jefferson Clinton

Right now, today, hundreds, no thousands of people
are stressed out. The most common reason for this
stress? Worry over money! Who are these people?
While they come from all levels of society, most of
them are people of color! Stress and worry debilitate
their health. They fall ill. Without money or health
insurance, their worry increases, their health decreases.
They become entrapped in an unbeatable cycle. But
is it, really? Do you really need money to get ahead?
Sure, money makes it easier to get an education, but
lack of money does not make education impossible.
Sure, money allows you to purchase the "right" clothes
to get the "right" job but there are ways to earn, borrow, or buy second-hand outfits that will get you in
the door. *Your best assets are absolutely free.* Your
intellect, your ability to think and plan, to solve problems, to work around obstacles — these talents you
already own. All you need to do is learn to use them.
You can activate them right now to help you overcome poverty and open closed doors. Another important free tool is the vote. Our foreparents worked and
sacrificed to open the doors of the polling places of
our great land. We owe it to them to vote, and vote
wisely.

I hold the keys to unlock my own future.

DAY 152

"I have a strong suspicion . . . that much that
passes for constant love is a golded-up moment
walking in it's sleep."

—Zora Neale Hurston

A woman friend of mine had just become engaged
to a wonderful man. It was to be a second marriage
for both of them. At a small celebration, I overheard
this conversation: "How did you manage to meet someone so great?" the bride-to-be was asked. "Yeah," remarked another, "no matter how hard I try, I just keep
coming up with losers." With a smile my friend
replied, "I wasn't trying. I didn't think much about
marrying again. I just kept on with my own life — my
job, my kids, my hobbies. I was too busy to look for a
man. Then it simply happened. Actually, we met at a
little league game. We were both there with our kids,
just being parents." Marriage is one of the most pro-
found experiences in life, but it is not the only pro-
found experience. True happiness comes from pursuing your own interests and goals. If someone comes
along whose love will enhance your already fulfilling
life, you have the potential to create a true marriage.
A happy marriage is the icing on the cake of a successful life; it is not life itself.

I'm leaving all my options open.

> "What makes 'great' great?"
> —Dorothy Height

Pick any prominent figure either from history or the current scene. Ask a random number of people of different race, religion, educational, and social levels their opinion of this person. Chances are the answers will range from great to inconsequential, from excellent to evil. What we think depends upon where we stand. Of course, no one can please everyone; human nature is too diverse to allow unanimous societal opinion. True greatness is defined by the ability to transcend personal ideology and act for the good of another. This "other" may be an individual, as in the case of the 16 year-old young black male who captured public esteem by caring for his young brother while remaining in school and working part time. The other may be a group of people, such as those who benefited from the revolutionary teaching methods of Marva Collins — highly successful methods which set a new standard for educating inner city children. The other may be an entire nation, as demonstrated by Dr. Martin Luther King, Jr. and other heroes of the civil rights movement. The common denominator of truly great people is their unswerving loyalty to their personal moral code.

I am great and becoming greater as I define those things that are dearest to me.

Day 154

"Ignorance is no excuse for failure."
—Dennis Kimbro

The secret of success is not how much you know, but how much you *know about yourself.* Knowing yourself is the key to overcoming all the obstacles, opening all the doors in your life. If you know you need more education, more training, more skill development, you can take steps to get it. If you know you need to improve your image, you can face the mirror honestly and make adjustments. If you know yourself to be unreliable, selfish, a procrastinator, jealous, hot tempered, closed minded, or to possess any negative trait, you can guard your actions. It's human nature to take the easy path. Identifying your strengths helps you to choose pursuits that complement and utilize your abilities. By knowing yourself — your good points and your bad points — you become more conscious of your behavior. When you're conscious of your behavior, you can take steps to change it. There are none so ignorant than those who are ignorant of themselves. There is no surer road to failure than practicing self-deceit.

Today I will listen to my own words and watch my own actions. By tonight I'll know myself better.

DAY 155

"Poverty is a disease of the mind."
—S.B. Fuller

We are what we think we are. When our mental image of ourselves is positive, we become more positive. Conversely, if our image of ourselves is negative, we become more negative. If you see yourself as poor, downtrodden, oppressed, suppressed, you probably are; you've accepted your lowly position. If you see yourself as a victim, you're probably allowing yourself to be victimized. It is only when you see yourself as a positive person, an overcomer, a free creature with free will, that you grow. You become the person you believe yourself to be; the real you begins to match your self-image. When that self-image is formed by other people's ideas, opinions, and judgements, it is bound to be inaccurate. Doubtless the input of others influences the development of your self-image. That's why it's so important to provide others, specifically children, with positive reinforcement. But the input of others is only one ingredient in the success formula. True self-image must come from within the self. There is no more powerful force in your upward journey than an image of yourself as the successful achiever you were created to be.

Today I will get rid of any negative images I hold of myself.

Day 156

> "A man's mind, once stretched by a new idea, never regains its original dimension."
> —Oliver Wendell Holmes

Somewhere between childhood and maturity, something terrible happens to the human mind. We lose that wonderful capacity to drink in new ideas, new concepts. The joy of learning from everything we encounter leaves us. Consider a child who has just learned to read. The child devours book after book. The child's mind has stretched to grasp the wonderful concept of written communication. It will never shrink back to its original shape. Once a child learns to talk, walk, reason, decide, you can't stop them. Their mind keeps on stretching to include new vocabularies, new actions, new powers. It's one of the greatest miracles of the Creator. Those people that you find most interesting, study their lives. Chances are they constantly seek out and absorb new knowledge. They have hobbies and interests. They travel either physically or mentally through reading, watching, and communicating. They are excited by new ideas.

Today I will stretch my mind by engaging in one activity I find exciting and challenging.

DAY 157

> "It takes a village."
>
> —African proverb

During the 1996 national presidential conventions, first lady Hillary Clinton was criticized for stating that it takes a village to raise a successful child. "It doesn't take a village," sneered the presidential opponent. "It takes a family." The question is: What constitutes a family? No one would argue that the nuclear mother/father family has the first and greatest impact on a child. But a child's world quickly grows beyond this hopefully loving, nurturing unit. Neighbors, baby sitters, day care workers, and extended family members figure prominently in the pre-schoolers's world. Soon teachers, pastors, scout, and your group leaders become adult role models. From the police officer who protects his home to the sanitation worker who keeps her sidewalk unobstructed, from the doctor who treats his illnesses to the business owner who gives his first after school job, adults beyond mom and dad exert tremendous influence on the child. In a very real sense, every adult has a hand in raising the world's children; every adult becomes their "family." Creating a can do atmosphere for children requires the dedication of can do adults. It's pointless to create opportunities for success unless we equip children to embrace those opportunities. Raising successful children does take a village.

I am my brother and sister's keeper — especially those brothers and sisters who are the children in my "family."

DAY 158

> "Dreams! Big dreams!"
> —Rev. Jesse Jackson, Sr.

You will only get as far as your dreams. If you dream small, you'll stay small. You'll opt for little victories. You'll be satisfied with getting by. If your dream vacation is a week sitting undisturbed in front of the TV set, you'll probably get there. It's not a real hard place to get! Likewise, if your dream vacation is to tour the U.S. or visit Europe, you'll probably get there, too. Your dreams, coupled with hard work, can take you anywhere you want to go. If you dream big, you'll get big — big results, big gains, big achievements. When you dream big, you'll appreciate little victories but you won't be satisfied with them. Big dreamers are never satisfied with just getting by; they want their share of the abundance of life. Big dreamers never lose sight of their dream — big things are highly visible — but they don't sit around dreaming all the time. They work hard at making their dreams come true. Because big dreamers have such big goals, they may never achieve all of them. They may dream of a year's vacation in Europe and achieve only six months there. But one thing is certain: big dreamers get much closer to their goals than small dreamers. Even when big dreamers fail, they end up way ahead of small dreamers who succeed. How big are your dreams? Is it time for an up-sizing?

If I can dream it, I can have it.

Day 159

> "Whatever we believe about ourselves and
> our ability comes true for us."

> —Susan L. Taylor

It's December 24th. Around the world children sleep securely in the knowledge that Santa will come. They don't doubt; they believe. Is it logical that an old man in a red suit driving a sleigh across the sky pulled by a team of reindeer could actually visit every house in the world? It doesn't matter; logic has no place here. Children simply believe. And because they believe, their world is filled with magic. Usually Santa Claus does come, to some homes more abundantly than others, but still he comes. Each year the magic returns, the dream is fulfilled, but only because they believe. Christmas is never the same once you stop believing. Nothing again will ever quite match the magic. The possibility of dreams coming true will never feel as close. All the presents you may afford in later life, the wrappings, the expensive gifts, the large tree standing in a new house, can't recapture those long ago moments that make up your fondest memories. Believing doesn't have to be limited to Christmas or childhood. All of life can be filled with wonder if you hold fast to a child-like faith. Good things can and will continue to happen, but first, you must believe-in yourself, your ability, your worthiness, your God.

I believe in myself, I can make anything happen.

Day 160

"The wise man must be wise before, not after, the event."

—Epicharmus

No athlete is as successful as the Monday Morning Quarterback. He never throws a bad pass. He never throws an interception. He's never sacked. The defensive line never breaks down, the offense never chooses a questionable play. Too bad life can't be played in rerun. We'd all be so perfect! In real life, we only get to live one moment one time. Whatever we decide to do, say, think, feel at that moment is a forever decision. We don't get too many second chances; instead we get experiences; it is up to us to learn from them. If you are to become a successful person, this is something you must learn to do well. Then, when a similar decision presents itself in the next moment, the next week, the next year, you'll have the wisdom to make the right call. Wisdom is gained not by avoiding mistakes but by learning from them. As you live moment by moment, day by day, experience by experience, your success depends upon your ability to gather wisdom to guide you through the future, whatever that future holds.

In the next hour I have sixty different minutes in which to learn.

Day 161

"Chill . . . Keep a non-anxious presence about your conflict."

—Odell Jones

If you can keep your head about you, you'll greatly reduce the times you say if only. "If only I had seen the danger, I wouldn't have gotten hurt." "If only I hadn't lost my temper, she'd still be with me." "If only I had . . ." You fill in the blanks. The bottom line is that keeping your head leads to a life long on happiness, short on regards. When you learn to keep your head, you are in control of situations. Outcomes, then, come under your influence. The driver keeps his head and avoids the pile-up. The mother keeps her head and rescues her child from the burning building. We even see cases on television of young children who keep their heads in emergencies and dial 911 for help. None of us will get through life without regrets. There will always be many things you would do differently if only you could do them over. The secret of success is to learn to keep your head no matter what is going on around you. You may not always make the right decision, but you'll sure make a lot fewer wrong ones.

Instead of dwelling on the past, I'll cope with today and learn for tomorrow.

DAY 162

"Keep Hope Alive!"

—Jesse Jackson, Sr.

Perseverance is more powerful than violence. The violent person endangers himself and those around him. The persistent person safeguards herself and others because she never lets go of the goal. Giving up is not the same as changing plans. Giving up is quitting; changing plans is positive adaptation. Sometimes there are ways around obstacles that we don't see at the moment, but that soon becomes apparent. The person who quits doesn't hang around long enough to benefit from new insights. One of the best ways I know to keep from giving up is to break the problem down into smaller pieces. Maybe you can't solve the entire problem at one fell swoop, but you do know the answer to parts of it. It's a lot like learning higher math. At first glance, the problem is overwhelming. Then you look at the equation and solve the parts you can. Next you put all the solved parts together and balance them against the unsolved parts left. You arrive at the answer because you refused to give up. Quitters miss out on the joy of overcoming. They never know the thrill of victory over impossible odds. They never advance because they never move forward. You can't choose to be both a success and a quitter. It's one or the other. What's your choice?

Today I promise never to give up on myself and my goals.

Day 163

"In a society that still more often thwarts black ambition than encourages it, black success is rarely accidental or ever a matter of simple blind luck."
—Audrey Edwards & Craig K. Polite

Children keep at things until they've mastered them; only adults give up. Have you ever known a baby to quit trying to walk because he fell down too many times? Or a child stop trying to learn to ride a bike because it was too hard? Even a dog will work and work to dislodge a bone that's stuck under the table. What do children and animals have that adults seem to lack? Persistence! No amount of money, resources, or intellect can take the place of persistence in achieving success. You can sit around and rationalize, hypothesize, moralize, fantasize, and justify your reasons for quitting, but when all is said and done, when all the internal arguments have been exhausted, all the excuses made, the obstacle will still be there, the problem will remain unsolved. When it comes to problem-solving, nothing can take the place of persistence. Persistent people may not know all the answers, but they're finding some of them. Persistent people may not totally obliterate the obstacle, but they'll move it enough to get around it. If I had to choose between a brilliant person and a persistent person, I'd take the persistent person every time. Our team may not win, but we won't be left at the starting line.

Today I'll keep working on that problem until I find the solution.

DAY 164

"Coulda Woulda Shoulda"
—Lou Rawls

You've heard the expression, "I would if I could but I can't so I won't." The only thing missing is the "I will." Maybe that's because "I will" people are too busy getting things done to give excuses for why they won't or can't. You know what I'm talking about. You see it everywhere. Is there an office anywhere that doesn't have both a doer and a slacker? Is there a job site without both a performer and a coaster? Thank God there is always a dedicated band of "I will" people to carry out the tasks. Ironically, it's the "I can'ts" and the "I won'ts" who have the audacity to complain that the "I will" people get all the recognition! What kind of person are you? You can't say "yes" to everything, but you can say "I will" to something. Choose your "I wills" carefully; they are a personal commitment and a reflection of your priorities. Choose your "I won'ts" with discretion; they delegate responsibility and give control to someone else.

Today I will find one thing I can "yes" to; I'll follow through on my commitments.

Day 165

"You can hear other people's wisdom,
but you've got to reevaluate the world
for yourself."

—Mae Jemison

Sally and Selma are cousins. Sally could do most anything. She was beautiful and bright. She was the soloist in the choir. She was the first in the family to go to college. She had a great job, made great money, bought great clothes, and took great vacations. All her life Selma longed to be like Sally. As children, Selma pretended she didn't care about Sally's talents. "I'm too busy to sing in the choir," she would say. As teenagers, she pretended she could outdo Sally. "I was invited but I think the prom (the date, the contest, the award, whatever) is silly." Even as adults, Selma continued to try to compensate for her poor self-image by mocking Sally's accomplishments. "Did you see what that show-off has gone and done now?" became her frequently repeated comment. As a result, a great deal of animosity grew up between the two women. When Sally got the job Selma intended to apply for, it was too much. Selma fell into a deep depression. It took months of therapy before she began to feel better and to develop some coping skills. That Christmas Selma encountered Sally at a family dinner. Instead of making snide remarks, Selma complimented Sally on her dress. The gap had been bridged. "No one can make you feel inferior without your own consent."

I know who I am and what I believe, I count!

Day 166

"If I were you, I would stand for something.
I would count!"

—Benjamin E. Mays

What do you believe about the world you live in? Do you really know? Do others know your beliefs? Do you feel strongly about anything? Would an outsider observing you for a month know what you stand for? As you look around at your community, your schools, your work place, your family, your own home, do you see things you wish were different? Are you doing something to bring about change? Not playing is the surest form of playing it safe. If you don't play, you can't lose; you can't even come in second or third. If you don't play, no one will know how well or how poorly you can play. Of course, if you don't play, you can never win. You risk nothing and nothing is exactly what you get. If you never stand for anything, it's tough for anyone to stand against you. Likewise, no one will ever be able to stand with you either. Life is made up of a series of choices. Deciding not to decide is a decision. Standing for nothing is as much a decision as standing for something. The choice is yours.

I know who I am and what I believe. I count!

Day 167

> "Self-hate is a form of mental slavery that results in poverty, ignorance, and crime."
> —Susan L. Taylor

When we hate someone, we wish that no good comes to that person. We judge the hated person as unworthy. We avoid or ignore the hated one. We become so obsessed with the hated one that we are enslaved by our hatred. Sometimes our hatred goes beyond thoughts and feelings. When our hate flows over into actions, the result is crime. When hate is turned inward, the same feelings and actions result. We judge ourselves as unworthy to receive good minds and thoughts. We are unable to work, to play, to form relationships, to grow. Self-hate is self-destructive. It destroys the individual from the inside out. It destroys love. It destroys the life of the hater and impacts the lives of those around him. Self-hate is the rawest form of slavery — slavery of the spirit. It is the greatest impoverisher; it robs the individual of human potential. It is the deepest well of ignorance; its' source remains undetected. It is the subtlest form of deception; it practices self-delusion. Self-hate is a crime against humanity. Those who hate themselves are criminals; they pillage the human spirit and destroy God's plan for individual success.

I am a beautiful person. I will treasure and nurture myself with love.

Day 168

"I am somebody!"
—Rev. Jesse Jackson, Sr.

The person you are today has nothing to do with where you live. The heart and core of your truest self are lived inside your mind. It is there that you make all the decisions that determine who you are. You are the person you know yourself to be. You are not someone else's perception of you; no one knows you better than you know yourself. When your actions reflect your own truest thoughts, you are happy with yourself. When you act contrary to your own best ideals, you betray yourself. If you act or speak in any way that falls short of the standards you set for yourself, you decrease in self-worth. Every time you break a promise, fail to honor a commitment, every time you lie, cheat, steal, or commit passive or aggressive acts of violence against another, you devalue the "somebody" you are. With every word you speak, every thing you do, you proclaim to the world that reflects who you really are — inside, in the deepest recesses of yourself, in the precious "you" only you know.

I am who I think I am. I am wonderful!

Day 169

"God bless the child who's got his own."
—Billie Holiday

Did your parents ever tell you, "I hope someday you have a child just like yourself?" If they did, they probably said it at times when you were misbehaving. If you have children of your own now, do your parents' words seem to be a self-fulfilling prophesy? All families have certain ways of speaking, doing, and interacting that carries down from generation to generation. Whether you like it or not, your own childhood is very present in the childhood you're creating for your kids. If your own childhood experiences were happy, positive, loving, success-oriented, you already know how to recreate these experiences for your children. You have the pattern; you've lived with the role models. If your childhood was violent, abusive, insecure, unloving, failure-oriented, you carry that pattern with you. Does that mean that you're bound to recreate your own unhappy childhood for your children? No. Patterns can be altered. First, you must be aware of the behaviors you carry over into your adult life. Then you must consciously go about making alterations. Ideally, this should be done before you become a parent, before you are responsible for creating the childhood of the next generation. But it is never too late to start. It won't be easy; you're behaviors were forged in the cradle. But by confronting your past and refusing to repeat your parents' mistakes, you can stop the cycle of destructive parenting. God will bless your effort. Your children and your children's children will be the ultimate beneficiaries of your success.

Today I will start to have presence in my child's life.

"I want to stay as is."

—Janice Hale

A recent favorite of talk shows is white kids who "act black." The host asks the frantic parents: "What do you call acting black?" The answers range from speaking or walking a certain way to poor grades, delinquency, dropping out, violence, and crime. Even today, this is how much of the world views people of color. Unfortunately, it's also how many people of color perceive themselves. Sure, we can continue to cry "poor me." We can blame others for what we fail to become. But blame hasn't worked in the past and there's no reason to believe it will work in the future. Blame is a fruitless waste of collective energy. It is time to end the blame game. It is time for black men to stop blaming black women for emasculating them. It is time for black women to stop blaming black men for abandoning them. The strength of character we develop as individuals and as a race must come from within. No one can give it to us. We must believe it about ourselves. We must adopt it for our own. We must earn it through our actions and lifestyles. Only then will we stand, head high, tall and proud among all the diverse people of this nation. Only then will we achieve the purest form of success.

Today I will set standards for myself. I will never lower them.

Day 171

"In knowing how to overcome little things, a centimeter at a time, gradually when bigger things come, you're prepared."
—Katherine Dunham

Have you ever watched true artisans at work? Their hands glide smoothly and capably over their project. There are smiles on their faces. They love what they're doing and it shows! Your work is your art. Whether it's fixing cars or fixing computers, building houses or building young minds, when you love your work, it shows. It shows in your face; it shows in your speech; it shows in the enthusiasm with which you approach your tasks. Maybe you can't do the work you'd most love to do right now, but you can work toward that goal. Maybe you can change your present job for one that relates to your chosen field. If that's not possible, think of yourself as being in a holding pattern. Say to yourself, "This is what I'm doing until I acquire the skills, education, opportunity, etc., to do the thing I long to do." Begin preparing yourself for your desired future. Constantly watch for opportunities. Be practical enough to meet your responsibilities and idealistic enough to put your butt on the line to achieve your dream.

"A can do attitude is necessary in a can't do atmosphere."

DAY 172

> "If it's hard, then do it hard."
>
> —Les Brown

Reaching the top is never easy; staying on top is even harder. There are no short-cuts to success. Success, however, has many levels. The level you attain is directly proportionate to the energy you expend. For example, if you sing, you can work at developing your voice until you make the choir. You will have reached a level of success at singing. You work even harder until you become a soloist. It's the same in any field. You can remain in the typing pool or shoot for office manager. You can stay there or work until you make middle then upper management. This choice is yours and yours alone. Sometimes moving up may mean changing jobs or changing companies. Believe in yourself. Never make a change unless it's an upward step or a move that offers more opportunities. Decide how hard you really want to work. Be honest with yourself. Target the level of success you will be able to achieve based upon the amount of hard work you're committed to expending. Keep your goal always before you and you're bound to reach it.

I am on target. I shall reach my goal.

"Since when did money become life?"
—Lorraine Hansberry

Some people believe that if you have money you can do anything. Some also believe that if you don't have money you can't do anything. Both beliefs are false. Certainly it's easier to do things when you have money, but there is always something you can do to get more money to enable you to do the things you want to do. You can watch the Help Wanted ads for a job or a better job. You can network with others who might be of help to you. You can go back to school, take a night course, borrow a "How To" book from the library. One free and even profitable way of building skills is to apply to a temporary agency. They'll help you gain experience in computers and office procedures. They'll place you a temporary jobs where you'll gain exposure, which often produces offers for permanent jobs. No matter how lacking in formal education you may be, there is something you can do to help yourself. The one thing you cannot do is to wait for something good to come your way. Waiting is inactive; it is counter-productive and a waste of time. Your self-respect and the respect of others are tied more to the efforts you make than to the gains you make. Your success is directly proportionate to your efforts. When you make the effort, the gains will come.

Today I will find new ways to actively pursue my goals.

DAY 174

"The best way to help the Poor is not to
be Poor."

—Rev. Jim Holley

Poverty is *not* piety. For too long opportunities to
prosper were closed to people of color. To compensate, we learned to view poverty as a sign of piety.
We couldn't get our rewards here, so we clung to the
belief that we would get them in the here-after. It's
time to abandon these outdated beliefs. We have the
opportunity to be anything we choose. Why not
choose to be rich? There is no guaranteed formula,
but there are certain objectives that must be met if
you are to have a shot at prosperity: 1) Decide what
you want; 2) Envision yourself attaining your goal; 3)
Analyze the steps you'll need to take to get there; 4)
Begin with a good education; 5) Continue learning and
extending your knowledge; 6) Stay on top of new
developments in your field — read; 7) Network with
others; 8) Believe in yourself enough to take responsible risks to achieve your dreams.

Today I'll write out a plan for achieving success.

Day 175

"Use your head before your heart uses
you."

—Ann Askmore

We all carry our own personal idea of beauty. For
some, the ideal woman will be tall and willowy; for
others, she will be tiny and petite. For some, the ideal
man will be broad-shouldered and slim-waisted; for
others, he will be large and brawny. This doesn't mean
we can't find beauty in someone whose physical image is quite different from our ideal. Many people are
surprised when they fall in love with someone who's
the exact opposite! The beauty of other people, other
places, other things comes from inside us. Some find
an automobile to be a thing of beauty; others, a building, a poem, a song, a scene. It is what we bring to
our experiences that make them beautiful. When
we close our eyes to the potential for beauty in anything or anyone different from our ideal, we are limiting ourselves. We are also devaluing the ideals of another. When we look to outside sources to define
beauty, we are missing out on our own interpretations. When we strive to fit into someone else's mold
of beautiful, we are denying our own significance. Limiting what we conceive of as beautiful, desirable, worthy, good, or valuable is limiting our chances for success.

I am beautiful — inside and out!

Day 176

"The mind is the standard of the man."
—Paul Lawrence Dunbar

As we grow, we develop certain standards. What these standards are is greatly influenced by those around us. Parents, teachers, friends, relatives — everyone important in our lives helps determine our personal standards. When we live and work and play among people with high moral, social, and educational standards, we develop high standards ourselves. The opposite also is true. As adults, we have the power to evaluate our standards and to change them as we see fit. It is when we allow others to determine our standards that we become disjointed. We are separated from who we are inside. The who that we are inside is divided from the who we are on the outside. Disconnection leads to brokenness in body, mind, and spirit. We were created to live in unity with ourselves and with God. Achieving personal peace, happiness, and success depends upon living up to the internal standards we set for ourselves.

I am who I am today, not who I was yesterday.

Day 177

"... for whatever the mind can conceive
and believe, the mind can achieve."
—Dennis Kimbro & Napolean Hill

Everything boils down to belief and action. One follows the other as surely as night follows day. They cannot be separated. If you believe yourself to be capable, you will be capable. You will act in ways that demonstrate and increase your capability. The image of yourself that you hold in your mind prompts your actions. You act in accordance with your self-image. Athletes know this. A great deal of training time is spent developing winning self-images. Runners are trained to mentally run the race, to hear the starting gun, feel the ground beneath their feet, sense the curves and turns, see the finish line ahead, and know the thrill of being the first runner to cross the line. In their minds, they go over and over the race. It becomes part of them. When it's time to compete, they know the course; they've run it a thousand times.

I am who I believe I am. I believe I am great!

"Greatness is not measured by accomplishments but by the opposition one overcomes."
—Dr. Dorothy Height

Greatness is different for each of us. Therefore, it is achieved in different ways. The genius must make an outstanding contribution in his or her specialized field to be called great. A learning disabled person achieves greatness by learning to read and conquering job skills. The athlete must break records to be great. For the physically impaired, greatness comes with each independent step. Obstacles are opportunities to achieve greatness. Likewise, overcoming obstacles is the achievement of greatness. Because obstacles and greatness are different for each of us, we cannot compare ourselves with anyone else; we would get a false reading. What's easy for me may be difficult for you. Therefore, the only standard for greatness by which we can measure ourselves is our success in overcoming our personal obstacles.

I have come far; I still have far to go.

DAY 179

"Good functions as God talk."
—The Frugal Gourmet

Frugal Gourmet and Methodist minister Jeff Smith, reminds us of the importance of food in Bible times. In the Bible, Smith says, "Food functions as God talk." No wonder our churches have so many chicken dinners and pot luck suppers! Feeding is the essence of nurturing. It is the first and foremost need of the newborn. It is a need that remains with us all our lives. The ancient Israelites had a custom that required people to share food with strangers, even enemies. The book of Ruth tells of the ancient custom of leaving something for the poor to collect when the fields were harvested. In the new testament, Jesus made provisions for feeding the crowds that came to hear Him preach. He also commanded His disciples, "Feed my sheep." There is something intimate, something divinely human, in the sharing of food. Unfortunately, today we forget the lessons of Jesus and our biblical foreparents. We exclude rather than include those who are different from us. How many "undesirables" were invited to your last holiday table or church dinner? Food is both a symbol of needs being met and a vehicle for bridging differences. A shared table is a sacred table. Providing food links us *back* to the past, *out* to the present, *up* to God.

Today, I will share and care for someone in the community of the human race.

DAY 180

"Not all black people can sing and dance."
—Niara Sudarkasa

Life is not passive recreation. Living requires movement, change, action! There are many things that are beyond your control; your life is not one of them. It is always your decision to change your own life or continue as you are going now — even to choose to go nowhere at all. Sometimes things happen to us or are done to us by others that we can't avoid or prevent. Usually these are not things we like or want. While we can't escape them, we can control how we react to them. Perhaps your neighborhood is riddled with violence. Maybe you can't yet afford to move, but you can choose not to be part of that violence. You can guard against violence in your home, in your family, in your mind. You can join with others to work against violence. In every situation in life, positive or negative, you are in charge of your reactions. You can let things get to you, or you can get to things before they get to you. You can be hit by the bat or you can move out of the way — mentally, spiritually, physically. You can change the course of your life by changing your actions and reactions.

Today I will think before I react.

"I had spent my life always becoming the woman, men I loved needed me to be etching my shadow inside the curve of their love."
—Marita Golden

People who come into your life unexpectedly come for a reason. When the time comes, they go out of your life for a reason, too. In between, they answer a specific need, help you through a difficult time, or teach you some unforgettable lesson. These people may be as transitory as a clerk in a store who goes above and beyond to help you find what you need. It may be someone you meet on a trip, someone you'll never see again but who makes an impact on your life. It may be a chance encounter with a neighbor who provides assistance during a difficult time. Whoever they are, these people appear at just the right moment, do for you what needs to be done, then go out of your life as quickly as they came. You desperately want to hold onto them; you cannot. They have fulfilled their purpose; it's time for them to go. Make them a model for your relationships with others. Angels always come in disguise. They leave behind the potential for you to be an angel to someone else.

I will treasure my special relationships. I will let go when the time comes.

"If you are willing to deal with the past,
you can make the moment you are in rich."
—Oprah Winfrey

Nothing blocks a successful future as much as an unacknowledged past. We've all made mistakes; we all need to admit them before we can move on. Some of us have had terrible things done to us; facing them is the first step in banishing them. This may mean confronting someone or something that is terrifying to you. Confrontation conquers consternation. This may also require that you learn the hard lesson of forgiveness. Is there someone in your life you need to forgive? Forgiveness is a double edged action; it blesses both the forgiver and the forgiven. Is there something you need to confess, someone from whom you need to ask forgiveness? Past issues obscure future opportunities. We all develop sophisticated methods for handling our pasts. The only method for putting the past behind you once and for all is to face it. Spend some time in self-examination. List emotional baggage that is weighing you down. Find a safe, satisfying way to dispose of it. Clean out the storeroom of your heart and mind. Clear the way for moving forward unhampered.

Today I will face my past with honesty and confidence in myself.

DAY 183

> "God is a verb."
> —Buckminster Fuller

How do you define God? Do you think of God as the Creator? Creating is an active process. Do you think of God as the Protector? Protecting is the process of preserving someone or something. Do you think of God as the Supplier? The Overcomer? The Savior? Supplying, overcoming, and saving are all action words. Do you think of God as Love? Love is an action word, too. Love *does* for the beloved. Love *takes care* of the beloved. Love *works* on behalf of the beloved. Love shelters, protects, provides, guides, encourages, helps. Love is never passive because our God is never passive. When we love we are like God. Therefore, when we love we act. We act and interact for and with those we love. Whether or not you recognize it, God is working in your life. Whether or not you recognize the impact of your actions, you are working in and on the lives of your loved ones. God's work is always good. God's actions bring good to His beloved. How do your work and actions measure up?

Today I will love actively and responsibly.

Day 184

"It doesn't matter how may times you fall down.
What matters is how many times you get up."
—Marian Wright Edelman

What are your beliefs about money? Many people
believe that they will never have enough. They have
resigned themselves to always living on the edge — or
below it. They blame the rich, the government, big
business, whatever, for their poverty, dependence,
welfare. Unfortunately, many of these people are
people of color. They have adopted their attitudes
about money or the lack of it, from their parents, grandparents, or the "hood." The 21st century belongs to all
people. You and I will make the decisions concerning
our futures. You can decide that it's useless to try,
that you'll never get ahead, so why bother. You can
decide that your lack is someone else's fault; blame
can carry you along for quite awhile on a self-righ-
teous wave of misplaced indignation. Or you can decide to go after your rightful share of this country's
riches. You can make or remake yourself into an em-
ployable person who will be an asset to any company. You can choose to fill your life with moaning or
with meaning. The choice is yours.

Today I will develop my talents. I am responsible.

Day 185

> "Respect comes with integrity that comes
> with character . . . all must be earned."
> —Hugh Price

   Respect cannot be demanded; it must be earned.
Respect has little to do with money or position; it has
everything to do with actions and attitudes. The respected person respects others. The respected person stands for something and doesn't waver despite
what others may stand for. The respected person has
established a code of morals and will never deviate
from them. Respected persons hold themselves in high
esteem, value themselves, care for themselves. The
respectful person honors God, life, and others. Respect is never gained at the expense of others. Respect grows out of self-respect. Respect is never demanding, never violent, never boastful. Respect comes
from seeing the good in self and others, acting to nurture that good, recognizing that we are all different,
and acknowledging that sometimes there can be no
compromise. To earn respect, choose carefully — your
friends, your mate, your occupation, your involve-
ments. If you would be respected, act considerately,
say nothing that erodes the self-respect of another,
do nothing that compromises who you are and what
you believe.

*I will respect myself and others as persons within
whom God dwells.*

Day 186

> "Children are not ours, nor we theirs, they are future, we are past."
>
> —Nikki Giovanni

Do you find your children hard to understand? To know your children you must first know yourself. Your children are never deceived. They hear the unspoken words, they feel changes in the atmosphere, they sense when all is not what you're pretending it is. When your children act — or act out — in ways you find incomprehensible, examine yourself. When you wonder where they possibly could have learned a certain behavior, look inward. When they lie, ask yourself if you're always honest. Do you say one thing but mean another? Do you conceal the truth from them? From yourself? Do you "snap out" at home but work against violence elsewhere? Is your behavior consistent with your words? There comes a time when all children will push against parental limits. Successful parenting is a growing process. Children try out behaviors on their parents because parents are safe victims. Pushing and trying and testing are a necessary part of growing. If you've provided consistency and unconditional love, you and your children will both survive intact. They will be equipped with the tools they need to grow into their God-promised success.

I see myself in my children. I will work to be sure I'll always like what I see.

DAY 187

"Every race and every nation should be judged by the best it has been able to produce, not by the worst."
—James Weldon Johnson

Unless they're athletes or entertainers, people of color seldom are seen on television except when they've done something wrong. Turn on the news. What do you see? Reports of black-on-black crime, black-on-white crime; reports of blacks rioting, blacks standing in welfare lines, blacks in every negative position imaginable. Is this an honest portrayal of our race? It's a question that must go beyond the individual insult and consider the collective image we portray. Sadly, in many cases we have earned our reputation. Black prisoners outnumber white prisoners three to one. This cannot be blamed on a biased judicial system. The number of black households headed by women greatly outnumber those of white female-headed households. The number of school drop-outs, pregnant teens, and welfare recipients is consistently higher for blacks than for whites. Certainly, there are societal factors for all these things. We can point to oppression, rejection, racism, denial of educational and employment opportunities. These are valid reasons for where many of us have been or are now. They are not valid reasons for remaining there. We are a successful people who come from a rich heritage of achievement. We have among us some of the greatest achievers of the twentieth century. We have worked and we have overcome. It's time we were judged not by the worst among us, but by the great multitude of the best this world will ever see.

My conduct reflects who I am and where I'm going.

> "Getting to know someone, entering that
> new world, is an ultimate, irretrievable
> leap into the unknown."
>
> —Eldridge Cleaver

Developing a new relationship is impossible if you are still drowning in the dregs of an old relationship. Developing a healthy relationship is impossible if you are not emotionally healthy yourself. We draw to ourselves people who are much like ourselves. Angry people draw angry people; lonely people draw lonely people; lazy people draw lazy people, etc. Likewise, successful people who have high self-esteem and high expectations of themselves attract the same kind of mates. It's inevitable. Every new relationship is bound up with who you are at the time the relationship is forged. Never accept in another what you would not accept in yourself. Remember, you are not in a relationship to save your partner from him or herself. If you can't love someone the way he or she is right now, don't count on changing him or her into someone you can love later. Getting your own emotional house in order is the surest way to a healthy, satisfying relationship.

I deserve the best; I will accept only the best for me.

DAY 189

"Change is certain, progress is not."
—Hillary Clinton

"If you're waiting for someone else to get you out of a predicament, you'll wait forever. You are the only one who can help yourself. No one else cares as much about you as you do yourself. No one else knows you as well as you know yourself. You alone know your dreams. It doesn't matter what someone else thinks your goals should be. It doesn't matter what anyone else thinks of your potential. You know! You have the power to decide! You are the best judge of your performance! There is no disappointment as great as disappointing yourself. When you disappoint yourself, there is no one else to blame. No one can make you do anything against your nature. No one can make you abandon your dreams and goals. No one can cause you to fail. Others may erect obstacles, construct detours, or cause delays. Only you can choose to abandon your plans and forfeit success.

I am the key to my own success.

Day 190

> "Of all weapons, love is the most deadly and devastating, and few there be who dare trust their fate in it's hands."
> —Howard Thurman

You are a part of every other human being. The world you inhabit is co-inhabited by every other person living in your time. The earth bears the imprint of your predecessors; your own footprints are stamped upon the future. You are created by the same Creator, modeled after the same divine image as every other person. You cannot learn to love yourself until you let go of hating others. Everyone has somebody who has done him or her wrong. Continuing the hate keeps the wrong alive. Continuing the hate extends the victory of the hated one. It's time to let it go and move on. Love truly will take you places — good places, positive places. A mind and heart steeped in hate will not allow you to grow. Hating, like loving, takes a lot of energy. Energy expending in hating is energy rendered unavailable for loving. Love is the way to success. Self-love is the motivator and encourager. Love for others allows you to share the burden of the journey. Love for others guarantees there will be someone to celebrate with when you achieve your goals.

My time is too important to waste in hating.

Day 191

"If you don't dream, you might as well be dead."
—George Foreman

Where do you see yourself being next year? In five years? Ten years? The vision you have of yourself is your greatest asset in reaching your goals. If you envision yourself moving onward and upward, you will! If you envision yourself in a fulfilling relationship, you'll have one! If you envision yourself living in a nice home, making good money, doing something you like, you'll get there! People with vision are a hundred times more likely to succeed than those with no vision. That's because people with vision see what needs to be done to achieve, and then they do it! The plan for the future. They plot the course they must travel to reach their goals. People with vision are disciplined. They have "stick to it tive ness." They not only work hard, but also take time to reflect on where their hard work is getting them. They are not afraid to evaluate and reevaluate their progress. They learn from their experience; they apply what they learn. Through discipline and hard work, reflection and experience, they move onward through life to fulfill their vision, to realize their individual dreams of success.

I'll keep the vision of where I'm going ever before me.

Day 192

> "What you do today will determine what
> you do tomorrow."
>
> —Frank Chikane

Life is a series of cause and effect. For every action we take, there is a reaction. Likewise, for every action we fail to take, there is a reaction. What you will do tomorrow has a direct link to what you decide to do today. Today is the day on which you lay the groundwork for tomorrow. Tomorrow you'll lay the ground work for the next tomorrow, and so on. Often we plan the little things of each day with tomorrow in mind, yet we fail to plan for the big things that will have a long-term effect on our futures. You shop on Thursday for a dinner party you're giving on Friday. You take the suit you plan to wear Saturday to the dry cleaners on Monday. You buy rock salt in October so that you'll be prepared for the icy days of winter. What about things like education, career training, preparation for marriage, parenthood? Aren't these more important than rock salt and a clean suit? What you do about these things today will determine if you succeed tomorrow.

Today is the tomorrow of yesterday and the yesterday of tomorrow. I won't be caught unprepared.

DAY 193

> "All beauty comes from beautiful blood
> and a beautiful brain."
>
> —Walt Whitman

Once elephants freely roamed the plains of Africa. Then the hunters came. They slaughtered the elephants for their ivory tusks. Soon the tusked elephants learned to fear the hunters. They no longer roamed freely and proudly but hid themselves in the darkest, deepest parts of the jungle. Gradually they recognized that it was their tusks the hunters wanted. It was their tusks, the very part of them that made them beautiful and valuable. But they couldn't eliminate their tusks. The tusked elephants could not breed tuskless offspring. Their frustration at not being able to change the essence of who they were caused them anger and pain. Their self-hatred grew; their pride diminished. Elephants are incapable of thinking, reasoning, and problem-solving beyond the most elemental level. Thankfully, we are not elephants.

I am bright! I am beautiful! I love who I am!

Day 194

"No God no peace. Know God know peace."
—Dorothy Stubbs

What will your day be like today? Most of us work because we must earn money to meet our needs. But God did not create us as one-dimensional creatures. Therefore, fulfillment and inner peace cannot come from one-dimensional activities. Maintaining personal satisfaction, fulfillment and inner peace require that we maintain a balance in our lives. Work must be balanced by play. Togetherness must be balanced by solitude. Introspection must be balanced by interaction. When we take time to reflect on our inner selves, we find God. Only God can bring peace to the workplace. Only God can bring peace to the home. Only God can bring peace to the community. How does God bring His peace into our hectic, stress-filled lives? By bringing inner peace to our souls. When we know God, we know the only kind of peace that's truly lasting.

Today I'll take time to balance my life from the inside out.

DAY 195

"I started with this idea in my head, There's two things I've got a right to . . . death and liberty."

—Harriet Tubman

God created you free. The law guarantees your liberty. If you feel enslaved, perhaps *you* are the task master. I know a couple who worked hard for years to buy a second home on the coast. When they at last fulfilled their dream, they were astonished to find that a second home was a real burden. They constantly worried about storms, break-ins, power failures, etc. They turned down invitations from friends because they had to spend their weekends traveling back and forth, even in winter, to check on their property. Their dream had become a nightmare. If you're feeling trapped, who is the trapper? Have you become a slave to your own possessions? Are you sacrificing time for yourself, your friends, your family in order to get or keep something that's really not so important after all? Is your identity tied to what you have rather than who you are? Are you measuring success by what you won rather than by the pleasure your possessions bring you?

Today I will begin to clear the clutter from my life.

"Our Father-Mother God."
—Maroba Jean "The Queen"

Genesis tells us that God created us in God's own image — male and female. Why then is there this constant power struggle between the sexes? We are all created in the image of God. God makes no distinction. We are created with differences, not inequalities. The sexes are meant to compliment one another, not compete with one another. Men, be proud of your manhood, but recognize that women are just as proud of their womanhood. Women, be proud that you have the ability to be anything you choose, but recognize that men have the right to choose also. It's time we stopped defining expectations and behaviors by gender. It's time we stopped setting one another up to fail. It's time we learned to live in harmony with one another, as brothers and sisters, as co-heirs to heaven. It's time we defined success not by proficiency in traditional gender roles but by individual achievement in any role.

I am proud of my body; I am proud of my brain.

DAY 197

> "A dream doesn't become reality through magic; it takes sweat, determination, and hard work."
>
> — Colin Powell

Every invention was once an idea. Every accomplishment was once someone's dream. There is nothing you will use today, no product you will purchase, no goods you will consume that was not first conceived in someone's mind. God gives us ideas so that we can progress. Along with each idea, God also gives us the ability to bring it to fruition. How many times have you seen some new invention and said to yourself, "I could have thought of that." How many times have you found that a product is something that you thought of long ago but never acted on? What's the matter? Have you no faith in your ideas? Have you no faith in God who gives you your ideas? Have you no faith in yourself and your ability to get things done? Doing is the result of dreaming. Action is the result of idea. Do you have a good idea? Are you acting on it? What are your dreams? What are you doing to make them come true?

Today I will dream and do, conceive and commit.

"Stress can be a silent killer — if I allow it."
—Rev. Jim Holley

Understanding stress is the key to coping successfully. The key to your house gets you in the door. What you do once you're inside is up to you. As individuals, we live out of several relational dimensions. We wear many hats. We wear the hat of parent, child, spouse, sister, brother, boss, employee, etc. Each hat casts us in a different role. Each role brings us opportunities to learn and to teach, to grow and to nurture. What we can do depends, in great part, on what we're willing to do. What we're willing to do — for ourselves and others — determines whether family stress will be a poison that destroys or a spice that enhances. Good cooks take great care to add just the right blend of spices that will make meals not just a means of physical sustenance but a source of pleasure and gratification. Good family relationships require a careful blend of tolerance, wisdom, love, and stress.

Today I will manage my stress with style. I choose to make stress my friend.

Day 199

"Much prayer, much power, little prayer, little power, no prayer, no power."
—Rev. Clay Evans

A close friend and true prayer warrior was worried about her husband's health. She prayed daily that somehow he would be given time to take a break from his hectic job to relax. Last week she called laughing. "I know God has a sense of humor," she said. "Bob fell off a step ladder and sprained his ankle. He has to stay off it for a week!" God is never malicious, but God is often subtle. Another friend once told me she was praying that she would learn patience. A few weeks later she confided somewhat wryly that God had definitely answered her prayer. "Nothing's been going smoothly, "she reported. "I've been granted innumerable opportunities to develop patience." God always answers prayer. Wise people are careful about what they pray for!

A successful prayer life will bring me a successful daily life.

> "The comic in this country united the
> tragic as well as the mindful."
>
> —Ralph Ellison

Would you laugh if you were poked in the eye, flipped your car, or had your toilet explode? Of course, these things are comedy, and the world sure has need for laughter. Unfortunately, laughter at someone's expense isn't confined to entertainment. One of the earliest lessons children learn is how to ostracize the fat, slow, uncoordinated, or otherwise different kid in the class. Teaching our children that laughter at the expense of someone else's feelings is never funny. The best method of teaching is by example. We must all guard against ridicule in our words and deeds. Even the inflections in our voices, our body language, or our facial expressions can undermine another's self-esteem. We must learn to put ourselves in the other's shoes. Ask yourself how you would feel were you the other person. If the situation no longer seems funny to you, it's not funny to the other person either. In seeking success, be sure to seek success in growing more sensitive to the feelings of others.

Today I'll seek greater sensitivity in my dealings with others.

Day 201

"The bee that robs the flower fertilizes the egg."

—Rev. Jim Holley

Life is an investment: you only get something out if you put something in. I'm not talking in terms of dollars. I'm talking about one world-effort! You've got one life to live, don't waste it. Don't settle for a cheap thrill; insist on the genuine high of success. Sharpen the skills necessary to make your dreams come true. With that kind of character, you will be on top of circumstances, not under them. If you want to see it through, you will; it's up to you. If you want to go from now to the end of your life healthy, happy, and successful, it's up to you. Right now I am asking you to do one thing: turn your life to at least one project that benefits someone else other than your family. Invest, plant, sow, and watch the increase. It is the law of the harvest. If you do, you will find a thrill that will fulfill you beyond your dreams.

Today I will make a deposit in my life investment account.

Day 202

> "Courage is the price that life extracts
> for granting peace."
>
> —Amelia Earhart

As you travel your personal road to success, there's one thing you can count on: you will experience times of great discomfort. That's just the way it is! It's human nature to want to cling to the comfortable, the familiar. Like a child on the first day in kindergarten, we face new experiences with fear. No matter how much we may want what's on the other side, it's the going through that tempts us to forego the experience. It takes courage to move forward, but forward movement is necessary for progress. The courage to move ahead despite our fears is basic to inner peace. You will never find inner peace without courage. You may avoid fearful experiences, but you will never be at peace with yourself. There will always be a restlessness, a nagging feeling of something left untried and undone. Which would you rather have: temporary fear and discomfort but eventual success or comfortable escape from fear but eventual stagnation? It's your life. The choice is yours!

I'll forego temporary comforts to achieve permanent success.

Day 203

"Man, if you gotta ask you'll never know."
—Louis Armstrong

"Do you love me?" It's a question that should never need asking. When someone loves you, you know it. You will be able to feel it. You'll be surrounded by that love; it will pervade each and every day of your life. When couples begin to ask one another, "Do you love me?" something has gone dreadfully wrong in their relationship. One or the other, most often, both mates have failed to meet the responsibilities of a loving relationship. This doesn't mean that loving partners never disagree. It doesn't mean that loving partners never disappoint one another, misunderstand one another, or let one another down. When love is the bottom line, it can be felt despite misunderstandings and disappointments. Love precludes disloyalty, dishonestly, and disintegration of the relationship. Love begets love. It is continually creating and recreating experiences that reveal its depth. Love establishes an open line for honest, forthright, communication. Love speaks in a language that leaves no doubt in the mind of the beloved. In successful relationships, love answers the question so that it need never be asked: Do you love me?

My actions today will tell the ones I love how very dear they are to me.

"I will not eat until I see progress in the feeding of the poor."

—Dick Gregory

There are certain needs basic to life. The need for shelter, food, water, clothing, and air to breathe are common to all creatures. Specific to human beings is the need for contact with other humans. No one is free to pursue more sophisticated goals until these basic needs are met. It's useless to talk about striving for success to a hungry person. The growl of an empty stomach drowns out all words of encouragement and motivation. Jesus knew that. He tells us in James 2:15 that it does no good to speak loving words to a sister or brother until we first meet their basic needs. This advice has not changed over the centuries. As long as there are people in need of the very basics of life, no one is free from want. No one is free to pursue personal success at the expense of the universal to overcome success. There is an inter-connectedness among all people that makes it immoral to ignore the basic needs of others. When it comes to basic human needs, we *are* our brothers' (and sisters') keepers. Their welfare *is* our concern. None of us can be truly filled while others are empty.

Now I lay me down to sleep, but not until I have helped create a safe place for my sisters and brothers to sleep.

Day 205

"It is a need of the spirit not to forget who ever has let you feel beautiful and safe. But the past is not the next amazing possibility."
—June Jordan

The university was pleased that a student with such a fine academic record as E. Blackwell had applied to their medical school. Had they known the "E" stood for Elizabeth she never would have been accepted. Thankfully, we've moved beyond sexual barriers, on the surface at least. Still, if we examine our consciences, we're forced to admit that sexual bias does both exist and persist. Why is pink for girls and blue for boys? Why do we give little girls dolls and little boys tools? Why are little girls sent to ballet classes and little boys shunned if they want ballet lessons? The mind is not intrinsically sex-typed. It is the lessons we both reach and are taught that create the barriers that continue to judge people on the basis of their sexual organs. Success includes successfully breaking through the glass ceiling. Only by our conscious effort will success become an equal opportunity employer.

My freedom ends where my sister's bondage begins.

Day 206

"Change produces stress. Stress produces change."

—Rev. Jim Holley

Graduation brings the inevitable question: What are you going to do with your life? Marriage demands that you merge two lives into a cohesive whole. The birth of a child, the death of a parent, the loss of a job, whether through firing, downsizing or retirement — all these changes produce stress. Stress is part of everyday life; no one can escape it. It is how to handle the stress in your life that determines whether you will be a *can do* or *can't do* person. Stress doesn't have to be negative. Creativity can transform the potentially crippling effects of stress into the empowering forces of positive change. By facing the stresses in your life head on, you can learn to greet the changes stress rings with open-minded enthusiasm. Rather than allowing stress to reduce you as a person, you can elevate stress to its proper role, that of stretching you to a higher level of personhood. Stress, and the changes stress brings are woven into the very fabric of life. What you do with stress and change involves a conscious decision to make the fabric of your life strong, durable, quality material.

Everyday in every way, I am changing for the better.

> "What happens to a dream deferred: Does it dry up?"
>
> —Langston Hughes

She dreamed of going to law school. She worked hard in college and had excellent grades. Then her mother fell ill and died. Suddenly, there were younger siblings to care for, housework and shopping to do. Soon her grades began to fall; there was simply no time to study. In her senior year she dropped out of school and went to work. "I'll go back," she told herself. "I can still go to law school when things get a little better." She continued to work hard; the family desperately needed the money. As her brothers and sisters grew, she instilled in them a dedication to education. One after the other, she helped them through college. With each passing year, her dream grew dimmer. She lived vicariously through the siblings she had raised; she watched them become successful professionals; she made their achievements her own. Gradually she felt them grow farther from her until she barely saw them at all. They had gone on with their own lives. She had deferred her dream so long it had dried up. Some people have few choices. Others have few goals. In which category do you fall?

Today I'll search for alternative ways to make my dream come true.

Day 208

"He can run, but he can't hide."
—Joe Louis

You were not made to live as a fugitive. You especially were not made to live as a fugitive from yourself. When you run from yourself, from who you are and what you value, you are making an important statement "I don't like myself." If you don't like yourself, how can you expect anyone else to like you? If you can't stand your own company, why would anyone else want to spend time with you? You may be able to minimize your contact with others, you may even be able to devise a style of living that lets you hide from the world, but you can never find a way to hide from yourself. No matter where you go or what you do, you take yourself with you. In the final analysis, you are all you've got. If you're destined to spend your lifetime being and being with yourself, why not make yourself into the best self you can be? Develop your talents. Pursue your interests. Work on overcoming your negative traits and replacing them with positive qualities. Like the Army slogan says, "Be all that you can be." After all, you deserve the best *you* for a lifetime companion!

Today I'll begin becoming a person I'd like to spend my life with.

DAY 209

"And that's the way it is."
—Walter Cronkite

As you move forward toward your goals, you'll encounter some things that can't be changed, at least not now, or not by you. They just are; that's all there is to it. Sometimes these unchangeables may appear as obstacles in your path. These are the times that separate the strong from the faint-hearted. Nothing can keep you from achieving your goals unless you let it. When you run into a person, place, thing, or situation that you can't change, stop wasting your time and energy in futile efforts. Channel your power instead to find creative ways to overcome the obstacle. If you can't move it, perhaps you can go around it. If you can't change it, perhaps you can find a new way to use it that will actually foster your progress. Ask yourself why you're bumping into this obstacle. Maybe you've taken a wrong turn and are off track. In that case, the obstacle serves as a reminder to check your map. Could it be that the barrier is meant to teach you something necessary to your journey toward success? Might it be there for a positive purpose you've yet to discover? Remember, when you run into a solid wall, God is always there to open a hidden door.

Today I'll accept the obstacle I can't change and find a way around it.

"The new frontiers of which I speak . . . sum up not what I intend to offer the American people, but what I intend to ask of them."
—John Fitzgerald Kennedy

You will receive success in direct proportion to what you give to achieve it. It's the old law of supply and demand: if you supply the energy, you can someday demand the rewards. Every successful person knows that you only get out of something what you put into it. Take a business. In order to grow, part of the profits must be reinvested in new equipment, new buildings, new technology. The business cannot stay afloat and remain competitive if the owner draws off all the profits without putting anything back. The trick is in deciding how to best reinvest, how much to put back in, and when to do it. This will be attained in direct proportion to the amount of time, energy, and funding the owner puts into the business. All of life is like a business. Relationships, education, social and political organizations, churches, communities — all require reinvestment in order to succeed. All give back to the investor proportionate returns on the investment.

I will invest my time and talent wisely; I will choose one activity and really get involved.

> "I didn't know I was so powerful until people
> began to tell me."
>
> —Eseola McCarty

I read an interesting philosophy on child rearing. During the first few months of life, a baby should be picked up as soon as it begins to cry. This is how a baby learns trust. Somewhere around the fourth or fifth month, a baby begins to learn cause and effect. "If I cry, mommy or daddy will come. Therefore, I'll cry to make daddy or mommy come. Just five months to learn about power and control! Some people don't seem to learn these lessons in a lifetime. They live as if they have no power at all. Everything that happens to them is someone else's fault. They lose job after job because the boss is unreasonable. They fail in relationships because the other party expected too much. They are poor because they come from poor families. They lose because the system has failed them or they're stuck in a losing system. Each of us has the power to take responsibility for our own lives. Each of us can begin exercising that power through responsible living. If you're stuck, get unstuck; don't blame it on someone else. If you need money, get a job. If you have no skills, get training and education. If relationships continually fail, look inside yourself. Take responsibility now for your own problems. Remember to take responsibility later for the wonderful way you've turned your life around.

I am powerful enough to control me.

DAY 212

"A person is a person through other persons."
—Bantu Proverb

If anyone had reason to see the world as filled with hateful, evil people, it was Anne Frank, the young Jewish girl who perished at the hands of the Nazis. Yet the journal she kept during her years in hiding prior to her discovery and death is a legacy of hope, faith, courage, and positive feelings. Despite persecution, deprivation, and constant terror, Anne Frank never lost her belief in the innate goodness of the human spirit. Many of us have lived with hardship and some form of injustice. Yet I doubt that any of us have been subjected to the systemized persecution Anne Frank suffered. Why, then, was Anne Frank able to write with such conviction, "I still believe that people are really good at heart?" Why do so many of us see only the bad? Anne Frank had faith. She believed that no matter how much evil surrounded her, good would prevail. She refused to accept that all that was good, all that was positive, all that was loving, all that was right had disappeared from the world. She looked for the good in herself; she found the good in others. Developing a can do attitude requires that we see the can do abilities in ourselves and in others.

I am a good person, I see others as good persons too.

"Who is my neighbor?"
—Bible paraphrase

No matter how widely traveled you may be, you still belong to a community. Your community is your home. It is where your house is, where you eat, where you sleep, where your children go to school, where your neighbors live. It is the place where you celebrate holidays, the place to which you invite relatives and friends. Even if you have a huge mansion with many acres surrounding it, you still identify with the community nearest your mansion. Doesn't it make sense, then, that you would work to make your community the best of all places to live? Most of us will not make a sweeping change in the world, but we can make important changes in our communities. We can take time to volunteer in a community organization. We can make the effort to develop friendships with our neighbors. We can support local businesses and patronize local stores. We can organize efforts to improve neighborhood schools, to eliminate neighborhood gangs, to eradicate violence in our neighborhoods and to make our streets safer. Not only are we a nation of communities, we are a world of communities. Successful living begins with living in a success-oriented environment. Maybe we really can make a sweeping difference in the world by making a difference in our neighborhoods, one community at a time.

I __can__ live in a successful neighborhood — my own!

Day 214

> "The thing that makes you exceptional. . .
> is inevitable that which must also make you
> lonely."
>
> —Lorraine Hansbury

God created us for His own benefit. He wanted someone with whom He could commune, someone to keep Him company. The human race was created to fill the void between the animals and the angels. If God needed companionship, you can be sure you do too! Choosing your companions is one of the most important decisions you will make. Your companions are a reflection of yourself. God created us in His own image to reflect His own qualities. Your friends mirror the qualities you most admire. This doesn't mean you should only choose people like yourself to be your friends. Diversity adds richness and color to life. What you should look for in people you choose as friends is morals, standards, and ethics. You want your friends to be honest and trustworthy. You want them to be interesting and fun. You want them to be kind, courteous, sincere, warm, considerate, and open. You want them to be as dedicated to achieving their own individual goals as you are. Once you have determined that a potential friend possesses all these characteristics, take a look at yourself.

A good friend is a good person. I'm a good person.

Day 215

> "No poor, rural, weak, or black person should ever again have to bear the burden of being deprived."
>
> —Jimmy Carter

Politics has been called "the art of the possible." However, for too long the possible has remained the impossible due to the focus of elected officials on getting reelected rather than on bringing about positive changes. We should not rely upon government to bring us success in life. However, the power of government to secure opportunities for success cannot be ignored. Developing a can do attitude in your personal life will allow you to extend this attitude to public life. It is vital that you exercise your voting power. Not only must you vote, but you must vote wisely. Being informed about candidates enables you to help elect officials who will act to make the possible happen. The poor, the weak, those in the minority must no longer be deprived of equal opportunities. As you grow stronger, as you learn through overcoming your own deprivations, you must not turn your back on those still coming up the ladder. Get involved and stay involved at every level, both for your own good and for the collective good of all people.

Today I will begin reading the daily newspaper and tracking the records of those who represent me.

Day 216

"It ain't over 'til it's over."

—Yogi Berra

Faith is the foundation of power. The path from where you are now to where you want to be is not straight and level; it often runs uphill. It takes many curves and turns. Sometimes it even seems to double back on itself so that you feel that you're going in the opposite direction. Don't give up! Don't lose your faith! This is the most important advice I can give you. Your life journey ain't over 'til it's over. The human eye is powerful, but our vision is limited. We see our lives in sections — the past and the present only. Our glimpses of the future are subjective and can be inaccurate. But God sees our entire lives, from beginning to end, in one glance. He knows where you are, where you've been, and where you're going. Your future is full of wonderful surprises. Walk toward your future with faith. Make wise choices. Prepare yourself for the unexpected. Hold on to your self-confidence. Look for the positive in the midst of the negative. Always remember, It ain't over 'til it's over.

Today is the first day of my future. I'll use today wisely.

> "My right and my privilege to stand here
> before you have been won — won in my
> lifetime — by the blood of the innocent."
> —Rev. Jesse Jackson Sr.

What does it mean to be a winner? Is there a difference between being a winner and winning? Little children want to win. They want to win the first game; they want to win every game. Winning is an action; being a winner requires a winning attitude. Winning takes place one action at a time, one victory at a time. The winning attitude is a continuous, positive way of looking at everything and everyone in your life and evaluating how they fit your game plan. A winner is constantly moving forward in positive ways toward success. A winner is able to accept defeat when it comes, learn from it, make it part of his or her personal history, and keep on moving forward. Winners are sought out and respected by others. Winning doesn't require that someone else lose; winners know there are plenty of routes to success with plenty of room for plenty of winners. Winning brings momentary victory. Winners live the victorious lifestyle day after unending day.

I'm a winner — today, tomorrow, forever!

DAY 218

The sun is up there, yes, it truly is. Reach for it!

—Rev. Jim Holley

I was leaving from the Detroit airport. Five inches of snow had fallen the night before and an ice storm the morning of the flight. I was slipping and sliding all over the road. The airport was crowded with delayed passengers; confusion reigned at every gate. Snow on the ground, an icy environment, crowds, delays — it didn't bode well for the flight. Finally, we took off. As the plane fought to break through layer after layer of clouds and turbulence, the pain in my ear drum was excruciating. Suddenly we reached our altitude and there was the sun! My attitude changed immediately. Life is like that flight. The project may get off track, the relationship may go wrong, but somehow you must continue to remind yourself that through it all, up there is the sun! Wealth, success, happiness, blessings, a better job will not come to you. You must go to it. It is up there. Yes, it is up there and once you realize it's there, what could concern you? Nothing! Go for it!

Today I'll reach for the sun!

Day 219

"I refuse to accept the idea that the 'isness' of man's present nature makes him morally incapable of reaching up for the 'oughtness' that forever confronts him."
— Dr. Martin Luther King, Jr.

You've heard the saying, "Nothing lasts forever." Usually this is applied to good things as a warning not to get too comfortable; bad things are just around the corner. A great commentary on the need for positive thinking! But remember, bad or negative things don't last forever either. While we all may get stuck sometimes, none of us has to remain stuck. You can move forward if you want to badly enough. You can change yourself; you can change your present situation; you can change your outlook for the future. Education, effort, perseverance, hard work — these will move you forward toward your economic and lifestyle goals. Networking can be a big help, too. On a higher plane, prayer, faith, adoption of high moral standards — these can move you mentally and spiritually from the "isness" of the present human condition to the "oughtness" of human achievement. You can change yourself. You can change the world. You can change the world by changing yourself. The human condition is changed one person at a time.

Today I'm growing. Today I'm changing. Today I'm becoming the person I want myself to be.

DAY 220

> "No person is your friend who demands your silence, or denies your right to grow."
> —Alice Walker

Remember "The Newlywed Game?" I was always fascinated by that show. Here were newly married couples, so fresh and alive and in love, readily disclosing the most intimate facts about one another on national television. And for what? A set of luggage? A new washer? A weekend get-away? Personally, I don't think I'd want to get away with someone who so easily betrayed my confidences. Essential to developing a can do attitude and successful relationships is simple courtesy and thoughtfulness. This means treating others as you would like to be treated. If getting ahead requires stepping on someone else's head, find another way. Now I'm not talking about fair competition. We all must compete for jobs, promotions, sales, etc. We should and must do all we can to land that position, make that sale — all we can within the limits of honesty and fairness. The road through life can be long and lonely; God puts others in our lives to become our fellow travelers, to share for awhile whatever distance is common to our personal journeys. The relationships we form are precious blessings. Treat them lovingly. Handle them with care. And if they should end, treasure their memory.

I am a good friend. I will remain a good friend. I will treasure my friendships.

DAY 221

"Is this happening because I'm a woman? Or is this happening because this is how it happens?"
—Charlayne Hunter-Gault

Relationships between the sexes will never improve until we do two things: women must forgive men for not being there for them; men must forgive women for surviving without them. You must take responsibility for where you are and where you're going. The past is gone. Examine it, learn from it, then let it go. Welcome new relationships for the opportunities they bring. Everyone who comes into your life comes for a reason. Sometimes it's to act as our mirror. It is easier to see faults in others than in ourselves. The faults most easily seen are those we, ourselves, possess. When we set high standards for our relationships, we achieve a higher standard of relationships. Setting standards means choosing for yourself the kind of relationships you judge right for you. Think of all the time and energy you'll save by not wasting yourself on sub-standard relationships! Instead of cluttering your life with people who don't meet your standards, free yourself to live and give to those where there is potential for a ten relationship.

My pursuit of success is too valuable to settle for substandard.

Day 222

"The wisest men follow their own direction."
—Euripides

You know when you're going in the right direction! Yes you do, you truly do! You have the complete road map for your life deep inside you. This may be hard to believe considering all the road blocks and detours life presents us. Buy this and you'll be more pleasing. Wear this and you'll be more popular. Change your looks and you'll be more successful. But why all these detours? Are they for your good? Of course not! You know that. They are for their own good, not yours. What you buy, wear, or use will benefit them, not you. You have the wisdom to discern the right direction for you in any situation. Listen to yourself. Be still and listen. Reflect. Look inward. Follow your own direction.

I carry inside me the complete road map for my life. Today I will find and follow it!

DAY 223

> "This is a country that regards it's woman as it's
> monsters, celebrating wherever possible the
> predatory coquette and carnivorous mother."
> —Toni Code

One of the greatest differences between men and women is that women have been taught that they must be everything to everyone. They have learned to subjugate their own needs in favor of meeting the needs of others. Part of this may involve the maternal instinct. Part, I believe, involve the survival instinct. If you think it's hard to succeed as a man of color, consider what it's been like to survive as a woman of color. Historically, the power of sisterhood is directly responsible for the survival of women of color. From sharing child care to sharing living quarters, from sharing meals to sharing chores, earnings, clothing, and furniture, sisterhood has been proven to be a powerful source of strength. Today we've finally reached a point where women are doing more than surviving. They are taking their rightful leadership roles in all areas — business, education, society, government, etc. Not all women, mind you, not even enough women, but they're making steady progress. Much of that progress continues to be supported primarily by sisterhood. Men, respect this unique relationship and be thankful that it was there for your women when they needed it. Women, never grow so successful that you forget the chain of women who helped you fulfill your dreams. People helping people create the greatest opportunities for success.

I know where I came from and where I'm going.

Day 224

"Anticipate the good so that you may enjoy it."

—Ethiopian Proverb

Every decision you make is a reflection of what you believe about yourself. If you believe you're strong, you will be strong. If you believe you can make it, you'll make it. Perhaps you're in a bad relationship. Ask yourself, "Why am I staying here?" Are you afraid to leave? Do you believe yourself incapable of making it on your own? You will never achieve more than you believe you can. You will never get better than you believe you deserve. You will never have more than you think you're worth. Begin by working on your self-esteem. See yourself as a cherished child of God. You are a child of the King. Know it! Believe it! Then act on your beliefs. We form relationships to grow, not to wither. Good relationships are supportive, energizing, growth-promoting. If yours is not, get out. Bad relationships sap your strength and stunt your growth. Women (and men) remember: If you have to, you can do anything. Do the things you must do to make you the person you were born to be.

Quitting is not failing. I am a child of the King. I cannot fail.

"Success is about dreaming big dreams,
setting specific goals, and realizing them."
—Darnell Sutton

Have you ever noticed how some people seem to have been born with a cloud hanging over them? No matter what they do, they encounter trouble. No matter how hard they try, they always fail. Often these are nice people, sweet people. Always, however, they are people off-track. When you're off track, nothing fits. The gears just don't mesh. There may be movement, but there is no forward progress. Time seems to slip away. While you're still trying to figure out what to do today, today becomes yesterday and another tomorrow is wasted. If you're off track, it's time to get back online. Stop whatever you're doing and take time to evaluate your actions. Have you formulated a plan? Are you sticking to it? Is it time to change course, devise a new map, or modify your plan? Think things through clearly. Write out your answers. Keep an accurate written record of everything you do every day for a week. Are your actions in harmony with your goals or are you just spinning your wheels? You can do anything you want if you want it badly enough. Know it! Believe it! Act on it today!

Today I'll act to get myself back on track.

DAY 226

> "Most people go through life with their boat tied up next to the pier. What made me a hero was that I weighed anchor."
>
> —Bill Pinkney

Each of us comes to today, to this place, at this time, with a history. No other, not even those who have shared your history, can fully understand the impact our pasts have on the present person you are. Your history is your most private possession. What you do to control the impact of your history on the person you are is your most private action. This control begins with acknowledgment. Parading your private past for public review is not necessary, but acknowledging your scars and admitting that your wounds exist is necessary. Expose them to the healing light of self-love, self-nurturing, self-appreciation. You are worthy of healing. You are capable of healing. You can begin the healing process by recognizing the ghosts of your past in your actions of the present. This recognition is not an excuse for negative behavior. Rather, it is the launch point of self-knowledge and positive self-transformation.

The past is past. Today I will take responsibility for my behavior in the present.

> "This is our family hour."
> —Rev. Jesse Jackson Sr.

Today we hear a lot of talk about families and "quality time." There's even a commercial that features a kitchen table and urges families to eat dinner together once a week! Have our families really deteriorated? Are our schedules so busy that we must pencil in a night with the family? Do we really believe that quality time can replace quantity time in the lives of our children? Anything worth having takes time and nurturing. A garden doesn't grow overnight. It won't flourish if neglected. Time spent smelling the roses can't replace the time spent on the hard work of planting, watering, weeding, and pruning. None of us gets to choose our families of origin. We do, however, get to pick our mates. Choose wisely. If you don't want to put in the time required to nurture a family, don't have children. Don't just drift into situations; make conscious choices about lifelong decisions. No one succeeds if the family fails. Work for your family. Be an example for your family. Take responsibility within the family. Make every hour family hour.

I am both whole and a part of a whole.

"All the lonely people, where do they come from, where do they go, where do they belong?"

—Dr. Arlene Churn

We were created as social creatures. We were placed in this world to live in community with one another. We were given the gift of language so that we can share ideas and feelings. We were filled with emotions that keep us striving to understand and to be understood. We were blessed with the capacity to love God, self, and others. Why, then, are there so many lonely people? Why do we ourselves often feel lonely? It's important to realize that there's a difference between being lonely and being alone. All of us need and deserve alone time — time to meditate, reflect, and commune with ourselves at the deepest personal level. None of us deserves loneliness — the prolonged sense of being unconnected and out of place. Setting high personal standards may cause times of temporary loneliness. That's okay. Stick to your standards; the loneliness will pass. For the young and strong, loneliness can usually be solved by making new friends and forming new relationships. For the old and weak, loneliness is not so easily solved. All of us have a responsibility to provide a sense of community for the frail, the weak, and the elderly among us.

Today I'll take time to listen to someone whose voice is seldom heard.

DAY 229

"More and more as we come closer and closer in touch with nature and it's teachings, are we able to see the Divine."
—George Washington Carver

Nothing brings about talk of change so much as a presidential election year. Out march the candidates, each calling for a change of the old order and the commencement of a new way of doing things. Ever notice how hard it is to get an exact picture of what each candidate is proposing? There's a lot of talk, but not much is said. Real life isn't like that. Things don't happen in the abstract. Change comes through concrete, identifiable actions. Life moves in an orderly progression of days, months, years. The calendar is unstoppable. You can idly flip the pages every thirty or so days, or you can fill in the blocks with scheduled activities and deadlines that give a framework against which progress can be measured. Presidents are elected for a four-year term. If their actions please enough of the people — or if their opponents alienate enough of the people — they may be elected to another four-year term. You, on the other hand, have been "elected" to be you for a life term. The actions you take affect your entire future. You can chart your course, change your course, or get off course. You can accept the current order of things or you can help shape the rapidly changing times you live in.

I am a part of the time in which God has placed me. I'll make my influence felt.

Day 230

> "I see the face of America, red, yellow, brown, black and white. We are all precious in God's sight . . ."
> —Rev. Jesse Jackson Sr.

We have come to a point in America today where politically correctness is a priority. We are careful to avoid "isms" in our speech and actions. But has anything really changed in our thoughts? I believe it has. I'm not saying racism, sexism, anti-semitism have been abolished. And I'm not saying that hate groups don't continue to exist. But I am saying that we can no longer use "isms" as excuses for personal failure. We are all precious in God's sight. We are learning to be precious in the sight of one another, too. That lesson becomes easier to learn as we become easier to love. Angry people are not easy to love. Violent people are not easy to love. Dishonest, rude, arrogant, or "poor-me" type people are not easy to love. Being loved, being accepted, opening the doors to educational and career advancement depend more on who we are on the inside than on the color we are on the outside. Today, the face of America is made up of many faces, many colors. If you can't find a place for your face, maybe it's time to examine your attitude. "Can Do," "Can't Do," or "Won't Do" — the choice is yours.

Today, I see the world with the eyes of God . . . Colorless.

Day 231

"Find the good and praise it."
—Alex Haley

All of us are constantly bombarded with a steady stream of both positive and negative impressions. Why, then, are some people able to maintain a happy, positive outlook while others are mired in misery and depression? The answer, I believe, lies in which impressions we allow to be implanted into our conscious and subconscious minds. We become what we believe. All of us have the ability to choose what we will believe, what thoughts and beliefs we allow to become part of ourselves. No matter where you are or what your circumstances, you can choose to find beauty, truth, light, and happiness. This is not the same as adopting a Pollyanna attitude toward life. Rather it is making a conscious effort to find the good in yourself, in others, in situations and circumstances. Choosing to be happy means taking positive steps toward happiness. It means having the courage to act in your own behalf, to adopt your own standards and goals, to put yourself and your own well-being first. Only when you, with faith and courage, become a happy person yourself, can you begin to bring happiness to others.

I deserve to be happy. Today I will seek out those things that bring happiness to me.

Day 232

> "Public Assistance = Public Dependence.
> Public Dependence = Public Resistance."
> —Anonymous

All problems are solvable. It's true. *You* may not be able to solve every problem, but then, isn't it great that no one's asking you to? When was the last time you were asked to solve the problem of global warming? Of rain forest preservation? Of economic development in the former Soviet Union? See how lucky you are? The problems you're asked to solve <u>do</u> lie within your ability. Are you caught in the endless cycle of public assistance? Get off it! Now I know the excuses. "The only job I can get doesn't pay as much as welfare does." "I can't afford day care for my kids." "I'd lose my medical assistance if I got a job." *Public Assistance = Public Dependence. Public Dependence = Public Resistance.* What happens to self-esteem when you become part of a public problem? How can you develop a can do attitude when the part of the public that is paying your public assistance turns into a stronger and stronger public resistance force? You *can* get out of the welfare trap! All it takes is believing that you can and a little creative thinking. Network with others in the same situation. Share child care. Explore new job placement incentives such as availability of low/no cost medical insurance. Learn to rely on yourself. After all, who is a more reliable person?

Today I'm becoming part of the solution.

> "Love is my inspiration and talent is my
> motivation to do good."
>
> —Camille Cosby

People respond to you according to the way you present yourself. If you are open, smiling, warm, receptive, you will be received with openness and warmth. If you exude confidence, people will trust you. If you are friendly, people will want you for a friend. Likewise, if you are closed, wary, distrustful, insecure, people will be wary of you. They will question your motives, doubt your abilities, and close themselves off from you. Life is a mirror reflecting your own attitudes about yourself and others. Why not make it a positive attitude? You're growing in self-love, self- esteem, self-respect, and self-reliance. Make sure these are reflected in your attitude. Let your attitude shine forth from your private self and become your public image. This new, positive can do public image will attract people who are also self-confident and self-reliant. By proclaiming in actions and deeds that you're somebody, that you're worthy of respect and love, you'll attract respectful, respectable, and self-respecting people. You'll be surrounded by loving people — people who love themselves in the best positive sense — people who are open to loving you — people who are worthy of receiving your love in return.

Today I'll polish my mirror to reflect my can do attitude.

Day 234

"You must focus on what you can do."
—Wally "Famous Amos"

A January night in the city. The temperature is ten degrees. On the streets, a "Code Blue" has been declared. A social worker, accompanied by a police officer, is attempting to move the homeless into a nearby shelter. One man refuses to be budged. "It's a free country, man, and this is a free street," he shouts. "I'm a free man and I'm staying here." Overnight the temperature plummets. By morning the man is dead. Ever notice that those doing the most shouting about freedom are often the ones with so little to lose? The teenager with failing grades declaring her freedom to quit school. The drug addict proclaiming his freedom to abuse his body. The father asserting his freedom to walk away from a failing marriage — and from his dependent children. The addicted, the abused, the pusher, and the abuser. When did freedom begin to be more about self-destruction than self-fulfillment? When did we trade the right to life, liberty and the pursuit of happiness for the freedom to destroy life, find liberty in a bottle or syringe, and pursue happiness at the expense of individuals and society? If you have nothing left to lose, then you have everything to gain! You can gain everything worth having by believing that you can, working so that you can, and doing all that you can to reach your goals.

I have too much to lose to waste time on negative behaviors.

> "He's a God of a second chance."
> —Bishop Paul Morton

As you move forward toward your goals, it is good to look back sometimes to where you've been. Your past is your personal history. In the final analysis, it is the only history that really matters to you. Pause for a bit to consider some questions. How far have you come from your starting point? What have you learned along the way? If you had it to do over, what things would you change? What would you do differently? I reflected on these questions recently and found that all of the changes I would make had to do with other people rather than myself. I would listen more carefully, love more freely, serve more willingly. I would reserve more of myself and my time for my family. And I would spend that time with my family being the best person (rather than the sometimes too tired, too grumpy, too demanding person) I could be. Looking back gives us a clearer picture of who we are and what is important to us. It highlights our priorities. If you find that your priorities sometimes have been misplaced, do not grieve. None of us can change the past, but all of us can change the future. Write down those things you wish you had done differently. Incorporate them into your overall plan for success. Check periodically to see how well you're meeting your revised goals. Maybe you can't re-write history but you can write your role for the future, the future that will someday be your personal history.

Today I'll view my future as a second chance

Day 236

> "Through the process of amendment, interpretation and court decision, I have finally been included in 'We the people.'"
> —Barbara Jordan

"They say that . . . " "Everybody knows . . . " "Everyone tells me . . . " How often phrases like these pepper our speech. Yet note the pronouns. All are vague, non-specific, non-personal. Have you ever stopped to wonder who the theys are? Who is everybody? How many people make up everyone? Think of how many things you do or don't do because of what "they" say. Seems silly, doesn't it, when they isn't even a definable group. As you develop your self-esteem, the opinions of others will have less impact on you. You'll learn to trust your own judgement and not rely less on the beliefs of others. Learning to trust yourself requires taking a chance on yourself. Acting on your own beliefs and convictions produces a positive outcome, and you'll grow in self-esteem. Your trust in yourself will increase. Of course, this doesn't mean no one's opinion should ever be taken into consideration. If you choose your friends carefully and surround yourself with people you respect, you'll want to seek their advice when you're unsure. This doesn't mean you don't trust yourself. Rather it proves you trust the judgement you exercised in choosing your friends. So consult them in times of doubt, but always remember, the bottom line for you is you.

I know what's best for me. I know who's best for me.

Day 237

"You can't completely control whether you're beautiful or popular. But you can control how you spend your time and whom you spend it with."

—Dr. Mary Pipher

All of us can't be raving beauties, but we all can be neat, clean, and well-groomed. Most of us will never have hordes of adoring fans, but all of us can cultivate loving, honest relationships. Each of us is given one lifetime to spend on earth. How we spend it is a very personal choice. Marketers, advertisers, and media experts compete in telling us how to spend our time. "Buy this and you'll be more attractive." "Stop here for awhile and you'll meet a crowd to hang out with." Your time is your most precious commodity. Will you let others choose for you how to spend it? Do you really want to spend countless hours in front of the mirror trying to look like someone you're not? Do you really want to hang out with people you don't care about and who you know don't truly care about you? Personally, I'd rather be alone with a good book than be at the center of a crowd of people with whom I have no common interests or goals. Spend reasonable time on your appearance. Give generously of your time to friends and family. Take time to explore new relationships and interests. Reclaim your time from unsatisfying pursuits. Yes, all of us are given just one lifetime to spend on earth. When you come to the end of that lifetime, who and what will really matter? Your looks or your legacy?

I have one lifetime. I won't waste one day.

DAY 238

"Like a bridge over troubled water, I will lay me down."

—Aretha Franklin

Do you have relatives who only contact you when they're in trouble? As long as everything is going smoothly in their life you don't hear a word from them. But let something go wrong, and they're on your doorstep. They expect you to provide the bridge over the troubled waters they've gotten themselves into. They call up all the old times and remind you that blood is thicker than water. Because they're family you take them in, lend them money, do whatever you can for them. Then when the crisis passes, they're on their way, never to contact you again until the next time they need help. Does their behavior cause you to feel hurt and used? If they were to come again begging for help, would you remind them that "once burned, twice shy" and send them packing? God has a family — a family that includes you and me and every person living on this earth. Some are close family; they speak to God, listen for His voice, remember to say thank you, and try to live the way He directs. Others only call Him when they're in trouble. Then they beg or try to make deals with God. "If you'll help me just this one time, God," they say, and then go on to make promises they'll never keep. They claim kinship when they need God to lay a bridge across the troubled waters of their own creation. They claim independence once they've crossed over. Ever wonder how God feels?

Today I'll remember that a bridge is for two-way crossing.

"You don't have to be an athlete to be a
good sport."

—Mildred Morgan Ball

Have you ever noticed the vastly different ways
people handle adversity? Some are so totally devastated that when troubles strike — and strike they do
in all lives — they never recover. Others keep bouncing back despite the worst difficulties life hurls at them.
What's the secret of not only going on but of continuing to thrive no matter what hurts and hurdles come
your way? The secret is inside yourself! You already
possess the power to overcome any obstacle. Tap into
that inner power. Become your own enabler. While it
may be a solitary process, continue to walk, head high,
through the thousand obstacles that try to block your
way. Be your own cartographer. The path you carve
out for yourself is the only true road to peace, progress,
and prosperity for you.

*I am my own best advocate. Today I will become my
own enabler.*

Day 240

> "I'm poor, I'm black, I may be ugly and
> can't cook, but I'm here."
>
> —Alice Walker

No matter where you are at this very moment,
you're here and you matter. If you're in a good place,
enjoy it. If you don't like the place you're in, today's
the day to move out. Every fact has a counter fact;
the two validate one another. The fact that you're here
makes the opposite true — you can be gone from
here. Wherever it is you want to go, you can get there.
Today's the day to start. Set an ETA (estimated time
of arrival). Plot necessary stops along the way. Then
get moving! Say your destination is the corner office
on the fifty-seventh floor of some corporate headquar-
ters. You calculate it will take two years just to be
hired by the company. First you have to go back and
finish your education. To do that you have to arrange
child care and transportation. Okay. Your destination
is that corner office. Your closest stops are child care
and education. Then you reach the junction of getting hired. From here plot out the next stops — more
education, special skills, networking, making yourself
known and indispensable, etc. By breaking it down into
goals, sub-goals, and small steps, the journey from here
to there is not overwhelming. But it does require that
you get started. Why not today?

Today I'll plan my ETA at the next stop.

"Hope I die before I get old. This is
my generation."

—Peter Townsend

Today, "over 65" is the fastest growing age group
in the country. Within the next decade, this population segment will soar. What's it like to be a senior in
a country and culture that worships youth? For many,
it's a lonely time filled with frightening changes both
inside and out. Spouses, friends, siblings pass on. Children move away. Everyday tasks become more difficult. Always lurking is the fear that the body, mind, or
both will fail, that resources will be depleted, that we'll
become a burden. Once again, those beautiful words
from First Corinthians speak to us. "Love never ends."
This is the beloved passage so often used at wed-
dings, when life is new and everything is just beginning. Yet read the words again. "Love never ends. As
for prophecies, they will cease." Prophecies — the
ability to predict what's ahead. Certainly this capacity
diminishes with age. "As for tongues, they will cease."
Tongues, the ability to speak and communicate, is lost
in old age. "As for knowledge, it will come to an end."
Knowledge — clarity of mind — this is a loss most greatly
feared. Only love never ends. Perhaps the best way
to prepare for old age is to practice love while we're
young. Perhaps the best assurance that we will be able
to cope with old age, no matter the condition of our
minds and bodies, is the undeniable fact that love —
God's love for us, our love for God — will never end.

God's love for me will outlast time.

DAY 242

> "I learned in moments of humiliation to walk away with what was left of my dignity, rather than lose it all in an explosive rage."
>
> —Arthur Ashe

From the day you were born, you were pressured to live for others. You were taught to deny yourself, your own inner needs, your own nature, and conform to the expectations of parents, teachers, neighbors. You were told that to put your own needs first was selfish and therefore sinful. Yet I tell you today that you cannot live for others. You can only live for yourself. You can't live a selfless life of love for others unless you first live for yourself. Get to know yourself and you'll find a wonderful person. You'll find a *you* you'll want to cherish, protect, and love. Please yourself and you'll find the kind of inner peace and happiness that spills over into true caring for others.

Today I will live for the wonderful, beautiful, unselfish person I truly am!

"The West is dying of the effects of its compulsive hatred, and it's obsessive wish for revenge."

—Allison Davis

Sometimes we find ourselves in such a state of need that it's hard to remember God's abundance. We blame other people, other times, other conditions, for our current situation. Yet we, as a people, rather than uniting to work for the common good, quarrel among ourselves. Jealous of one another, we waste our time criticizing, berating, and lamenting while the world unfolds around us. We cannot complain about what others are doing to us if we, together, are not doing for us. We, as a people, are blessed with an abundant quantity of gifts. Instead of quarreling among ourselves, we must use our gifts with creativity, forethought, and confidence. We are so many. Our talents are so great. We have the ability to make sure there is enough to go around.

Today I will tap into God's abundance for myself and others.

"Slaves, though we be enrolled / minds are never sold."

—David Ruggles, Appeals 1835

As you think, you are. The self-speak you talk to yourself all day long creates the respect you have for yourself all life long. Your thoughts are your personal form of mind control. By controlling your thoughts, you control your mind that controls your body that controls your actions. Positive thoughts bring positive control over your mind, body, and actions. Negative thoughts create the reverse. This doesn't mean you never should think about negative things. It is important to explore deeply hidden feelings, buried memories, reactions to past events. But you must learn to think about negative things in positive ways. What do I remember from that bad experience? Why did I react the way I did? What could I have done differently? What did I learn, or fail to learn, from the event? Negative thoughts left unexplored can gradually create a negative mind-set. Negative thoughts explored in light of positive questioning will bring forth greater self-knowledge. The better you know yourself, the more quickly you can recognize your own weaknesses and begin working on them. No one controls your mind but you. Make sure you're not the oppressor.

Today I'll use positive self-questioning to explore painful memories.

DAY 245

"I have made my choice. I had no alternative."
—Paul Robeson

The little girl was too young to read, but she certainly recognized the wonderful pictures on the colorful menu. "Mommy, can I have one of these and one of these and one of these?" she asked, pointing to an ice cream sundae, a slice of apple pie, and a whipped cream-topped brownie. Was it an accident that the dessert menu had such big, bright pictures while the entree menu was simply printed words? Marketing has become one of the highest art forms in today's culture. Billions of dollars are spent annually on efforts to affect your choices. It's easy to understand how someone who is not firmly grounded in a secure value system can be easily swayed. After all, the "swayers" get paid for swaying you; they're experts at it. What can you do to protect yourself? Know who you are and what you want. Don't worry about styles, trends, or what other people want for themselves. Form a picture of who you want to be and what you want to have. Hold that picture in your mind and don't let go of it. Visualize the steps you'll need to take and the choices you'll need to make to become who you want to be and have what you want to have. See yourself taking each step in order, methodically moving from step to step, choice to choice until you reach intermediary goals. Maintain the vision. Now start stepping and choosing. You can get anything you want! It's your restaurant! You can write the menu!

Today I'll take control of my choices.

Day 246

"I no longer need the past to stand up
in the present."

—Edward Maunick

No matter what your past has made of you, you
don't have to stay that way! All of us are products of
our pasts. None of us reaches adulthood without being accused, abused, rejected, dejected, unloved, over-
loved, oppressed, repressed, or any number of negative things. Likewise, none of us reaches adulthood
without some positive experiences, too. No matter
how bad your past has been, there must have been
some times, at least one time, when you had a friend,
won a contest, got a hug, found a love, were paid a
compliment, received an award, or just plain felt good.
Why do we place the blame for who we are only on
the negative things that have happened to us? Surely
the positive things have had an effect, too. Today is a
great day for unpacking your old baggage and filling
your traveling packs with all the good things from your
past. Toss out the hurt, put in the hug. Take out the
pain, put in the gain. You're going on from here any-
way. Why not be a little choosey about what you'll
take along? Make it easy on yourself. Discard all those
unwanted items. Travel light! Don't let your baggage
be a burden.

Today I'm repacking my traveling bags.

> Success is a journey, not a destination.
> —Rev. Jim Holley

In today's busy climate, it's easy to get the idea that success comes overnight. It doesn't. Success comes over a lifetime. The CEOs of major corporations will tell you three things they credit as major factors in their ability to get to the top and stay on top.

1. You need one day in seven to do nothing but think, get a shot of rejoicing, recharging, and renewing of powers. Your dreams and your ideas will be resurrected.

2. You don't need money, you need dreams. You must have a desire for something so strong you'd die to accomplish it. You must decide what you really want to do with the one life you have to live.

3. You must be willing to make an all-out commitment. If you are, here is what will happen. Commitment will produce energy. Energy will produce enthusiasm. Enthusiasm will produce a whole new way of living. Living will produce a whole new attitude.

Today I will decide what I want to do with my life and begin doing it.

DAY 248

"What matters is not to know the world, but
to change it."

—Frantz Fanon

A teacher who refuses to accept a "C." A modern
doctor who makes house calls to the elderly. A neighbor who shows up bearing a casserole on moving day.
A passing motorist who stops to render assistance.
We've all had wonderful people come into our lives
at the very moment we've needed them. Some stay
for a lifetime. Others move on without us quite knowing why. Have you ever questioned why these special persons turned up at exactly the right time with
exactly what you've needed at just that moment?
Could it really be coincidence, or do you see the hand
of God at work? Do you believe in angels? How about
saints? Whatever you call them, angels or saints, God
works through human beings to accomplish divine
purposes. Sometimes these human beings serve as
guardian angels. They help us, inspire us, believe in us,
encourage us, and meet our needs at the very point
and place of need. Sometimes we receive one-time
intervention from a stranger. Sometimes someone we
know performs an unexpected, even uncharacteris-
tic, act of kindness. The bottom line is, *God works
through people*. He uses people to answer prayers
and bring about His purposes. If God uses others to
answer your prayers, mightn't He use you to answer
the prayers of someone else? It's an exciting concept,
being a saint, an angel, or an answer to prayer. Keep
yourself open to the possibilities — of rendering or
receiving divine help.

God, use me today.

Day 249

"The enemy called *Average*"
—Rev. Jim Holley

Indifferent, half-way, mediocre, medium, middle of the road, ordinary, routine, second-rate, so-so, tolerance, typical, norm, and a lack of vision.

The difference between vision and dreams is that one you sleep and the other one you got to get up. Always understand there is within all of us a mixture of ability and opportunity. As humans, we are by nature short sighted. Even those of us with the vision to see our life plan unfolding into the future, can still see only the span of our own lives. A life, by God's timetable, is but a moment. God sees our lives from before birth to long after earthly death. God has a plan for our lives that supersedes our own plans. Working out His plan often requires some interesting and unexpected events. Does this mean we shouldn't plan our lives? Absolutely not! Life is God's greatest gift. He expects us to treasure it, to keep from wasting it, and to use it wisely. God also expects us to keep in touch with Him as we plan our lives and live our plans. By being open to His voice, we can hear warnings to change direction. By being open to His hand moving in our lives, we can avoid roadblocks, negotiate detours, and anticipate crossroads. In planning, we show gratitude for the gift of life. In trusting, we acknowledge God's kingship over our greatest gift, our very lives.

Today, I will conquer this enemy called average.

"People do not wish to be worse, they really wish to become better, but they often do not know how."

—James Baldwin

You were born from the union of two people. You have two parents, four grandparents, eight great-grandparents, and so on. You are linked with someone who is linked with someone who is linked with someone. You are a part of the human chain. You are "The People." When the people speak, governments must listen. When the people act, society must take notice. You are the people and the people is the only force that can change your community, your country, your world. The people hold the power to end poverty. The people hold the power to end homelessness. The people hold the power to recreate the world as we know it and refashion it into a place where all the people have the opportunity to get what they need. Now, having opportunities to get what is needed is not the same as having what you need handed to you. You already possess ability; opportunity must be created. Opportunity to exercise your own talents, to expend your own energy, to secure what is needed for yourself and your dependents must come without compromising the opportunities of others before success is possible. The people hold the power to end violence. The people have the power to stop crime. The people have the power to improve schools, make neighborhoods safe, ensure that the young, the old, and the frail are cared for. You are the people. And the people have the power!

I am a powerful person. I am a part of the people and all people are a part of me.

DAY 251

"I don't regret it one minute. I just wish
I had more to give."

—Eseola McCarty

When Cardinal John Krol of Philadelphia died in 1996, I watched in fascination much of the three-day TV coverage of the funeral. Here was a man who had lived his entire life for his church. Millions testified to his good deeds, unfailing faith, and deep love for all people. Over and over I wondered if, at the end of his life, in the final days when he knew death was near, he had any regrets. Were there things he'd left undone? Were there people he'd disappointed? What sins would be there for him to list in his final confession? None of us will ever know all the ultimate regrets of another. Each of us can begin now to shorten the list of our own final regrets. We can live each day as if it were our last. We can do those things we wouldn't want to leave undone. We can seek pardon of those we've injured and grant pardon to those who have injured us. We can take time right now, today, to express love, give praise, extend help, lend encouragement, provide an example. Today, this minute, is really the only time we're sure of. Make the most of it. Tomorrow may be too late to mend a quarrel, restore a friendship, say "I love you." Begin now to put regrets on your "short list."

Today is the only day of which I'm certain. I'll live it as though it were a legacy.

DAY 252

"No form of government make anybody omniscient."

—Thomas Sowell

One of the greatest problems that has continued to plague minorities in the United States is the failure of people of color to exercise the right to vote. As citizens, we have both an enormous blessing and an enormous responsibility. We are blessed with the right to cast our ballot for the candidate of our choice. We are responsible for exercising that right with wisdom, knowledge, and understanding. Yet year after year, despite mass voter registration drives, people of color fail to register and neglect to vote. The government that governs you is made up of people elected by the voters. Why allow others to have their voices heard while remaining silent yourself? If a law was passed tomorrow revoking your right to vote, you would revolt. Yet while you have this privilege and blessing, do you take it for granted, fail to exercise it, and allow others to choose those who will govern you? Developing a can do attitude means developing the political knowledge that is part of responsible citizenship. Read the papers. Listen to the candidates. Know what they stand for and hear what they're saying. Evaluate their positions. Make up your own mind. Register. Vote!

I trust my judgement. I'll voice my opinion. I'll cast my vote.

Day 253

"The road less traveled is the road less certain."

—Congressman Kweisi Mfume

A network of super highways links Philadelphia with the New Jersey shore, making it possible to travel the approximately 100 miles in about two hours. It wasn't always so. The old shore road used to be the only way to traverse. One woman had been traveling the old shore road all her life. It was the only way she knew to get to the beach. Her children thought she was crazy to stick to the old way. They would brag about the excellent time they could make on the super highway. She would smile and continue to go her own way. Eventually she grew too old to drive. One day her son offered to take her to the shore. Although now slow of speech and sometimes confused of thought, he knew the idea pleased his mother who so loved the beach. Part of the way down, the highway became a snarl of bumper-to-bumper cars. "I wish there were some other way to go," said the son, thumping the steering wheel. "There is," replied his mother. "Just take the next turn." Suddenly, they were out of the traffic and into the cool, scented air of the pine barrens. "Mom, this is great," exclaimed the son. "Why didn't you ever teach me this route?" The mother just smiled. She answered. "Sometimes, son, the road less traveled offers the most beauty."

Today I'm open to new experiences, new beauty.

DAY 254

"In the beginning God . . . in the end God."
—Desmond Tutu

In the Lord's Prayer we say, "Thy will be done."
Then we fill in the blanks with lots of suggestions just
in case God hasn't gotten the total picture. For most
of us, the hardest thing to do is nothing at all. When
something goes wrong — a relationship falters, a plan
goes awry — it's human nature to want to rush in and
fix things. We act without first stopping to assess the
situation. We act for action's sake, without a plan, without forethought, without taking time to evaluate the
total situation. This kind of action does not promote
can do progress. Rather, it renders us scattered and
unfocused. Our energy is diverted away from problem-solving thought processes and wasted in useless,
undirected activity. When we come up against a can't
do situation, often the best solution is to simply let it
be. This doesn't mean giving up. It means offering
the problem up to a higher power. It means recognizing that some things can't be changed except by time.
It means letting go — truly letting go — and letting
God have His way. It means trusting that God's way
will prove to be the best way for you if you just let
it be.

*For today, I'll give it a rest. Just for today, I'll let
it be."*

Day 255

"The constant virtues of the good are tenderness and love."

—Mahabharata, 5-1bc.

Wherever you are today, you'll be directly in the path of someone who needs you. It could be a co-worker in need of task-specific directions. It may be a spouse in need of appreciation. It may be a child in need of encouragement. It may be a neighbor in need of a tool. Don't wait for extraordinary circumstances to do good. Use the ordinary situations you encounter every day as an arena in which to perform little acts of kindness. Then remember, once performed, keep them to yourself; kindness, when boasted of, loses its shine. Whatever you're doing right now, think of how you could perform the same activity for someone else's benefit. As you're reading this book, is there someone who doesn't know how to read? Could you serve as a tutor? If you're preparing dinner, could you prepare a little extra and take a plate to a shut-in? If you're talking on the phone, is there a lonely person who'd love to hear from you? Random acts of kindness bring double blessings. They bless the one you help; they bless you with the good feeling of helping.

Today I'll perform a random act of kindness. (And I won't tell anyone about it.)

DAY 256

"A man who has no imagination has no wings."
—Muhammad Ali

Trading a can't do atmosphere for a can do attitude is a process that takes time and effort. You'll be busy setting goals and working to meet them. If the advice in this book sounds like it will create busyness, it will. But never confuse busy-ness with barrenness. The success-oriented life is filled with meaningful work. The barren life needs work to give it meaning. Can do people have deeply treasured relationships with other can do people. They openly give and receive love. Because they are whole and complete within themselves, can do people find that other people of wholeness gravitate to them. Their lives are rich in action and interaction. The barren life is loveless, empty of all but temporary relationships. It is shallow, filled with frantic scurrying from activity to activity with no focus or roots. As you move from can't do to can do, you'll be busy, but never too busy to spend time with yourself, with others, and with God. It is this grounding — from within, without, and above — that will keep you on the course of productive busy-ness, not destructful barrenness.

My life is full, but there's always room for more.

> "Happiness is perfume, you can't pour it
> on somebody else without getting a few
> drops on yourself."
>
> —James Van Der Zee

Happy people are people who share. We're simply made that way. Children bubble over with happiness, spreading it indiscriminately around to all they meet. The happiness of a bride and groom flows down the aisle touching everyone at the ceremony. How much coaxing does it take to get a proud grandparent to share pictures of a new baby? As you begin to find ever greater happiness through successful living, you'll automatically begin to share more of yourself with others. The new, confident you won't be timid about approaching others with warmth and openness. Your can do attitude will radiate outward, drawing others to you, causing them to want to be in your company. Don't be afraid of spreading yourself too thin. Your good judgement will keep you from wasting time in unproductive pursuits and relationships. Rather than taxing your strength, your happiness will strengthen you to share even more generously. Best of all, you'll hardly know you're doing it! Since God built the sharing mechanism into your human character, you'll be acting more in sync with your true self, the happy, sharing self you were created to be.

Happiness is within me. I don't have to search for it.

"If you would reap praise, sow the seeds:
gentle words and useful deeds."
—St. Francis de Sales

You never know what another is made of; handle all human beings with care. It's so easy to alter the future. A word, an act, even a look can make so much difference in the outcome of another's life. This is especially true with children. They are so anxious to please, they so hunger for your attention that they'll even act up and risk punishment rather than be ignored. You never can give a child too much praise. Praise builds confidence, self-esteem, and, in turn, respect for others. You never can give a child too much attention. Positive attention tells a child she's important. Handle children gently; they are so fragile. They're so newly come into this world that they haven't yet built up defenses. Speak to children gently, frequently, lovingly. Remember, communicating is as much about listening as it is about speaking. In dealing with children, keep three goals in mind: Give them roots, give them wings, set them on the can do journey a little further along than you were when you started.

Each time I speak to a child, I hold the future in my hands.

Day 259

"A dream is the bearer of a new possibility,
the enlarged horizon, the great hope."
—Elizabeth Barrett Browning

Whatever you want, God wants something even better for you. Whatever your goal, God has a higher prize. Whatever you dream of, God's dream for you shines brighter. I'm always amazed that we can live in this world, so full of beauty, and fail to see God's gifts. "My world's not beautiful," you might be saying. "You ought to see where I live!" It doesn't matter where you live. Your world is filled with God's gifts. If you're in a lousy neighborhood, use God's gift of creativity to bring about improvements. Or, use God's gift of intelligence and ambition to move up and out. Even if you're living in the worse ghetto while you're working to bring about change, use God's gift of discernment to seek out beauty. Look for it in those around you. Surely there's a neighbor who's been kind, a teacher who's been encouraging, a pastor who's reached out. Turn off to the ugliness of situations and things, and turn on to the beauty of God's gift of other people. Continue to dream, but don't sleep. Work on changing yourself and changes in your situation will follow. Make a plan. Put it into action. Don't be sidetracked. God has given you so many wonderful gifts. Why would He stop now? He's waiting to bless you with the gifts that will far surpass your dreams.

If I can dream it, God and I can do it.

> "Find the good. It's all around you. Find it, showcase it, and you'll start believing in it."
>
> —Jesse Owens

Are beliefs fact or fiction? Do we believe only what we can prove? Or can we prove anything we believe? I think a little of both is true. For example, I believe that although my parents had a bitter divorce, at one time they loved each other. I can't prove it. My mother would never admit it and my father's dead. But because I exist, I believe that at some point there was love. Some things just have to be taken on faith. I believe that no matter how bad life is, changes can occur. And because change is possible, life is worth living. This is an especially hard belief to hold on to in some of my pastoral duties. Sitting by the bedside of a cancer patient wracked by pain . . . standing by a family whose child has been killed in a drive-by shooting . . . counseling a woman whose husband has deserted her and their five children — these are times that test my belief. Yet over and over I've seen miraculous changes come out of the direst of situations. People do find release, grief does subside, hope does renew itself. Wherever you are in life, believing that it's worth going on is the first step in making it so. Couple your belief with action, and you've taken the second step. Soon you'll be making visible progress. In time, you'll wonder why you ever doubted. New beginnings have to start somewhere. Believing is as good a place as any to begin.

If I believe it, God can prove it.

"There are no accidents with God, only purpose."

—Althea Gibson

Maybe you weren't planned, but you were no accident. God doesn't make accidents. Your birth date was the exact date He planned for you to enter the world. You were created by the divine hand according to His divine plan to accomplish divine purposes. If God put you in the here and now, how can you feel like you don't belong? You are a child of the King, living in your Father's kingdom! How well are you representing your father? All families have skeletons in their closets. When something base or immoral occurs in a prominent family, it doesn't stay in the closet; it's front page news. Everyone runs around saying, "How could this happen in that family? What a shame." We say, "How disgraced the family must feel." What about God's family? Do we worry about bringing shame or disgrace upon our Father's kingdom? Your actions reflect your relationship with your Father. Your behavior, your moral code, your standard of integrity — everything you do and are — is front page news when you're a child of the King. What are you doing to make sure it's good news, for yourself and your Father?

Today I'll make sure my life reflects my Father's glory.

"Life is a short and what we have to do
must be done in the now."

—Audre Lorde

The Procrastinator's Club is such a popular group there are chapters throughout the country. Members celebrate the fine art of delaying. Of course, there are never any meetings; meetings are always postponed. Without meetings, there's really no time to hold a celebration, so there's no celebrating. Procrastinators are always in a hurry to catch up with yesterday. What a waste! Life is simply too short to delay living. No matter how long you live, there will never be enough time to do all that you want to do. No matter how short your life span, there is always enough time to do something you want to do. Feeling complete has little to do with time and lots to do with action. The complete life is filled with meaningful actions — actions meaningful to the person living it. What makes me feel complete might make you feel empty. Don't worry about what's meaningful to others, fill your life with relationships and activities that are meaningful to you. Stop lamenting the shortage of time and start enjoying the length of time, however long it is. In the final analysis, it is what you lived for, what you accomplished that was important to you, that will make your life complete.

Today I'm complete. I'm doing something I want to do.

Day 263

> "Muffle your rage. Get smart instead of muscular."
>
> —Roy Wilkins

Jason was so angry at his boss he couldn't hold it in. "I hate this job," he whispered to a co-worker. "I hate getting up in the morning to come to this crummy office to work for that unreasonable man." Jason's boss overheard. That afternoon, Jason was fired. After their first argument, Brenda couldn't help pouring out her anger at Robert to her parents. "He's small-minded and selfish," she sobbed. "I don't know why I ever married him." Long after the newlyweds had made up, Brenda's parents were cool toward Robert and worried about their daughter. We all have some things in our lives we wish we could change. Perhaps this is a blessing in disguise. Discontent motivates us to change and grow. It presents us with challenges that prompt us to stretch our limits to find positive solutions. Grumbling is never a blessing. Grumbling asks other people to find solutions for us. It is a lazy person's way of avoiding positive action. Grumbling brings discontent to others and stirs up trouble in otherwise peaceful situations. If you're discontented with a situation, change it, don't grumble about it. New horizons await and you don't want past words to come back to haunt you.

Today I'll quietly seek a change.

Day 264

"If at the end one can say, 'This man used to the limit the powers that God granted him'; then that life has been lived well and there are no regrets."
—Eleanor Roosevelt

Each of us stands on the shoulders of those who have gone before. We are where we are because others made sacrifices. If you think you're nowhere, look around. There are limitless opportunities and resources available to you. They are available to you because someone in the past made a sacrifice, took a chance. This legacy should create in each of us a desire to, in turn, accomplish something for those who will come after us. Every window we crack lets the air of change enter and blow on the door of opportunity. Every block we cement in place forms a foundation for the next level. Every time we attain a personal goal we mark a trail in the path of time. No life is so wasted as the life that leaves nothing behind. No life is so well lived as one that uses to the fullest its God-given powers to complete God-given tasks and pave a road for the next generation.

I'll live worthy of those who went before and those who will come after.

Day 265

"We bake the bread, they give us the crust."
—Traditional

Asked to speak at a worship service in a shelter for the homeless, the young chaplain shocked the audience by beginning his message with "Live in gratitude! Accept life with joy!" Yet that is one of the most important — and most difficult — lessons for us to learn. Perhaps it's our history of slavery and servitude that clouds our ability to see clearly all that we have received. It's a fact: we were denied in the past. It's a fact: we still are fighting discrimination. It's true, too, that more white people than ever before are on our side. Today's world is filled with opportunity. We have received God's gifts and combined them with the gifts willed to us by the blood of our forbearers. We have risen to new heights of limitless possibilities. Our horizons are clear. If there is a shadow, we are the main ones casting it over our own path to success.

Today I'll check to be sure I'm not standing in my own way.

"The word will never be short of work or adventure."

—A.G. Gaston

Do you want to discover the wonders of the world? Spend time with a young child. To a child, all the world is new. There is wonder in the dust motes floating in the sunbeams. There is wonder in the purr of a cat, the sticky lick of a dog. There's wonder in the way a vacuum cleaner works, a telephone carries Grandma's voice, and a radio "talks." As adults, we long to see the wonder of beautiful beaches, majestic mountains, golden sunrises, and purple sunsets. We crave the experience of riding in a limousine, drinking at the posh bar, dining in a roof-top restaurant, and living in a penthouse. As you realize success after success by living with your new can do attitude, many adult dreams will come true. They represent the peaks of your journey through life. They're wonderful when they come; you earn them and you deserve to enjoy them. But between the peaks are many valleys. Valleys hold wonder, too. Make sure you're not walking blindly past the wonders of your everyday world. If you think you might be missing something, ask a little child to guide you. Enjoy the journey, not just the destination.

Today I'll rediscover seven lost wonders of my everyday world.

"What parents need to give children is presence not presents."

—Rev. Jesse Jackson Sr.

The young parents were nervous. It was the first time their son was attending church with his Sunday School class. "What did you do in church?" his father asked. "We had to sit very quiet and think beautiful thoughts," replied the little boy. "What did you think about?" asked his mother. "Oh, 'bout beautiful things like elephants," answered the child, the wonder still apparent in his voice. Reverence is one of the greatest gifts we can bequeath to our children. In order to bequeath it, we must first possess it ourselves. A synonym for reverence is respect. We show respect for God by reverently caring for all of His creation. We show reverence in the way we treat the environment. We show reverence in the way we interact with others. We show reverence for ourselves, for the body He has given us, and the life He has breathed into that body by treating ourselves lovingly and respectfully. No one can revere God and not hold in awe all that God made — yes, even elephants. What is more awesome than you, just the way God intended you to be?

God made me for myself. I will respect His creation in me.

"The child looks out and sees naught, but the old man sitting on the grounds, sees everything!"
—Senegal

Along with racial integration, it seems we've achieved generational segregation. Old folks are shut away in retirement communities and nursing homes. Neighborhoods are dubbed "new," meaning filled with young families. We are the only country in the world that reveres youth and fails to venerate age. God save me from a world where all my neighbors are the same age! No matter how hard we exercise, how carefully we watch our diet, how precise we are about our medical care, we can't deny the slowing of our physical bodies. Even an adult in the best of shape can't compete with the energy of a child. As the body ages, the mind triumphs. What a wealth of wisdom is stored in those nursing homes and old age facilities. Our older people have already traveled the road we're now walking. They hold the gems of wisdom gathered on their life journeys. Their treasures can be ours; they're ripe for sharing. All we need to do is ask. The hands that hold so many secrets of success may be withered and wrinkled, but they're open and ready to clasp and to share. Take those hands. Let's re-integrate our homes, families, and communities with intergene-rational living.

I'm getting older, but wiser, every day.

DAY 269

"Beauty is God's signature."
—Traditional

On *Sesame Street* they do this little skit about a child who has lost her mother. She keeps telling those who try to help that her mother is the most beautiful woman in the world. One by one the *Sesame Street* characters bring beautiful women to the child. Over and over the child says, "No, I told you, my mother is the most beautiful person in the world." At last an old hag wanders by. "Mother," the child cries, as they are reunited. "Beauty is God's handwriting," and God's handwriting is easy to decipher. All it takes is the ability to look beyond "face" value. True beauty is a gift of the heart. When a person has a beautiful heart, his or her entire body seems to shine. Kind eyes filled with compassion, willing hands extended to help, sturdy feet ready to move into positive action — these are some of the most beautiful features a person can possess. It's true that "pretty" people have an easier time, at least at the outset. There's no denying the attraction of physical beauty. But pretty people also run a greater risk of getting stuck in shallow places. Outward beauty is the one asset you won't improve as you travel life's journey. Inward beauty, drawn by God's own hand, increases in direct proportion to can do living. A can do attitude reflects a light so bright it becomes a welcoming beacon to all you meet.

I'm beautiful inside and out.

"Lord, when we are wrong, make us willing
to change. And when we are right, make us
easy to live with. Amen."

—Rev. Peter Marshall

One of the greatest temptations in a successful life
is to say, "I told you so." Take heed now and don't
yield to temptation. No matter how successful you
become, if you turn into an "I told you so" person,
you're a failure. Never forget that your achievements
are personal victories. Never measure your victories
in terms of another's defeats. There's plenty of room
at the top. Your winning doesn't require another's losing. We all can take time to help another without jeop-
ardizing our own progress. Jealousy, failure to help
one another, are major causes of minority setbacks.
Successful living means learning to live with your own
success as well as your own failures. Be proud of your
successes, but never become haughty. There will always
be someone who knows a little more than you do, who's
climbed a little higher than you have, who has a little
more than you possess. Proverbs 11:2 warns us, "Pride
cometh, then cometh shame." This doesn't mean generous, positive pride, but rather false, boastful "I told
you so" pride. The achiever who takes quiet pride in
personal successes will be surrounded by admirers even
in times of failure. The boastful achiever will stand
alone.

I'm proud of who I am and who I'm becoming.

Day 271

Satisfaction is the one thing in life only you can give yourself. The key to success is not so much what you do as how you do it. When you give yourself whole-heartedly to a task, satisfaction comes with the doing. As you do, you grow. Your best becomes even better. We tend to think only rich or brilliant people can achieve true satisfaction. Satisfaction cannot be bought or sold. It is the by-product of your own efforts. When you've given something your very best, the final outcome becomes less important. Whether or not things turn out exactly the way you hoped, you'll have the satisfaction of a job well done. Satisfaction can be found in little things as well as big projects. When you give your best to the smallest details of your life, the smallest details can bring big satisfaction to you. Approach every task as if it were the most important project. After all, it *is* the most important project at the exact moment you're doing it. Give your best to every task. Enjoy the satisfaction that will come every day with every job well done.

Whatever I do today, I'll give it my very best.

> "Faith is not belief without proof, but
> trust without reservation."
> —Rev. Johnny Youngblood

Faith is tricky business. If you place your faith too readily in someone or something, you run the risk of being disappointed. If you withhold your faith in anything that can't be proved, you'll live a shallow life. Some people say their belief in God rests totally on their faith. Look around. The existence of God *can* be proven! God is evident in every plant and tree, in every ocean and mountain, in sunsets and clouds, rain, snow, and sunshine. Cradle a newborn, and you'll see the face of God. It is when we place faith in people that we're taking a risk. There are no perfect people; each of us disappoints someone sometime. Even love is no guarantee against disappointment. What, then, should we do? Are we to go through life never trusting anyone? Trust and faith means risk and chance-taking; risk and chance-taking means living. Choose carefully those people in whom you place your faith. Pray for guidance. Then love them, trust them, and have unreserved faith in them. If they disappoint you, you'll be no worse off than every other human being who ever took a chance on love. If your faith and trust are valued, you will be rewarded with a rich life filled with loving, deep relationships.

Today I'll think before I speak.

"Age is nectar."

—Wole Soyinka

There are no guarantees in life, but it's certain that unless you die young, you will age. You may not like the idea of getting older, but it sure beats the alternative! Aging is a natural part of living. If you live well during youth and middle age, you'll have a storehouse of resources to call upon in your later years. Retirement brings the gift of more free time — time to spend doing those things you were unable to do when you went to a job everyday. There will be time to deepen friendships. Time to pursue a long-postponed hobby. Time to study a foreign language, become computer literate, or learn any subject you've often wished you knew. There will be time, too, to give back more to your church, your community, the organizations and institutions that made a difference in your life. Your later years will bring a harvest of choices. Exactly what those choices will be depends, in part, on the way you live in the years leading up to retirement. Begin now to plan for later. Make financial plans; financial security makes everything else possible. Make spiritual plans; if you're close to God now, you'll draw even closer later. Make goal-oriented plans; the need to accomplish doesn't cease when work-for-pay stops.

Today I'm one day older — and one day wiser — than yesterday.

DAY 274

> "To know the 23 Psalm is one thing, to know the shepherd is another."
>
> —Traditional

Whether or not you realize it, you are a spiritual being living in a spiritual universe. Spirituality has little to do with religion. Spirituality has everything to do with God. It is in the spirit, the deepest core of your being, that your values and standards are lodged. It is in the spirit that you experience all of the emotions that make you human. God is a spirit. God created you in His own image, therefore the essence of you is spirit. When you pray to God, you communicate spirit to spirit. Often our most sincere prayers are prayed with no words at all. Instead it is like the tide of our souls flowing completely and inexorably outward to our creator. When our spirits touch and commingle with the spirit of our creator, we know that we have touched God. Communicating in the spirit, like other forms of communication, requires speaking and listening. It also requires waiting. Flip, smart-alecky, off-the-cuff answers are cheap. When friends listen patiently and consider their responses thoughtfully before speaking, you know you have their full attention. Their words have value. God is like that. Sometimes you have to wait for God's answers. But when they come, they'll be precious and positive and help promote your personal progress.

Today I'll celebrate my spirituality.

Day 275

"I kneel and pray before new Gods come
into a godless age."

—Jean Toomer

People often ask, "If God knows my every thought and desire, why do I need to pray?" We pray for our own good, not for God's. Prayer helps us to define our goals. Through prayer, we acknowledge that there is a higher being who loves us and wants the very best for us. God wants us to succeed. Prayer is the method we use to permit God to have a hand in attaining our success. By utilizing the three components of prayer — speaking, listening, waiting — we allow time and space for God to work out our success. We tell God our goals and our plans for achieving them. We tell God what we think needs to happen in order for us to reach our goals. At the same time, we acknowledge the possibility that the goals we've set may not be those God has in mind for us. We leave ourselves open to a better way to get where we want to go, a better destination than the one we've chosen, a higher level of achievement than we've set for ourselves. Like little children, we have a limited capacity for planning, working, and problem solving. In prayer, we tap into the limitless capacity of God to give us even more than we ask for.

*Today I'll acknowledge my limits and God's capacity
to stretch me to new heights of achievement.*

"Persistence and a positive attitude are necessary ingredients for any successful venture."
—Douglas Wilder

As a pastor, I attend more than my share of meetings. One thing is common to them all: every committee has at least one member who constantly points out the difficulties of every project. That person will tell you all the reasons why you can't accomplish whatever it is you're trying to achieve. She or he will dredge up all the failures of the past, all the horror stories of others who have tried what you are attempting. For every good reason to do something, the naysayer will give you ten reasons for not doing it. If left unchecked, that one person can change the course of the entire committee. Everyday life is a lot like those committee meetings. There is always someone waiting to tell you why you can't succeed. He'll point out the risks; she'll enunciate the pitfalls. These negative people will do everything in their power to make you second guess yourself and your own good judgement. Don't let these people get you off track. Believe in yourself. Make your decisions thoughtfully and prayerfully. Then move ahead. Begin to view the glass as half full instead of half empty, and fullness is exactly what you'll get.

I believe in myself. Nothing can happen that God and I can't handle.

> "Most people in actuality are not worth very much, and yet every human being is an unprecedented miracle."
>
> —Ibid

Even as you're reading this book, a thousand miracles are taking place right there inside your body. Your heart is beating, pumping blood throughout your body. Your lungs are exchanging life-giving oxygen for life-robbing waste products. Your brain is translating the jumble of lines that make up this printed page into understandable words and sentences. The planets are traveling in their prescribed orbs. The earth is rotating at exactly the right distance from the sun. The tides are flowing, plants are growing, rivers are running — all without human intervention. We recognize miracle breakthroughs in science. Unexplainable "miraculous" happenings are touted in the media. All this, and the miracle of human progress is overlooked. The big miracles are celebrated; the quiet miracles go unnoticed. Every time a human being overcomes the odds and achieves success, it's a miracle. Every person who rises above poverty, ghetto life, the heritage of a dysfunctional family, epitomizes a triumph of the human spirit. Miracles come from God but they're activated by humans. Unleash miracles in your life. Choose to live a life of miracle experiences. Believe, plan, act. Miracles of achievement will follow.

Today I'm my own miracle-maker.

"Humor cleanses the heart and keeps it good."

—Alfred Paster

When all else fails, laugh! One of the greatest gifts God gives us is a sense of humor. Every truly successful person has cultivated a sense of humor. When we are able to laugh at ourselves, we are able to accept ourselves as the wonderful, imperfect creatures we are. A sense of humor keeps things in perspective. Laughter brings out the child in all of us — the long-lost child that is the essence of ourselves in our former innocent state, free of guile and self-righteousness. On the road to success, we all make mistakes. We can let them get us down, throw us into depression and defeatism, or we can learn to laugh at ourselves, to find enjoyment in our journey despite our periodic setbacks. Laughter truly is the best medicine. It cures pompousness, eliminates arrogance, and unstuffs the stuffy. In short, a sense of humor makes us all more human. It is contagious, spreading to all we meet. It attracts others, giving us good company to share our journey. A sense of humor saves us from the sin of taking ourselves too seriously.

Living is fun! I'll fill today with laughter.

Day 279

> "One's work may be finished some day,
> but one's education never."
>
> —Alexander Dumas

Have you ever heard someone with a college education say she wishes she didn't have one? Going to school is a lot like learning to play the piano. It can be pure drudgery at times, but once mastered, no one ever wishes he couldn't play. Success is about getting the things you want most — real life material things: a new car, a nice house, stylish clothes, etc. Material things in and of themselves are not evil unless you become enslaved to them. But success encompasses much, much more. Success includes the attainment of wisdom. It requires being knowledgeable about your particular field. It means being well-read and well-rounded. When you've acquired wisdom and knowledge, you've attained success. When you invest as much time, energy, and money in gaining knowledge as you do in purchasing cars, houses, and clothes, you are building up equity in the only asset that can't be taken from you. Houses can burn to the ground. Cars can be totaled in accidents. Your body can outgrow your stylish clothes. Knowledge can never crash, burn, or cease to fit. If you should lose all your material possessions, it would be a sad and sorrowful experience. But as long as you have wisdom and knowledge, you have the tools to rebuild.

I'll put education at the top of my shopping list.

> "I don't allow anyone to put a limit on
> my dreaming, and I dream big, Always."
> —Gordon Parks

One couple I know came up through the ranks. They had worked hard and achieved a comfortable level of success. Each summer they took their children to the seashore where they especially enjoyed long walks on the beach. Remembering the lean years, the father taught his children to look down, to scan the sand after the bathers had gone for loose change, jewelry, or other valuables that might have been dropped. The mother, on the other hand, taught her children to look up, to track the tides by the fullness of the moon and predict the weather by reading the skies. As the approaching autumn shortened the summer days, the mother would measure the sunset from the time the sun first touched the horizon until it disappeared from view. She taught her children to identify the constellations and differentiate between twinkling stars and steadily glowing planets. By the time the children grew to adulthood, the loose change and trinkets they had found on the ground were long spent and forgotten. The lessons learned from their mother remained with them to enrich their lives.

Today I'm moving up, up and away to where I'm meant to be.

Day 281

"A man must saddle his dreams before he can ride them."

—Traditional

Some people believe they get birthday presents only once a year. How silly! Every day is a birthday present — a present in honor of another day in your life. Each day is a gift to use, to enjoy, to spend with people and places of your choosing, experiencing things of your own choosing. Wasting a day is like discarding a gift without even opening the box. You rob yourself of discovering what's inside. Perhaps not every birthday present pleases you. There are always the outlandish ties, the footed pajamas, and the purple throw pillows with the orange tassels. Not exactly the gifts on your most wanted list! Yet even these misfits have value; they are valuable because they represent the caring, love, and esteem the giver feels for you. Successful people are able to separate the gift from the giver. They value the thought behind the gift. In the same way, successful people value the gift of each new day. They are able to separate the day's events from the day's potential. Successful people look forward to each new day. They're not naive. They accept the fact that the day may bring problems, challenges, and even temporary defeats. Yet they never lose sight of the potential that the new day begins.

Happy birthday to me!

> "Ask for what you want and be prepared
> to pay for what you get."
>
> —Maya Angelou

Find a stingy person and you'll find an unsuccessful person. Success comes through giving — the giving of those things that are yours and yours alone. The unique gifts, instilled in you by God himself, are the divine spark that makes you different from every other individual. No one else has God-given gifts exactly like yours. While your actions, thoughts, and beliefs may be similar to those of others, they are not identical. You could say that when God made you, He threw away the mold. You are one of a kind, a unique creation made for a unique purpose. True success comes from fulfilling that unique purpose. What is your unique purpose? Usually you won't discover it until you start giving of your unique gifts. What are your unique gifts? You'll discover those, too, by giving what comes naturally. Perhaps you love books and reading. Your unique gift may be giving your time as a volunteer tutor. Do you love entertaining in your home, having people over for dinner or dessert, going all out to prepare special foods that look as good as they taste? Perhaps you have the gift of hospitality. Success will be yours when you contribute from your personal store of talents to help bring success to others.

I'm a limited edition masterpiece. I cannot be duplicated.

Day 283

"A wise man sips the elixir of life, circumspectly, slowly, and heedful."

—Panthatantra, 2 AD

Karen and Gary Smith had achieved success. They had purchased a single home surrounded by a large yard. They owned two cars, their tailored suits bore designer labels, and their friends belonged to the "right" club where Karen and Gary were taking golf lessons. Recently, they had begun collecting antiques and signed oil paintings. From all outward appearances, Gary and Karen were the picture of a successful couple. At home, it was a different story. The large house came with a large mortgage. Designer clothes, club dues, and pricey possessions all carried high price tags. Their two paychecks barely covered their bills. Their dream of starting a family was put on indefinite hold. In addition, the Smiths soon discovered they hated yard work, were more comfortable in jeans, and had little in common with their new friends. Frustration led to bickering; soon their marriage was on shaky ground. Fortunately, Gary and Karen had the wisdom to call a time out and reevaluate their priorities. By making a list of the people and things they truly cared about, they were able to rid their life of the nonessentials that were robbing them of joy, satisfaction, and money. Today, they are back on track. They are living a successful life brimming over with treasures — the treasures of being true to themselves and their own values.

I've set my own standards and am meeting them.

Day 284

> "The best thing about the future is that
> it comes only one day at a time."
> —Abraham Lincoln

Only God can see the future. That's a real blessing because only God is big enough to handle knowing the future. Even the smartest human being, the person with the very highest IQ, has a mind too finite to cope with the knowledge of all the future holds. Of course, it is wise to plan for the future. Planning and preparation increases the probability of success. Yet, despite all our planning and preparations, the future unfolds one day at a time. This day-by-day knowledge is another of God's gifts to us. It keeps us from being overwhelmed; it protects us from discouragement and despair. Developing a can do attitude requires that we also develop a sense of the unpredictable. As we move from can't do to can do, we equip ourselves with the ability to handle whatever may come our way. Can do people recognize that they will never know with certainty what the future holds. However, can do people also recognize that while the future may be uncertain, their ability to succeed is not. Can do people possess the strength to handle whatever comes their way, and to handle it in positive, successful ways. After all, isn't the ability to forge positive outcomes from unpredictable circumstances the true measure of success?

Today I'm busy preparing for the unpredictable.

"Happiness comes of the capacity to feel deeply, to enjoy simply, to think freely, to risk life, to be needed."
—Storm Jameson

What does it take to make you happy? Money? Fame? A trim body? A big house? A flashy car? All these things certainly can bring happiness. They help make life pleasant and are symbols of success. But what happens when the money runs out, the fame fades, the body ages, and the car gets a few dents? You'd be pretty unhappy, wouldn't you? But would you be so unhappy that you'd never bounce back, never start over, never try again? If the loss of material things would plunge you into deep, insurmountable unhappiness, perhaps you're putting too much value on possessions. Possessions are simply things you own. When your possessions begin to own you, to control your actions and attitudes, your life is off balance. To get back on an even keel you need to rethink your values. Think of a time when you felt great happiness. Remember that time; relive it in your mind. What is the memory? What made the experience so memorable? You'll find that the things that matter most involve more people than possessions, more feelings than things. Only when you learn to treasure the simple joys of life will you be free to risk deep emotions. Only when you freely risk your deepest emotions will you be truly and lastingly happy.

Today is an adventure; I'm taking a chance on life.

Day 286

"Pain is another word for fear. True believers
have no fear."

—Marvin Gaye

The value of every emotion is measured by its
opposite. The height of joy is measured by the depth
of pain. The delight of laughter is measured by the
depression of tears. The exhilaration of victory is
measured by the difficulty of the challenge. No happiness is so sweet as that which follows grief. No success is so fulfilling as that attained after many failures.
Often we question why God allows pain, sorrow, and
failure to touch our lives. One answer is so that we
may know the fullness of pleasure, joy, and delight.
To live without pain is to live without risk. To live
without risk is to live without possibilities. Risk involves leaving ourselves open to the possibility of
pain, while believing in the even greater possibility
of attaining pleasure. As you develop your can do
attitude, you *will* achieve success. However, along with
that success you'll probably experience some painful
defeats. Look at them as stepping stones. When you
try something you always move forward. Even if you
fail, you never slip all the way back to where you
were in the beginning. There is progress simply in
the attempt. Accept a reasonable amount of pain as a
consequence of successful living. Recognize that each
painful experience increases your capacity for the joy
that will soon be yours.

Today I have to hurt a little; tomorrow I will heal a lot.

> "Life doesn't run away from nobody.
> Life runs at you and brings the best
> out of you . . . or the worst."
>
> —Joe Frazier

I know people who seem to have everything — good jobs, happy marriages, health, looks — yet are always unhappy. And I know people who have very little — poor health, lost jobs, addicted spouses — yet never seem to be down. As a pastor, I've spent years dealing with both kinds of people, and I've learned an amazing thing. Usually it's the people who seem to have everything that come to me for counseling, advice, help, and comfort. It's the people who have little, those whose lives seem filled with an unfair measure of trouble, who are always there to pick me up! The very ones I should be comforting are comforting and encouraging me. It's all a matter of attitude! Some people just don't know how to appreciate what they have. Other people don't know how to feel sorry for themselves and to complain about what they don't have. I'll take the second group any time! They're the real winners. They have the winning attitude and nothing or no one is going to defeat them. They look their problems squarely in the eye and keep smiling. They defy trouble. Whatever is happening to them, they believe in themselves and their ability to get through it. They have no illusions. They know life can be tough, but they also know life can be beautiful.

I have a positive attitude and will never give in, despite the negative atmosphere that surrounds me.

> "To live is to suffer, to survive is to find
> some meaning in the suffering."
> —Roberta Flack

What's outside your window? Do you see rows of brick and concrete, locked doors and broken windows encasing hordes of faceless people? Or do you see the raw materials for building homes and businesses and communities? Do you dream of someday escaping the neighborhood? Or are you actively involved in reshaping the neighborhood? Nothing is as tragic as a life put on hold. Yet, so often, that's exactly what we do. We put off doing things, getting involved, making a difference because we're afraid, or because we feel incapable of changing things. We let the impossibilities of our situation blind us to the wonderful possibilities inherent in every situation. Action, involvement, making a difference, bringing about change — that's what can do people are about. With a can do attitude, you'll see gardens blooming in wastelands, people growing and thriving in caring, nurturing communities. With a can do attitude, you'll live life in a present filled with such excitement and enthusiasm you won't want to miss a minute of a single day.

Today I'm living each moment to the fullest.

DAY 289

"Do what you can and God will do what you can't."

—Rance Allen

Sometimes it's difficult to determine the will of God; sometimes it's impossible. A child is born brain damaged and deformed. "Is this the will of God?" we ask. A random shot rings out in the street and an elderly woman is killed. "Is this God's will?" we demand. An earthquake topples a building or a hurricane devastates an entire village. Immediately we wonder, "Can this possibly be the will of God?" Questions like these haunt our minds, affect our prayer life, and even undermine our faith. I've never found the answers, but I have come to terms with the questions: In God's will we find perfect peace. We don't have to understand the situation. We don't even have to accept the situation. We simply have to remember that God understands the situation and our feelings about it. Then we turn the situation over to God. This doesn't mean we give up or stop trying to bring about change. Rather, it reminds us to turn to God first, to seek God's guidance in our actions and reactions. A can do attitude doesn't automatically empower us to change the unchangeable. A can do attitude empowers us to accept the things we cannot change, and to move forward, at peace with ourselves knowing God is in control.

Peace is God's will for my life, God's gift for my day.

> "Don't tell God how big your problems are,
> tell your problems how big your God is."
> —Traditional

From the day we're born, most of us are taught to be nonconfrontational. We are told "don't make waves." We're taught to buckle in and buckle under, to be peace-makers at all costs. This is a good and proper philosophy. Even the Bible tells us "Blessed are the peace-makers." Jesus himself gives us the direction to "turn the other cheek." But the Bible also tells us to stand up for what we believe in, to speak out, to act boldly. How are we to deal with this dichotomy? The difference, I believe, is between aggression and assertion. The aggressive person is pushy and rude. Aggressive people demand their own way and trample upon others as they seek to fulfill their own ends. The assertive person, on the other hand, is not discourteous or demanding, but speaks honestly and forthrightly. The assertive person climbs the ladder of success, but never on the backs of others. The aggressive person is ill equipped to deal with problems, but will try to dodge them or place blame on others. The assertive person acknowledges when a problem exists, faces it, and deals with it until a fair and equitable solution is found. Success is won by overcoming problems, not avoiding them. Learn early to face up to your own mistakes. Mistakes are part of the learning, growing process that leads you to your destination.

It's better to risk making a mistake today than to remain "safe" by doing nothing.

DAY 291

> "We get what we deserve and we live by
> the Grace of God."
>
> —Benjamin Mays

Life is like a bank account. Each day represents a transaction. Some are deposits, some withdrawals. We deposit what we learn from every day of living; wisdom, experience, understanding, perception. We can then draw on these deposits as needed. We spend from our account for all kinds of purposes. We spend from our experiences so that instead of constantly starting over, we build on what we've already learned. We spend from our store of wisdom to help us make present choices. We use the perception and understanding we've gained from the past to help us navigate the future. All of us spend our lives doing various things. Wise and successful people make sure at least one thing they spend their life on will outlast life itself. They spend a portion of their lives building or developing something lasting that will benefit future generations. Sometimes this lasting thing is as visible as a skyscraper. Sometimes it's as fragile as an idea. Sometimes it's a revolutionary breakthrough that brings the person great fame and wealth. Sometimes it's the quiet passing down of values, the setting of moral codes, the unspoken example of a loving marriage, wise parenting, the respect for education that will serve as a benchmark for generations to come.

My life savings are earned by toil and spent with care.

"The purpose of life is to know oneself."
—Richard Wright

Everyone is someone. Everyone is something. Often it's hard to tell the difference. Ask a person to describe who he is and you'll often get a description of what he does. "I'm an accountant, a carpenter, a baker, salesman." Probe further, and you might get, "I'm a wife, a husband, a mother, a brother, a sister." The first definition describes job or career choices. The second describes relationships. Who you are is not defined by what you do for a living or how you're genetically linked with someone else. Who you are goes to the very essence of you, to that inner core or soul that makes you unique and different from everyone else. Who you are resides in the place from which self-respect, pride, and personal success spring. Who you are is formed by your relationship to God, to all of life, to yourself, and to others. Who you are exists even while what you are is still developing. Who you are is the person few will discover and only you will truly know. Who you are is the person you'll live with the rest of your life.

I treasure who I am; I work on what I'm becoming.

"There is no power on earth that can neutralize the influence of a high, pure, simple, and useful life."

—Booker T. Washington

In Lancaster County, Pennsylvania, there is a pocket of people called the Amish. They refer to themselves as the "plain people." They live simply, without benefit of modern conveniences including electricity and automobiles. They dress plainly, in dark colors undisturbed by jewelry or frills. Yet these are some of the happiest, most long-lived people in the nation. They have learned the secret of maintaining purity of thought and a high moral and ethical code. Every moment of their lives is spent in useful work or worship. They are pacifists; in their community, violence is unknown. They place a high regard on family; they care for one another, both the young and the old. They respect the environment and love the land that they've farmed for generations. These people are a model of successful living of the pure, simple, and useful life. I'm not suggesting that we all go join the Amish. However, some of the secrets of their success— purity of mind and thought, devotion to God and to one another, respect for self, others, and the community—might prove keys to our own success as we seek to live life in our own chosen ways.

On my journey through life, I'm sticking to the high road.

Day 294

"Jesus, Savior, pilot me over life's tempestuous sea."

—Robert Hayden

How close we pull toward God when we're desperate! How far away we push God when things are going fine. Talk about feeling used! We're certainly a bunch of unappreciative, thankless, willful children! If God were an earthly parent, He would have kicked us out of the household long ago. It's no accident that the more we need the more we pray. In His infinite wisdom and complete knowledge of our human nature, God gave us prayer as the bottom line. When all else fails, we still have prayer. Prayer truly is need finding a voice. But prayer is so much more! Prayer is our strength to meet all the little needs of everyday life. Prayer is our armor that protects us against the bumps, bruises, and pitfalls of living. Prayer is our voice saying thank you for all things great and small. Prayer is the way we articulate our desires, goals, and dreams to our God who has created these desires, goals, and dreams within us. Prayer is the way we gain direction. Prayer activates our God-given power to achieve the desires, goals, and dreams He promised to bring to fruition in all of our lives.

Whatever I need today, big or small, I'll get from God.

Day 295

"I want the right to be Black and me."
—Margaret Wright

Have you ever experienced complete connectedness? You do something and it clicks. It's right on! You think it, do it, complete it, and you just know it's right! It's the greatest experience on earth. Nothing gives you such a sense of power, of control, of positive energy directed at positive goals. This true sense of right always involves action. It's not enough to think of what's right; you must carry the thought into action to truly experience its power. Often this action involves risk. You risk trying something new, different, and challenging, and come out finding you've connected with something that's exactly right for you. One woman described the sense of right she experienced when she risked volunteering to teach a class. She was scared and unsure, but she did it and did it so well that now she's teaching on a regular basis. Our past is populated by people with this sense of right. They are the ones who risked taking stands for ideas and ideals. They succeeded because first they made sure they were right, then they went ahead. They put it all on the line and came out winners. Developing your sense of right is an important element in developing your can do attitude. As you decide on who and what you are, and who and what you will be, you'll see the possibilities.

Today I'm "right on." I'm standing up for myself. I'm connected!

Day 296

> "Be kind, for everyone you meet is fighting
> a hard battle."
>
> —Sandra Johnson

As you move through life, isn't it nice to know you're not alone? You're surrounded by fellow travelers. There are people who will walk beside you, some for a day, some for many years. All of us are traveling together yet each is on an individual journey. Be gentle, then, to your fellow travelers. We all have problems and obstacles. Just because you're having a bad day doesn't mean I'm having a better one. Be kind to all you meet, you never know how far they've come or how far they're going. The stranger you encounter today may be the sojourner who'll walk with you the longest. Why get off to a bad start? Share the road while you can. Take comfort and pleasure in one another. When the time comes to part, do so with good feelings, happy memories, best wishes for the next leg of the journey. Help where you can, but never hinder. Leave no one injured because you passes him on the road through life. We will all meet again someday. Anticipate that meeting by building friendships for the future. Remember, many of your fellow travelers in life will be sharing eternity with you.

I'll walk through my world kindly and gently today, being good to myself and my fellow travelers.

"Unconditional love not only means, I am with you, but also, I am for you, and the me included."
—Al Young

Sometimes it's hard to distinguish between like and love. Yet they're so far apart that a river runs through them. That river is called human emotion. We like someone because — he's funny, she's pretty, he's smart, she's ambitious, etc. We love someone although — she's gained weight, he's lost his hair, she's lost her job, he's changed his mind. In the marriage vows we say, "Until death do us part." Sometimes this just isn't possible. No one should remain in a relationship that has become dangerous or harmful. Yet more marriages could last a lifetime if they were entered with more care, wisdom, and forethought. Unfortunately, we often spend more time deciding on a car to purchase than we do choosing a mate presumably for life. Part of the problem is that marriage is usually entered by those too young to know themselves or to predict how their still-maturing feelings will change in the future. Often, though, it's simply a matter of not recognizing the difference between like and love. Our likes are temporary and ever-changing; love is unconditional and never-ending. Love, once found, lives forever, even if only in memory. Like attracts us to someone; loves keeps us there, "through sickness and in health," through all the "unattractive" times of life.

Because I love myself, I'll choose my life's love carefully.

Day 298

For the best advice, have a talk with self!
—Rev. Jim Holley

❖ Establish positive work relationships with those around you. It's up to you to take the initiative.

❖ Know your organization's goals and purposes so you can help achieve them.

❖ Build a network of constructive, successful people in your workplace; communicate with them frequently.

❖ Build your relationship with your boss on genuine mutual interests, abilities, and goals.

❖ Establish a reputation for reliability by completing assignments well and on time.

❖ Record and communicate your contributions and achievements. They are the building blocks of your career.

❖ Recognize the contributions of others.

*Today I will remember: There is always a **NEXT TIME!***

Day 299

"A man without questions is assumed that
he has all the answers. Thy Fool!"

—Niger

Teachers are fond of saying, "There are no stupid
questions." Then they often chastise a student for asking stupid questions. No wonder many of us learn early
on to keep our questions to ourselves. Yet some of
the most admired people in the world are avid question askers. Proof is the success of the recent Barbara
Walters Special, *Twenty Years of Asking Questions!*
Certainly Oprah Winfrey has asked questions that have
lifted taboos and shed light on situations that were
plaguing people around the world. Asking is learning.
We ask because we want to learn. This is different
from snooping or invading the privacy of others. Sincere questioning puts us on a lifelong search for answers. When we spend time questioning our motives,
our feelings, our beliefs, and our behaviors, we open
ourselves to inner growth. We force ourselves to plumb
for answers, some so deep-seated and long-indwelling
that we no longer remember how they got there. This
quest for self-knowledge leads to self-discovery.

I'm getting to know me better everyday.

> "Life commences not with birth, but with
> the onslaught of awareness."
>
> —W.E.B. DuBois

Do you remember asking to be born? Life is one of the gifts God gives without our asking. We have no choice in the matter. We are here, alive, with a life to live. Our only choice is how we will live it. This is a choice in which there is perfect equality. We all have the same freedom to choose how we will live our lives. Sure, being born into wealth, social standing, and a stable family may give you a jump on success. But you can choose to live as a winner or loser no matter what state you are born into. Consider: Millionaire John DuPont is in jail, a mentally-disturbed man accused of murder; Colin Powell, a self-made African American man, retired a hero and could probably win the White House if he chose to run. The accused Unobomber is a Harvard graduate; boxing champion Muhammad Ali grew up in poverty in one of the highest crime areas in our country. All around us we witness people making choices on how to live their lives. Would it be easier to make something of your life if you had a million dollars? Well, you have at least a million dollars worth of talents to spend making your life successful. How, when, and on what you spend them is your choice. After all, it's your life.

It's my life, my choice.

Day 301

"God's love is unconditional. He knows our weakness and strengthens us through his love."

—Bishop Paul Morton

It has been said that the only thing you can count on in life is change. I would amend that you say the only thing you can count on is the unchanging love of God. It's a fact. It's a certainty. It's unchangeable. There's nothing you can say or do to make God stop loving you. God's love for you does not depend upon your success. It doesn't depend upon your station in life. God doesn't love you more if you go to church and less if you don't. God's love doesn't even require that you love Him in return. God's love simply is. In a world where change is the only constant, the changeless love of God is a constant stabilizer. It also is the great facilitator. Because I know God's love for me will never change, I'm not afraid to try new things, to set new goals, to strive for new accomplishments. Whether I succeed or fail will have no effect on God's love for me. I can attempt all things because there is nothing I can attempt that will make one bit of difference in God's personal love for me. If you learn nothing else on your road to success, learn this fact: God's love for you is unchangeable.

God can change me, but I cannot change God.

Day 302

> "It is more important to be in time than on time."
>
> —Kelly Miller

What will you do with today? This may be the most important decision you'll ever make. None of us can see the future. We can plan for it, but we can't be certain of it. This is what makes our choice of what to do with each day so important. Will your day be filled with productive work? A good day's work brings satisfaction. Will your day include time with friends and family? Loving personal relationships make life rich. Will you spend some time alone with yourself? Knowing yourself is the day to fulfillment. Will you choose to make time for God? Prayer keeps you close to your creator and unites the present day with eternity. All these ways of spending your time promote personal success. Your day is such a precious gift. The freedom to choose what you'll do with each day is such a wonderful blessing. You take care of the things and people you love because they're important to you. Why, then, would you be careless with even one day of your own life? You make wise choices about how you spend your money. Why, then, would you give less thought to how you spend your time?

Time is on my side. I'll cherish this precious ally.

Day 303

"We don't have eternity to realize our dreams, only the time we have here."
—Susan Taylor

Have you heard the expression, "I'll be a long time dead?" People usually use it jokingly to justify making frivolous decisions about non-serious activities. Yet there's a lot of truth to the saying. Our time on earth is limited; our time in eternity is limitless. Our time on earth is marked by encounters with pain and sorrow. Our time in eternity is free of pain and sorrow. It is right that we begin preparing for eternity while we are here on earth. This includes not only developing our relationship with God, but also our relationship with ourselves. If heaven is filled with joy and devoid of pain, why not begin preparing for heaven by experiencing joy here on earth? Be good to yourself. Know what you like, what brings you joy, and make time for that activity. This may be as simple as walking in the woods, or as complex as skiing a glacier. It may be as calming as lolling on the beach, or as exciting as learning to fly. It doesn't matter what you enjoy, it matters *that* you enjoy — someone, something, some place. Success includes making time for these people, places, and activities on a regular and frequent basis.

I'm preparing for eternity. I'm spending this day doing what I enjoy.

DAY 304

"What then shall we say to these things?
If God be for us, who can be against us?"
—Romans 8:31

Are you ready for supernatural miracles in your life?
God's ready to give them to you. God is ready to go
to work moving every obstacle in your path. God can
open that door. God can change that "no" to "yes."
God can turn around hearts and straighten out situations. God not only *can* do these things but God *will*
do these things. What does it take to activate God's
power in your life? It takes faith, your faith in God.
(God already has faith in you. Didn't He provide you
with all the tools and talents to help you get what
you want?) Activating God's power also takes prayer.
Sure, God knows what you need, but God wants you
to come to Him and ask. He wants to talk it over with
you, to hear from you and allow you to hear from
Him. That how prayer works. Prayer proves faith. You
wouldn't talk to someone unless you believed that
someone existed and was listening, would you? Prayer
shows that, through faith, you know God exists and is
ready to listen to you. As you move from an atmosphere of "can't do" to the attitude of "can do," God
watches your progress with pleasure. Your positive
actions put you and God on the same side. And if God
is on your side, who or what can stand in your way?

*Nothing can keep me from making it. God is on my
side!*

Day 305

"I'm mad at God and we're not talking."
—Dr. Carl Spangler

Dr. Spangler is one of the medical personnel who worked round the clock during the rescue efforts in the days following the Oklahoma City bombing. If ever there was an event that prompted anger at God, it was this senseless act of violence. Dr. Spangler can verbalize his feelings. Perhaps you, too, are angry with God. Whatever the cause, remember: God is big enough to handle your anger. You're not. Your anger, directed at God, will eat away at you and erode your chances for happiness and success. Anger turned Godward is anger misplaced. We need someone to blame. For want of an obvious villain, we blame God. Like everything about us, God understands our anger, too. Even when we're so angry that we stop speaking to Him, God never stops speaking to us. His voice is the one constant in a world of turmoil. We may withdraw from God, but God never withdraws from us. God is both our greatest fan and our greatest facilitator.

Yesterday's storm severed the wires. Today's I'll reconnect.

Day 306

"Do not judge, so that you may not be judged. For with the judgement you make you will be judged, and the measure you give will be the measure you get."
—Matthew 7:1 & 2

As you move into the realm of can do, be careful not to judge others who may not yet have made the same progress. Each person must decide his or her own goals and strategies for achieving them. Unfortunately, some may decide not to decide. This, too, is a personal decision. Be encouraging but not judgmental. The high standards you set for yourself are for your own guidance. Don't apply them in judgement of others. At the same time, be aware of your standards and don't compromise your principles. If there is a person or a situation that will drag you down, avoid that person, get out of that situation. Knowing something is wrong for you is far different from judging what's right or wrong for others. As you move up, avoid the temptation to look down on others. Instead, celebrate your own successes and give thanks for your own progress. Your achievements are your personal victories; they are not gained by defeating others. Heed the warning in Matthew's Gospel. Be aware that there are times when you, too, will fall short, when you will fail to measure up to your own expectations. Seek no one's approval but your own and God's. Next time you decide someone — a family member, friend, or stranger — doesn't meet your approval, ask yourself, "Am I meeting God's approval?"

I'll practice self-evaluation and leave evaluation of others to God.

DAY 307

> "If you believe you have power, thus gives
> you power, and if you use it, act on it, you
> can make things happen."
> —Maxine Waters

Tomorrow you could become a millionaire . . . or a pauper. Tomorrow you could have a miraculous healing of some physical problem . . . or die of the same condition. Tomorrow you could meet the mate of your dreams . . . or have your dream mate walk out on you. Tomorrow is always uncertain. In fact, the only thing certain about tomorrow is that you can't be certain of what will happen then — you can't even be fully certain that tomorrow will come. Most of what we do in life is based upon our past experiences. Because a new day has dawned every morning of your life, you base your belief that tomorrow will also see the dawn of a new day. You can't be absolutely certain of it, but because this is what has always happened, it's reasonable to believe that this is what will continue to happen tomorrow. Therefore, planning for tomorrow is prudent, wise, and an important element in every plan for success. The danger comes when we worry so much about the future that we miss the opportunities of today or fail to enjoy the gifts of the present. "Take time to smell the coffee," has become a popular way of saying slow down, look around, enjoy today for today's sake.

I'll plan for the future but live in the present.

> "Ye shall know the truth, and the truth
> shall make you free."
>
> —John 8:32

Are you strong enough to face the truth about yourself? God is able to grant you that strength. Gaining the strength to face the truth about yourself is vital to achieving personal success. Are you a procrastinator? Are you easily distracted? Do you tend to be lazy, negative, or unprepared? Facing the truth about your personal weaknesses is the first step in converting those weaknesses into strengths. Ask God to open your eyes to the parts of you that need improving. Ask God to remove any bad habits or self-defeating behaviors. Next, acknowledge your negative habits to yourself and commit to improving your weak areas. Make a conscious effort to work on one negative behavior every week. Be sure to replace negative behaviors with positive actions. Thank God and congratulate yourself on each bad habit you overcome. Be willing to know the truth about yourself. Allow this self-knowledge to free you of weaknesses so that you can continue developing into the person of excellence God wants you to be.

I'll guard against lies, especially to myself.

DAY 309

"Don't buy where you can't work."
—Adam Clayton Powell

We all know the history of minorities in America. Thanks to those who have gone before — from all races, colors, and creeds — things have changed. Today there is no excuse for not moving ahead. Too many people who have had it just as bad as you, who have come from backgrounds even worse than yours, who have been given fewer talents than you possess, have made it. So can you. It's strictly a matter of attitude! Your attitude, the way you think about yourself, is the biggest factor impacting your success. It's not the neighborhood you live in. It's not the educational system you attend. It's not the family you come from. It's you, inside, the inner you, your own constant companion, the voice that talks to you all day long, the feelings you experience every day. That companion, that voice, those feelings are YOU. Who else and what else has a greater influence over you than you yourself? No one! Nothing! That's why your attitude is so very, very important. It's your attitude that will get you up and get you moving. It's your attitude that will keep you up when you're running, pick you up when you fall, stand you up when you face injustice, hardship, obstacles, and barriers. And it's all right there inside YOU!

Deep in my heart, I do believe I CAN!

> "To God be the glory, by whose power . . .
> we are able to accomplish abundantly more
> than we can ask or imagine."
> —Ephesians 3:20 (paraphrase)

What are your wildest dreams? You can go far beyond them. What are your greatest desires? You can have much more. What are your ultimate goals? You can far surpass them. God's power, working in you, can take you far beyond anything you can ask or imagine. First, you must believe that God has the power to do anything. Second, you must believe that God will put His power at your disposal to use for accomplishing positive growth throughout your life. Third, you must activate this power by living an active prayer and faith life. Ask, believe, have, do! These are the steps that will enable you to accomplish abundantly, more than you can ever imagine. Always remember, everything you are striving for has already been accomplished in the spiritual realm. It was accomplished through Jesus' death on the cross, a perfect act of salvation that covers all your sins and gives you God-power for life. Jesus paid the price; God redeemed your life. Through grace you're given the power to conquer every hour. Whatever you want, *go for it!* God's power will take you beyond your wildest dreams.

If I can dream it, I can have it.

DAY 311

"Tough times never last, but tough people do!"

—Rev. Robert Schuller

No matter how tough your situation is, you have the God-given potential to overcome it. You have the power to get from where you are to where you want to be. You have the innate ability to achieve health, happiness, and prosperity. Whatever your problem — unemployment, poor health, loneliness, fear, abusive/destructive behavior — you can find a way out of it. Name your problem and you name your possibility! You're loaded with positive potential. God put it inside you when you were created. It doesn't matter what's going on around you, it's what's going on inside you that produces positive change. God didn't just make you, stuff you full of potential, then send you off while He sits back to watch what will happen to you. God remains both active and interactive in your life. He constantly places in your path possibilities for using your potential. And He remains on call to help you recognize these possibilities and figure out the best way to use your potential to create positive change. In a way, you and God are partners in the task of creation: together you create the ways you live your life. Tough times call for tough people to fix tough problems. How you get through these tough times is up to you.

Today may be tough, but I'm tougher. I can conquer tough times.

> "I treasure your word in my heart, so that I
> may not sin against you. . . . I will delight
> in your statues; I will not forget your word."
> —Psalm 119: 11,16

Knowing God's word and God's promises is the greatest weapon you can have against those who would impede your progress and try to bring you down. My grandmother's Bible was marked with ink, pencil, and tear stains. Each one that I saw reminded me of the peace she felt in trusting God's word. This legacy of my grand-mother's was one of my greatest gifts in life. It set me on the path of regular Bible reading and memorization of scripture. It is those scriptures, committed to my memory, that I call on to see me through any situation. It is important that you, too, begin now to build up this arsenal of scripture. Find the verses that address specific situations. Seek out God's promises and commit them to memory. Hide them in your heart. Then, when you find yourself under attack, you can pull them out at a moment's notice. Even when you can't access your Bible, you'll have the Word of God at your finger tips. What better weapon could you want?

Today I'll ask myself, Where do I keep God's word?

Day 313

> "God our Savior, and His love . . . saved us, not on the basis of deeds . . . but according to His mercy."
>
> —Titus 3:3-6

Someone you know needs to be saved. Perhaps it's your parent, spouse, sibling, friend, or co-worker. Because you're saved, you have an obligation to reach out to them, to encourage them to come to their full potential by coming to Christ. They may be stubborn and refuse to hear you. Don't give up, but don't hound. Instead, show them what it means to turn your life over to Christ by being an example of what God can do. Live your Christianity. Remember, you weren't born saved. Someone spoke to you. Someone encouraged you. Someone prayed for you. Can you do less for others? Be patient with potential believers. You never know how close they may be to saying YES to the Lord.

Someone I know needs to be saved. Today I'll speak out.

Day 314

> "Except the Lord build the house, they labor
> in vain that build it; except the Lord keep
> the city, the watchman waketh but in vain."
> —Psalm 127:2

Whenever you are faced with choices that will affect you for the rest of your life, it is important that you consult with God, the Master Builder of the universe. Never attempt to do anything without prayer and consultation with God. Sometimes God will direct you to seek advice from Godly women and men who are knowledgeable in your area of concern. You must be assertive in seeking them out. Don't settle for less than Godly business or personal advice. Sometimes God will direct you to look deeper into yourself for guidance. Here, too, you must be aggressive. Don't let yourself off the hook. Look inside; look deeper; listen for your inner voice. Pray for help in getting in touch with your best self. God, the Master Builder, will enable you to lay a foundation with bricks of decision that are God's will. Whatever you are seeking, you will find. Whatever you are attempting, you will accomplish. God, the Master Builder, is ready to build a masterpiece out of you.

God is the master builder. I am God's masterpiece.

Day 315

> "Coincidence is God's way of remaining anonymous."
>
> —Anonymous

God is always working at teaching us something more about himself. Through coincidences, He teaches us about humility. Sure, He could have set things up so that whenever something good or wonderful happens to us, we'd see a big fluorescent sign flashing "God At Work!" Instead, God chooses to remain anonymous and to let us decide to whom we'll give the credit. Coincidences bring us a special opportunity to choose. We can decide that we just got lucky and give the credit for our good fortune to chance. Or we can choose to see the hand of God at work in our lives. Crediting your life's events to chance puts you on a par with a gambler sitting at the dice table. Choosing to see God in the events that make up your life puts you on an entirely different plane. The Creator, the Divine One who made you, did not stop His interaction with you at the act of creation. He remains with you, not as a spectator but as an active participant in your life. Viewing life in this way makes every moment exciting. You learn to look for the good in the bad, to search for the joy in the midst of pain. You learn to read coincidences as signs from God himself.

I may not have planned my day, but God has.

> "Where there is no vision, the people perish."
>
> —Proverbs 29:18

How many times has God given you wonderful dreams? How many times have you ignored the possibilities contained in those God-given dreams? Maybe you've shared your dreams with others, only to be told that your dreams were foolish, that they were too high for you, that you could never achieve those things you dreamed of. Don't let anyone discourage you! Don't let anything get in the way of your dreams! Right now, think back to a dream you've abandoned. Grab hold of it again. Let it pull you up above the level of mediocrity to a level of Godly excellence. Is your dream of a better education, a different job, a challenging career? See yourself achieving your dream. Picture yourself walking onto that campus, successfully going through that job interview, dressing for the first day of that new career. That dream didn't come to you by accident; God put it there and God's waiting to help you fulfill it. Cut the strings that are keeping you earth-bound. Unleash the energy that will carry you heaven-bound in your thoughts and actions. Give God a chance to give you a chance to make all your dreams come true.

I'm a dreamer. My dreams are alive in my life.

Day 317

"And Jesus increased in wisdom, and in
years, and in divine and human favor."
—Luke 2:52

Can you recall a time when you've asked a friend
or family member for a favor? They proved their love
and faith in you by granting your request. But first
that faith had to be earned. You earned their trust
throughout your ongoing relationship with them. When
you needed help, they knew you well enough to believe your request was genuine and founded upon
good reason. Well, God grants favors, too! When you
prove your faith by obeying God's commands, you
find yourself being highly favored by the Lord. When
you are obedient to God, your wisdom increases. You
begin to recognize God's plan unfolding in your life.
You see intuitively where you're going and the best
way to get there. You sense God's power surrounding you, enabling you to go farther, accomplishing
more than you ever believed possible. When you live
in obedience to God, you increase in human favor,
too. People will be drawn to you. They will respect
your lifestyle, your beliefs, and your achievements.
You will naturally find yourself in the company of others who also live in obedience to God — others also
wise in spirit and favored by the Lord. What wonderful company to keep! God's favorites living in obedience, drawing on His favors, growing in wisdom, success, and personal fulfillment.

I'm God's favorite; I rely on His favors.

> "Part of our problem with debt is that we have confused needs with wants. Yesterday's luxuries are today's necessities."
> —Rev. Billy Graham

Americans have more private homes, more two-car families, more expendable wealth than citizens of any other country. Americans also spend more on psychiatrists, counseling, anti-depressant drugs, and "How To Be Happy" books than any other group of people. If this seems incongruous to you, try explaining it to someone living in the slums of Calcutta or in a refugee camp in Africa. The very concept of unhappiness in the midst of plenty is unimaginable to more than half of the world's population. Yet here we are — well fed and, all too often, pretty well fed-up with our lives. Perhaps the root of our insatiable hunt for happiness lies in an unbalanced value system. Wanting more in and of itself is not a bad thing. The desire for more can be a positive motivator that leads to personal success. It is when the desire for more keeps us from appreciating what we already have that we get into trouble. We fail to see the progress we've made. We devalue ourselves, our relationships, and our successes. Left unchecked, the desire for more can outstrip our ability to achieve. Soon we are living on credit, in debt for things that lose their value to us long before we're done paying for them.

On the road of my life, I'll remain the driver not the driven.

DAY 319

> "We can say with confidence, 'The Lord is my helper; I will not be afraid. What can anyone do to me?'"
>
> —Hebrews 13:6

How do you approach people and situations? Do you lack confidence? Does your voice have a note of fear? Are your actions tentative and uncertain? God wants you to be so sure of His help and power that you can act boldly and with confidence. God wants your faith in Him to be so strong that you're never afraid. Imagine the freedom of a life without fear? Never again would you be afraid to try to accomplish anything. You'd be free to pursue your dreams with confidence. Your boss, your professor, the job interviewer, your spouse — no one would be able to make you afraid. This is exactly the kind of freedom God is ready to give to you. God wants you to have such confidence that you will be bold and forthright even in your prayer requests. After all, God already knows what's on your heart and in your mind. Why try to hide your needs or clothe your requests in less than forthright words? Boldness can be a mighty trait in committed Christians. God can accomplish mighty things with the help of bold Christians. Bold Christians can accomplish mighty things with the help of God.

I'll live this day free of all fear.

Day 320

"When you've exhausted all the possibilities, remember this: You haven't!"

—Rev. Robert Schuller

Humans are action-oriented animals. Everything in our make-up compels us to do something. When conditions in our external world would hamper our actions, we don't hibernate like the bear or migrate like the birds. Instead, we change so that we can keep on doing. No situation is harder for a human being to face than that in which there is nothing more to do. Nothing is so hard to face as the complete exhaustion of all possibilities. Thankfully, that never has to happen to us. For us, when we've reached the limit of human action, we find divine intervention. In short, there are miracles. We hear about dramatic miracles — miraculous survivals, unexpected discoveries, healing in the face of certain death. What we don't hear about are the quiet miracles that happen all around us everyday. The miracle of finding God even when you weren't looking. The miracle of faith restored even in the face of tragedy. The miracle of God's presence acting for us when we have run out of ways to act for ourselves. No matter what is going on around you, no matter what your situation, no matter that you've run out of options and exhausted all your possibilities, there still is God, waiting with endless possibilities, limitless options.

I'm never out of options. Prayer provides possibilities and potential.

Day 321

"But from the beginning of creation, God made them male and female."

—Genesis 1:27

The best thing you can do for your marriage is to ask for what you need. Being less than forthright is just playing games. Love and marriage is really about people coming together to support and affirm one another. When we ask for what we need, we honor and respect our own wants and desires. In asking honestly, rather than pouting and waiting for our partners to figure out what we want, we demonstrate trust. Like a muscle, trust grows with exercise. As we exercise trust, our trust in one another grows stronger. We cultivate an environment in which each partner can flourish. Honesty grows, too. We are able to accept the needs of our partners when they are expressed honestly and openly. When we know they are honest, we are more able to accept our partner's answer to our needs and requests. Sometimes those answers will be "no." When spoken honestly and with love, we learn to accept our partner's limitations as well as our own. Remember, marriage is seldom a fifty-fifty proposition. Sometimes you will need 100% from your spouse. Other times you must give 100%. Asking, honestly and openly, listening as well as talking, will give you both a better chance of maintaining a marriage filled with love, respect, and genuine passion.

Today I'll ask, then listen for the answer.

DAY 322

> "I used to ask God to help me, then I
> asked if I might help him."
> —Missionary James Hudson Taylor

Following the 1995 Oklahoma City bombing, rescue workers and volunteers told of discovering previously untapped sources of inner strength that kept them going through one of America's darkest hours. Combat veterans have shared similar discoveries. Nothing is so self-revealing as the experience of parenthood. Suddenly we are totally responsible for another human being. At the same time, we seem to lose responsibility over our own lives. We can no longer eat when we want, sleep as long as we want, go when and where we want. Likewise, many middle-aged adults struggle with the problem of assuming responsibility for aging parents. Suddenly the very people who provided strength and stability for us become weak and dependent. Life has come full circle. New coping skills are needed. If you've built a tradition of helping others, life's changes won't be as devastating for you. You'll have developed the fine art of helping God help others. Rather than be defeated by added responsibilities, you'll welcome them as new opportunities for learning more about yourself. Remember, you can get lost in yourself but never in someone else. When you give of yourself you'll always get more of your true self back in return.

I'm reaping the high returns of self-giving.

DAY 323

"Miracles are earthly impossibilities heaven's intervention."

—Rance Allen

Have you ever noticed how desperately we can pray for help and then, when it comes, chalk it up to everything else but God's answer? I was thinking about this while praying over a Prayer List recently. I realized that as needs were met, we never moved them to a "Thank you for the miracle" list. We simply explained how the problem had been solved. "She found a different doctor." "He met a friend who loaned him the money." "The Realtor found a buyer for their house." No wonder we miss so many miracles! We simply fail to see God's hand working out problems through everyday people and events! Most of us would agree that God works miracles through doctors, nurses, and teachers. But isn't it possible that God also works miracle through Realtors, bankers, grocery store clerks, landscapers, day laborers? Doesn't the "miracle worker" depend on the miracle needed? Once in awhile it's important to step outside yourself and conduct a reality check. What are the realities of your life? If things are going your way, is it simply a matter of good luck or is there divine intervention at work in your life? Being the all-loving God that He is, God doesn't need our recognition. He'll keep right on working His quiet miracles everyday. It's we who benefit from recognizing the miracles around us. By being aware of a higher realm of reality, we open ourselves to living with new excitement, possibilities, and potential.

Today, anything's possible!

DAY 324

"I will never leave you nor forsake you."
—Hebrews 13:5

God has created us to live in joy. But for many people, life is filled with loneliness and depression. These two emotions can influence them to seek advice from ungodly sources. Just look at the millions of dollars spent on fortune tellers, tarot card readers, and psychic 900 numbers. Horoscopes are so popular most newspapers publish them daily. What a misguided way to seek direction! God is waiting to deliver us from all bondage. This includes the bondage of loneliness and depression. If you are feeling lonely or depressed, call on God. Ask God to put Godly people in your life. Then prepare yourself to receive them. To paraphrase Proverbs 18:24: "A person that hath friends must first be friendly." Be sure you are not the cause of your own loneliness. Ask yourself, "How do I react to new people?" If you're not going to welcome them, it's wasteful to ask God to send them. But if you truly are ready to move from loneliness and depression to a rewarding, friend-filled life, ask God. And, while you're waiting for God to answer your prayers, remember His promise: 'I will never leave you nor forsake you.' God is the best friend you can ever have.

Today I'll talk with my best friend. Today I'll pray.

Day 325

> "Change has always been led by those whose spirits were bigger than their circumstances."
> —Jesse Jackson, Sr.

When I was a child, heaven didn't seem like a very exciting destination. From all the books I was read by my Sunday School teachers and all I heard in church, I thought heaven sounded a little boring. In fact, I thought it sounded a whole lot boring. I remember thinking the flying part might be neat, but I wondered how much time I'd really get for flying around, what with all that singing all day and everything! I remember being afraid that God would find out I didn't want to go to heaven and would send me to the other place. This was especially terrifying because I was taught that God knew everything; He could even read my mind. There was no way I could hide my thoughts about heaven from Him. It was quite a dilemma. Now that I'm an adult, I still don't know exactly what heaven will be like, but I'm sure it won't be boring. Everything I've seen so far in life promises that. My life experiences tell me that if this world, which is temporary, is filled with such beauty and excitement, the next world has to be at least as magnificent. In fact, I believe the biggest difference between this world and the next is that in heaven I'll live in the visual presence of God. And where God dwells, there can be no sin or sickness, no fear or failure, no broken promises and no potential left unfulfilled. Totally fulfilled potential is never boring. Try living to your potential here on earth and you'll have a glimpse of the unseen excitement of heaven.

Someday I'll see for myself. Today I'll prepare myself.

DAY 326

"... none of them received what had been promised. God had planned something better."

—Hebrews 11:39-40 (paraphrase)

Has someone you loved and trusted broken a promise to you? Have you been betrayed by a friend, let down by a child, abandoned by a spouse, abused by a parent? Every time we hurt someone in any way, physically or mentally, we break a promise — the common promise that binds all humans — the promise to hold life in sacred respect and to treat one another as we want to be treated. This is a command of God's, yes, but it also is a vow He placed inside of each of us on the day of our creation. Being part of the human race means being part of a higher life form that is entrusted with this promise. We become disengaged from our very souls. We are no longer able to live as whole persons. Instead, we become fragmented, and a person in pieces cannot accomplish wholesome, fulfilling purposes. God has so much planned for each of us *right in this lifetime!* God's plans are better than anyone's promises. Yet, in order to have God's plans work in our lives, we must be true to that human promise of respect and care for one another. True success is never achieved at the sacrifice of someone else's progress. If you do your part, God will do even more.

I am a child of God. So are others. God has enough "goodness" for each of us. I'll help spread it around.

DAY 327

"There are no mistakes, no coincidences. All events are blessings given to us to learn from."

—Dr. Elizabeth Kubler-Ross

Have you ever found yourself in the middle of a situation and you just don't know how you got there? Of one thing you can be sure: you're not there by mistake, you're not there by accident. God doesn't make mistakes and God doesn't have accidents. What I believe God does do is cause what we humans call "coincidences." The way I see it, even when we make our plans with prayer and stay in close touch with God as we carry them out, we are limited human beings. No matter how hard we listen, we sometimes fail to hear God's advice or misinterpret what we hear. This is when God steps in and causes coincidences. We might not recognize them at the time, but looking back, we can see that many coincidences in our lives have caused dramatic changes. This is God's hand — sometimes gently, sometimes urgently — turning us around, setting us on a different course, opening a new door, or pointing out an alternative direction. In coincidences, we glimpse the gentle humor of God as He works quietly, anonymously, but always powerfully to keep His plan unfolding for us. When you learn to look for God in coincidences, you'll be on the watch for new horizons, new vistas of success and happiness.

God wouldn't leave my life to chance and neither will I. Today we're taking charge.

DAY 328

"The light of God surrounds me. The love of God unfolds me. The power of God protects me. I can't get away from God's Everywhereness."
—Rev. James Perkins

This is a beautiful thought from one of America's more renowned preachers. I wrote it down and carry it with me. I pull it out and read it several times a day. In the course of a year, I must repeat it hundreds, if not thousands, of times. The light of God *does* surround me. I can see it shining in times of victory and in times of defeat. The love of God *does* enfold me. I can feel God's love even at times when I don't love myself. The power of God *does* protect me. Look at all the things I've faced and conquered! Look at all I'm willing to undertake because I know I can count on His protection! The presence of God *does* watch over me. There is nowhere I can go that God doesn't go with me. There is no place too far, too dangerous, too poor, too frightening for God to go to be with me. God is never too tired, never too busy, never too over-committed to accompany me. *Wherever I am, God is!* Knowing and believing all this, I still have one more question to ask myself: Am I sure that wherever I am and whatever I'm doing, God's presence is reflected by my presence, God's love felt in my actions? We can be very sure of God, but can God be very sure of us? Perhaps that's the question that must be answered at every step of our journey from "can't do" to "can do," from where we are now to where we want to be.

Everyday I count on God. This day I'll let God count on me.

> "'In God we trust,' it's right on the money!"
> —Anonymous

This book is about succeeding. Money is part of success. You might be surprised to hear a preacher say this. Well, I'm saying it, and I'll say it again: Money is a part of success. It's not the only part. It's not the most important part. But it is one of the important parts of success. Let's be real honest. It's hard to be generous when you're broke. It's hard to be caring when you're hungry. It's hard to be ambitious when you're homeless. It's hard to be motivated when, after working hard for years at a company, you suddenly find yourself unemployed because of restructuring or down sizing. Money is definitely part of success. If you believe God wants you to succeed, then you must believe God wants you to have enough money to meet your needs. If you believe God wants you to live abundantly, then you must believe God wants you to have enough money for abundant living. Oh, yes, there is one more thing: Trust in God. Remember, it's right on the money!

I trust God to help me succeed. God trusts me to help myself to success.

"People have to look at things for what they have, not what they haven't been given."
—Hakeem Olajuwon

"Every silver lining must have a cloud," says Lewis Smedes in his book, *A Pretty Good Person*. How true. As we pass from our can't do atmospheres to the blessings of can do living, we'll have many things for which to be grateful. At the same time, we'll be more sensitive to those around us who aren't making it. On a global scale, can a truly God-filled person be grateful for food, home, clothing, education, and health while half the world's population is starving, homeless, sick, and illiterate? We know that God wants us to recognize His gifts to us, be grateful for them, enjoy them, and acknowledge them with our thanks. We also know that God wants us to care about the plight of others and to act to alleviate their needs. It's a dilemma. When we look around and see how un-blessed others are, our personal gratitude turns to personal shame. Perhaps one answer is to acknowledge that our world is, and always has been, too blemished for perfect joy. The inequities have always been too glaring, the injustices too great.

Lord, make me a blessing to someone today.

DAY 331

"Increasingly, what we earn depends on what we learn."

—Secretary Ron Brown

Few of us would argue with this statement by the now deceased (and first African-American to hold the position) U.S. Secretary of Commerce, especially when applied to formal education. In fact, a recent survey shows that the average lifetime earnings of a college graduate over a non-college graduate jumped from 34% in 1978 to more than 52% in 1994. Education, then, is key to financial success. From the Bible we learn that we were created for successful living, that we are promised abundance, and that we have God's full support as we pursue God-pleasing plans. From God we learn unconditional love, uninterrupted companionship, unceasing victories, and unlimited blessings. By heeding well the lessons of life, we earn confidence, spiritual strength, increased self-esteem, the increased respect of others, and a host of other blessings — not least among these are the blessings of friendships, acceptance, love, and financial security.

Everyday I learn something that will increase my earning power.

Day 332

"There are two sides to life."
—Ray Charles

Life is multi-dimensional. These dimensions can most easily be seen in the many roles each of us fill. We are parents, siblings, spouses, friends, children, employees, employers, neighbors plus however else we describe ourselves in terms of our work, i.e., teachers, sheet metal workers, bakers, homemakers, preachers, construction workers, accountants, clerks, etc. Beyond these many roles, however, there are two sides or dimensions to life that encompass all the others: The side of life in which we function as children of God and the side of life in which we fulfill all of our other roles. How well we fulfill our worldly roles depends upon how well-rooted we are in our role as children of God. When we accept and celebrate ourselves as children of God, we function differently in all our other roles. We become more loving spouses, more caring children, wiser parents, more accepting siblings, more concerned neighbors, more honest, dedicated, and proficient workers. In short, we become more successful people in every role and in every way as we become more sure of our roles as children of God and heirs to God's eternal kingdom. It is your purpose for being and your inheritance from the one who created you.

I'm a child of the King; I'll fulfill all my other roles to the best of my ability, as an example for others.

"God can mend a broken heart, but first you have to give him all the pieces."

—Anonymous

Do you feel broken and battered? Has the very act of living become a painful ordeal? Are you merely getting through each day rather than embracing the daily miracles of living, growing, achieving? Is your heart so broken by someone or something that you're stuck in a can't do mind-set? Maybe for you, all the lessons in the world about developing a can do attitude are pointless; you're simply too beaten down to move forward. God, however, is never beaten. God truly can mend your broken heart and broken life. You don't even need the strength to enter into lengthy prayer accounts of the details of your position and how you got there. Remember, God already knows. All you have to do is acknowledge your brokenness to Him and ask Him to fix it. Your life-changing prayer can be a simple one-sentence plea. God doesn't demand eloquence. But He does demand sincerity. Ask Him to not only show you the path to successful living but to walk beside you as you go. Believe that He will strengthen you; also believe that He will carry you in His loving arms, that He will be your leaning post until you grow strong enough to walk upright and sure. Turn over to God all the pieces. Hold none, not even one, back. Allow Him to carry out His work of transformation.

I'll be patient with myself.

Day 334

"I don't have to bring my own into the world."
—Michael Jackson

Having children is an awesome responsibility. Not until you hold that newborn child in your arms are you struck with the realization of the life-long duty you have to this person who has been entrusted to your care. Unfortunately, society has placed parenthood on a pedestal, implying that to be truly successful and complete you must take on this role. At the same time, society has set few, if any, parameters for parenthood. There are no classes, no tests, no standards that must be met. In fact, it is easier to become a parent than it is to become a licensed driver. Having children is one of the most challenging and fulfilling experiences of life. It is one choice but only one choice. Of all the choices you make, it is the most serious. Once made, it cannot be changed or taken back. You don't simply wake up one day and find yourself a doctor, teacher, electrician, or secretary. You *decide* to become whatever and then take orderly steps to attain your goal. Each step must be conquered before you can move on to the next step.

Children are gifts from God, but not the only gifts God gives. I will pray long and hard before I choose to become a parent.

Day 335

> "God adds to the beauty of the world
> by creating friends."
>
> —Anonymous

It has been said, "You can't choose your family, but you can choose your friends." Friends bring beauty and truth to life. Who else but a friend can tell you those difficult to hear things? Who else but a friend knows what is so painful or so difficult to hear that he or she refrains from telling you unless absolutely necessary? Who else but a friend knows you well enough and cares for you deeply enough to judge the difference? Now I'm not talking about acquaintances and superficial friends. I'm talking about long-term, proven friends whose loyalty has withstood trials by fire. Can't do environments often include family members. Sometimes these are the very people who, usually unknowingly, will try to hold you back and drag you down. Not so with a proven friend. Friends have no hidden agendas. True friendships don't demand a balance of give and take; there is no score-keeping, only love. If you inadvertently do something that hurts a friend, apology and atonement are acts you should perform for your own sake; your true friend knows you didn't act out of malice or purposely cause hurt. Friends should be chosen wisely; they will be your companions for life.

To have friends, be a friend.

Day 336

"When growth stops decay begins."

—Anonymous

"Atrophy," the doctor called it. Lack of use had stunted normal growth. To live is to grow. When growth stops life ceases. We all know how quickly decay devours a dead body. The same is true for a dead mind and a dead spirit. When we choose to stop growing in wisdom and understanding, when we abandon our journey of growth in our relationships with God and with others, when we cease our quest for greater self-knowledge, meaningful life ends and decay begins. None of us can turn back the hands of time. While diet and exercise can help prolong physical health and strength, we can never recapture the vigor of our youth. Yet we can continue to grow in other, non-physical areas. Perhaps God slows us down physically so that we may redirect our energies to growth in more enduring pursuits — developing strength of character, respect for others, self-acceptance, and faith in the goodness of God and in the validity of His promises.

I'm growing stronger, wiser, older. I'm growing into God's image of me.

Day 337

"I believe the church is declining because it no longer costs very much to be a 'Christian.'"
—Anonymous

Once being a follower of Jesus meant putting your very life on the line for your beliefs. Discipleship then was a very costly vocation. Today there are few martyrs. We have so watered down the Gospel that the title "Christian" can be earned by spending an hour at church on Sunday (and not even every Sunday), by serving on committees, by being a good neighbor. Today we have become so afraid of offending others that we leave the proclaiming of the Gospel to the professionals — preachers, deacons, evangelists. And, if they proclaim it too loudly we dub them zealots and distance ourselves from their embarrassing behavior. The social aspects of the church are an important means for drawing members closer. But let's face it, when it comes to entertainment, television, videos, and the mall are more exciting than a church chicken dinner. Discipleship means witnessing to the risen Christ not only among those who already believe but among unbelievers. Following Christ is to be like nothing else we do in our lives. Being the Church, loving people we may not like, preaching, teaching, and living as God's people — this is what it means to be a Christian.

Today I'll become a better servant — to my God, to my church, and to activities that will help me achieve my own goals.

DAY 338

"I just think you should have some fun
with your life and not take yourself too
seriously."

—Hillary Clinton

The ability to laugh at oneself is one of God's greatest blessings. Life is meant to be productive, to be
lived in a Godly way, and to be fun. God could have
created the world as a drab, colorless sphere endlessly
spinning without rhyme or reason. God could have
created life devoid of excitement, challenges, opportunities, friendships. God could have decided to leave
out of human personalities the capacity for pleasure,
enjoyment, humor. Instead, God filled the world with
beauty. God made us creatures capable of enjoying
one another's company, of sharing laughter and good
times, of just plain having fun as we journey through
life. Remember, all talents come from God. This includes the talent of a stand-up comedian, a circus
clown, a juggler, a magician — all manner of people
whose talents bring fun and humor into our lives. What
is more beautiful than the gift of laughter, more heart-
warming than the gift of camaraderie, more life-en-
hancing than the ability to accept with humor our
human shortcomings? Fun times make sad times bear-
able. A life lived without humor, laughter, and fun is
shallow.

*Because I'm human, I sometimes make mistakes.
Because I'm human, I will find the humor in my shortcomings.*

Day 339

"If a man is called to be a streetsweeper . . . he should sweep streets so well that all the hosts of heaven and earth will pause to say, here lived a great streetsweeper who did his job well."

—Martin Luther King, Jr.

Becoming a can do person requires that you give your very best effort to every pursuit. If you don't care enough about something to do it right, don't do it at all. Half-hearted attempts earn half-hearted results. You won't be pleased with your achievements and you'll always be haunted by musings of how things would have turned out had you given more of your best self. It doesn't matter so much what you're doing as how you're doing it. Whether you're making a bed, cooking a meal, teaching a class, selling a product, do it to the very best of your ability. Then, and only then, will you know the joy of self-satisfaction. Success comes not only with the end result but with how you feel about the end result. You may be the best salesperson in the company, but if deep inside you know you could have done more or done it better, you won't truly feel successful. Likewise, if you choose an endeavor and give it your very best shot, you'll never feel like a failure no matter what the outcome. Choose your goals carefully, then, whatever it takes, do it right; otherwise, get out. Make different choices, ones you can pursue with all your heart, soul, talents, and enthusiasm. Success builds on success, one achievement after another. Don't become your own worse enemy by crippling your chances of succeeding. Whatever you choose to do, do it right, or don't do it at all.

Today I'll do my best at whatever I do.

DAY 340

"This is the real world."
—Bill Gates

Computer genius Bill Gates knows that your environment is your "real world." You can leave it; you can change it; you can accept it. But whether positive or negative, healthy or self-destructive, your world is your reality. It's a fact: can't do environments exist. It's also a fact that you have a choice to remain in a can't do environment or to get out of it. This book is about getting out. There are many ways to do this. You can remove yourself physically by relocating. You can remove yourself mentally by adopting positive can do behaviors. You can get out spiritually by knowing — really knowing — that who you are has little to do with where you live. Creating a real world for yourself in which you can become a success and realize your dreams takes hard work and a thick skin. No matter how you choose to escape from a can't do environment, you will be criticized. People will talk about you. Let them talk; you know who you are and where you're heading. You must create your own reality, your own world in which you call the shots. Your life is your real world. You can share your world with losers or winners. You can move through your world on a positive track or remain immobilized by hardship, injustice, laziness, defeatism. You can adopt a "poor me" attitude or develop a "successful me" attitude. The choice is yours. This is your real world.

I am not an address, I am not a victim. I am in control of my world, my future.

DAY 341

"What you ought to do, you should do; and what you should do, you ought to do."

—Oprah Winfrey

What's the difference between "should" and "ought?" "Ought" statements most often come from others, while "should" statements come from self. Throughout childhood, parents tell children what they ought to do. Successful parenting results in children internalizing the "oughts" and converting them to "shoulds." Successful adults no longer need parents, teachers, employers, etc. to tell them what they "ought" to do. They've developed their own sense of right and wrong. They know what they "should" do and act accordingly. Does this mean we must adopt all of the rules set down for us by others? No! A successful person has developed the ability to adopt the good, adapt the potentially good, and discard the bad. Successful people are like successful gardeners: they plant seeds that grow well in a particular soil, light, and climate; they transplant crops to different spots for better growth; and they weed out all that is unhealthy, unsuited, or harmful to the overall good of the garden.

Today I'll examine the "oughts" and preserve the "shoulds."

DAY 342

"Love is spelled T - A - C - T."
—Anonymous

I Corinthians 13, that famous passage chosen by so many couples to be part of their marriage ceremony, reminds us that love is patient and kind, never rude, never "puffed up." In other words, love is more concerned with *doing* right than with *being* right. Why is it then that we speak to and act toward our loved ones in ways we wouldn't dream of treating strangers? A co-worker gains weight, gets a new hair-do, or wears an outfit that you find most unflattering. Do you say "Gee, you're getting fat," or "Where did you get that hideous outfit?" Of course not! Now suppose it's your spouse whose appearance fails to please you. Are you quick to criticize, to condemn, to say hurtful words — words that can't be taken back? Sometimes it may be important to be honest with your spouse about your reaction to his or her appearance or behavior. But these times are far and few between. And, even during these times, you can be tactful. Tact allows your love to shine through even when you feel compelled to criticize. Tact leaves both parties with their dignity undamaged and their certainty of your love uncompromised. Tact, born of respect, is the most important way of succeeding in building enduring relationships that grow more precious and love-filled year after year.

I'll be careful to treat those I love the most at least as lovingly as I treat acquaintances.

Day 343

"Don't get involved unless you feel a call, but when you do, see it through."
—Mahatma Gandhi

Your old can't do environment is made up of closed doors. Your new can do attitude will bring you a multitude of choices, possibilities, and opportunities. As you grow into your new, self-confident can do self, deciding where you want to invest your energies will be an exciting adventure. A word of warning: Don't spread yourself too thin. Make your decisions with prayer and care. Set goals that will truly satisfy *you*, not someone else. When you feel called to some pursuit, some action, some challenge, step back for a day or two — or longer — and analyze your motives. Success comes in many ways. Always the successful life is one lived to the satisfaction of the individual. There are many noble causes, many important endeavors, many admirable careers. And there are many people capable of making these pursuits their life-long goals. Your life-long goal, God's plan for your success, has been specifically designed for you. It is perfectly matched with your innate abilities, talents, and interests. Take time to discover your true calling. Then give it all you've got. Let it be the crowning achievement of your life.

I can do many things. God and I together will choose from among them to form my priority list.

> "It is preferable to wear out than to rust out."
>
> —Sign on a Church Lawn

It wasn't a new car, but it wasn't really old, either. In fact, many older models were still on the road and running well, thanks to the regular maintenance they received. But this car sat unused, unprotected, and unmaintained. Now, it would never pass inspection. It had simply rusted out. People have much in common with cars and other appliances. Some can be used so hard that they wear out; others, due to lack of use, simply rust out. Can do people are much like well used and well maintained cars; they may get tired, their parts may even wear out. Can do people will never rust out. They are too active, too busy, too involved to corrode away. They are also too well cared for. Also, success-oriented people take care of their bodies, their minds, and their souls. Because they love life, they provide themselves with the preventive maintenance that helps prolong life. This is not to say a can do person will never suffer a heart attack, a stroke, or a debilitating accident. While can do people do all they can to maintain health, there are no guarantees. The only certainty is that can do people will never rust out. For can do people, life is a constantly unfolding adventure toward success. You'll never find them parked, abandoned, and rusting away.

Rust and decay can't catch up with me. I'm too busy pursuing success and taking care of myself.

DAY 345

"Faith is a journey without a map."
—Anonymous

A friend told me of a trip she made to Greece with basically no set itinerary, hotel reservations, or guided tours. She booked her outgoing and return flights and a hotel for her first and last nights. Otherwise, she free wheeled it all the way. This friend loves to travel and has taken many trips. However, she maintains that her trip to Greece was the best. Unfettered by time-tables and schedules, she journeyed at her own pace, visiting out-of-the-way spots, lingering in places she found meaningful. When a city, village, or town didn't feel right, she simply moved on, always believing that the next stop would provide a more positive growth experience. In a way, my friend journeyed on faith alone. Rather than being locked into pre-planned destinations, she adopted an open-ended, wait-and-see attitude. Negative, preconceived ideas had no place in her plans. She traveled as the spirit moved her, embracing the opportunities offered by each new stop along the way. The journey of faith is much like my friend's trip to Greece. The known destinations are success in this life and eternal fellowship with God in the life to come. Like the roadways in a foreign country, the Bible provides signposts and directions. Yet the true faith journey is one of adventure and surprises. God has your life all mapped out.

With God as a travel agent, I don't have to know every step along the way.

"Faith is a process, not a possession."
—Rev. Marybeth Asher

Faith is not something you own; it is a process you develop. Even people known for their great faith are continually perfecting that faith. They never say, "Well, I 'own' enough faith now. I will quit my faith journey. I'll stop seeking to grow in faith and be content to rest on my past achievements." God makes Himself known to you so that you may embark on a life-long process of growing in faith. Challenges, obstacles, and hurdles are placed in our pathway so that we may test our faith in ourselves. Relationships develop in our lives so that we may test our faith in others. When we fail to meet a challenge, when a relationship falters, we face the biggest test of our faith. It is then that the process of faith can either grow or be stunted. When a possession — a refrigerator, car, furnace, whatever — fails, we replace it. When we fail or others fail us, we have the opportunity to grow in faith by trying again. We also have God's promises that He will never desert us, abandon us, or demand more of us than He has given us the ability to handle. Reaching your goals and achieving success demands that you accept on faith God's promises and believe in your own your ability. The process of growing in faith is a life-long adventure in risking, trying, and succeeding.

My relationship with God and others is based on faith — faith in my ability to be an overcomer.

DAY 347

> "Get the presence of God fixed in your mind and fear will go away."
>
> —Rev. Jim Holley

Wherever you go, whatever you do, God is with you. Developing a can do attitude involves risk. As you move from the familiar, comfortable can't do environment, there will be change, which is always scary. In order to overcome this fear, you must believe in the ever presence of God. God will be with you as you change and grow. God will be with you as you risk the known for the unknown. God will be with you when you're on track and when you temporarily get off track. God will be with you as you set goals, change goals, achieve goals, and, yes, even fail to achieve goals. Fear is the enemy of success. God's presence is able to conquer every fear. Your job is to accept the truth of God's presence in your life. Fix this truth in your mind and heart. Successful living depends upon successful believing. You may live in a neighborhood that seems the most unlikely dwelling place for God. You may be stuck in a job, a relationship, a situation that appears devoid of God's presence. You're wrong. Wherever you are, God is. Wherever you want to be, God will help you get there. Everyday say "God is with me. God is present in my life." Say it until you begin believing it. Then never let go of that belief. Fear and faith cannot coexist. Once you fix in your mind the reality of God's presence in your life, fear will flee.

God is with me; who can stand against me?

DAY 348

"My message now is calmer, forever seeking
the transformation and reconciliation that
come from hope, love, and forgiveness."
—Barbara Reynolds

The more delicate the plant, the smaller and harder
to see are its seeds. Bigger plants tend to have bigger
seeds. Whether large or small, we plant seeds in faith,
believing they will produce positive results — a lush,
abundant garden. Problems, like plants, contain the
seeds that will result in growth. Sometimes the seeds
of problem resolution are difficult to see, but they're
there all the same. We may have to look longer and
harder to see them; we may have to exercise more
care in planting and nurturing them. Still, if we're willing to do the hard work of problem solving, the seeds
of solutions will reward us with success. We'll reap an
abundant harvest of obstacles overcome, victories won,
barriers toppled, answers revealed. When you encounter a problem, look first at the problem itself. Study
the situation. Search for the seeds of solution. You'll
become an adept problem solver and a success at
overcoming difficulties great or small.

*I have a green thumb when it comes to sowing the
seed of success.*

DAY 349

"Nothing is more powerful and liberating than knowledge."
—Congressman William (Bill) Gray, III

Knowledge is the most powerful and liberating force in your life. Likewise, lack of knowledge is the most enslaving force. When you have knowledge no one can take away your freedom. Knowledge is not the same as formal education. Book learning is one of the greatest assets you can possess, but it is not the only asset. Stay in school; go back to school; take night/weekend/summer courses. Get as much formal knowledge as you possibly can, but never ignore the development of your other knowledge bases. Develop your self-knowledge; you are the one who knows you best and knows what's best for you. Develop your people knowledge; throughout your life, others can open or close doors, make the going easy or rough. Develop your practical knowledge; you'll be able to pull it all together and live in self-advancing ways. When you have knowledge, in all its wonderful facets, you have it all. When you have knowledge, no one and nothing can ever enslave you.

" . . . *Wisdom and knowledge are granted to you. I will also give you riches, possessions, and honor.*" (*II Chronicles 1:12*)

Day 350

"Competence is proven through excellent
performance and God Almighty intending
for us to be here and to do some good."
—Rev. Jim Holley

The greatest sadness is the waste of human potential. When God's gifts go undeveloped and unused,
the world suffers. Think how much farther along we
would be in creating a can do environment if each
human being lived up to the very best she or he could
be. Excellent performance yields excellent results. It
doesn't matter whether you're replacing a car's engine or a human heart. When you perform any task to
the best of your ability, you grow. You become living
proof that God intended you to be exactly where you
are doing exactly what you're doing. To perform well,
grow continually, and do well the work God has created you to do is the highest form of success. Doing
good begins with doing well; nothing done in a half-
hearted, unenthusiastic, less-than-your-best fashion can
result in a job well done. You are a competent person. You possess skills and talents that allow you to
perform excellently. Your life is a journey in growth.
You are where you are because God put you there to
grow and develop, not to lie around complaining, not
to be lazy, negative, or unproductive. God put you
where you are so that you can experience the joy of
moving forward. Get moving! Embrace the adventure
of your personal journey toward success. And, as you
travel the road, be gentle with yourself, kind to others, and do some good along the way.

*I can do whatever I am called upon to do. I am at the
starting point of the journey; God wants me to proceed.*

DAY 351

> "I live in the fastest growing public housing
> tract in America."
>
> —Mumia Abu-Jamal

Mumia Abu-Jamal is not alone. Recent statistics show that one in four men of color are, have been, or will be incarcerated. What does this tell us? Many would say these men are victims of an oppressive society or a prejudicial law system. If so, why isn't the statistic four out of four? Why do three out of four survive, thrive, grow, and rise above their environments? The answer, I believe, is fairly simple: some want to rise above, believe that they can rise above, are willing to work, make sacrifices, and persevere to rise above. These are the people who have developed a can do attitude. They may be in a can't do environment, but they are not of it. They refuse to adopt the can't do mentality. They know that it's not where you are but where you're going that counts. They know where they're going, and it's not to prison. They live with dignity, showing respect for themselves and for others deserving of respect. They have no dealings with those undeserving of respect.

Who I am depends on me, not my environment.

Day 352

"Seven days without prayer makes one weak."

—Rev. Deborah Spink

Life is a constant lesson in opposites. I remember making a statement once something to the effect that while I wasn't spending as much time in formal prayer, I had an awareness of God's constant presence. It was a cop out. My prayer life was going through a weak stage and I was trying to justify my situation. Claiming to be close to God but not praying is like claiming to be close to your spouse but not talking to him or her. You may be aware of your spouse's presence, but you can't know your spouse's needs, wants, plans, or desires. For that, you have to talk. Just as a marriage grows weak when communication breaks down, so does a relationship with God. When your relationship with God grows weak, you grow weak as a person. Don't kid yourself. If you're not spending time in prayer, you're not only not talking to God, you're not listening to God, either. God has messages to impart to us each day. Some are life-changing; some are quiet reassurances, some announce new challenges. If you're not listening, you'll miss these messages. You'll be unprepared for an important event, a vital decision, a life-changing encounter. If seven days without prayer makes one weak, even one day without prayer must make one stupid.

To be prepared I must be in prayer.

Day 353

> "A person can have only one life, one death, one heaven, or one hell, and everyone is his or her own architect."
> —Anonymous

Have you ever watched a house being built, a room remodeled, or an addition put on? It's a complicated process. No one begins to build without first drawing up a plan. Even before the plan there are important questions that must be answered: What am I starting with? What do I want to achieve? What will my future needs be? What can I afford? If building a house, or even just a room, is given so much forethought, why do some people put so little thought into building a life? The start-up questions are the same: What do I want? What will I want for the future? What am I willing to spend to get what I want? We all are the architects of our own lives. Some of us take seriously the responsibility of becoming capable builders; others just float along letting things happen wily-nily. They never pick up the reins and take charge. What a mess a house would be if it were built without a plan! Why should an unplanned life turn out any better? Being an architect, a builder, a person who conceives, plans, and makes it happen, is exciting work! What could be more exhilarating than shaping your dreams into reality? It doesn't happen without a plan. It doesn't happen without cost. Oh, but when it does happen, it's worth all the hard work and sacrifice. You have only one life to live. Shouldn't you be the one to design it?

I'm learning to read maps and draw up blueprints!

> "It is the deed that teaches, not the name
> we give it."
>
> —George Bernard Shaw

We live in a society in which the names of deeds have been changed to make the deeds more acceptable. We don't kill the dog, we put it to sleep. We don't mutilate the frog, we dissect it. We don't lie, we simply stretch the truth. The state doesn't murder people, it executes them. None of these words change the meaning — or the impact — of the deed. Violence begets violence just as kindness begets kindness. It doesn't matter what word you give to a particular behavior or action, it is the action itself that will leave its imprint on you and everything around you. Walk gently, then, as you pass through this life. Be assertive but not aggressive, confident but not smug. Never fear you'll lose stature if you stoop to help another; no doormat has ever been woven out of kindnesses. Be thrifty but not cheap, careful but not penny-pinching. Say what you mean but listen to what others mean as well; God included hearing with our five vital senses for a reason. In everything you do, be careful — of yourself, of others; the strongest among us is still a fragile human being. Take care of the world you live in; you may pass this way but once, but others have to follow.

My actions speak louder than the names by which they're called.

"Don't look down on a man, unless you
are picking him up."

—Williams Brothers

When I hear someone whining about how he can't
get anywhere or all the doors are slamming in her
face, I say, "Look around!" Maybe things aren't perfect, but they're sure not impossible. Even in the bleak-
est of times, things were never impossible. Our an-
cestors proved that! Oppressed and enslaved, they
made advances. Newly freed and totally broke, they
continued to achieve. Through war years and depression years, in back woods and in teeming cities, nothing could hold them down. They have passed to us a
legacy of progress. How can you stand around whining and complaining? Whatever your situation, ask
yourself, "What would my grandmother or great-grand-
mother have done?" No matter how far you've fallen
in life, ask yourself, "How would my grandfather or
great-grandfather have pulled himself up?" Whatever
is there in your background, you'll see that your heritage is not made up of whiners. Today minorities have
more opportunities for success than ever before. Today there are more minority-owned businesses, more
minority executives, more women and people of color
in politics, government — every area of American life.
Are things equal? Of course not! But things have
opened up. Are things moving fast enough? Certainly
not! But things are moving — and they aren't being
moved by whiners. You're either part of the solution or
part of the problem. Which part do you want to play?

I'm starring in my life role. I'm playing for success!

Day 356

"World, I will not change you all by myself,
but I will contribute, and you shall remember
I passed this way."

—Rev. Jim Holley

You don't have to be rich to make a contribution.
You only have to be unselfish enough to give of yourself yet selfish enough to want to leave your mark.
You will pass through this world but once. When you
leave it, those who come after will either benefit from
your life or forget that you ever existed. Blazing a
trail for others to follow may be the most successful
thing you'll ever do. Think of the people whose
names and accomplishments are embedded in your
mind: George Washington Carver, Jesse Owens, Rosa
Parks, Martin Luther King. None of them changed the
world by themselves, but all of them make a contribution and the world will never forget that they once
passed through it. Think of a person who had the most
positive influence on your own life. Perhaps it was a
parent, grandparent, teacher, pastor, neighbor, or
friend. Perhaps they didn't change the world, but they
did change your world. The very fact that they are
remembered with love and appreciation make them
successes. They recognize that while they may not
be able to change the world single-handed, they can
give of their experience, their time, talents, concern,
and knowledge to one or to many.

*I matter to myself, to someone else, to my world. Be-
cause I'll leave something behind, I'm a success.*

DAY 357

> "I may have had some significance in my time because of the boundaries that I crossed that had not been crossed before."
>
> —Harry Belefonte

Who can forget the picture of the young Chinese student defiantly standing in Tianimen Square as the communist tank rolled toward him. The scene is etched into our minds. It has significance because that student crossed a boundary that had not been crossed before. Life is a succession of running up against boundaries. It's up to you whether these boundaries will serve as ladders or as fences. Those who occupy a place of honor in history are usually among the first to cross a boundary. You don't have to be the first in history in order to earn honor; each boundary you cross is a first for you! Maybe you come from a family that believes higher education is unimportant, too expensive, or simply not for us. You can cross that boundary by becoming the first college graduate in your family. Maybe you live in a neighborhood where single-mother families is the norm. You can cross that boundary by refusing to have a child before you're married and by creating, after marriage, a life-long, mutually fulfilling relationship. Every time you successfully cross a boundary you grow in self-confidence. It doesn't matter so much what boundaries you cross as that you have the courage to cross them.

I'll climb the fences. I'll use boundaries as ladders to a higher level of success.

DAY 358

> "I learned that if you manage to make a name for yourself, people will listen to what you have to say."
>
> —Jesse Owens

In 1996, when Colin Powell spoke, everyone listened. Colin Powell made a name for himself — a good name, a respected name, a name that many would like to see associated with the highest position in the land. When Maya Angelou speaks, everyone listens. Maya Angelou has made a name for herself — a name many hold up as an example of gentle power and sensitive insight. When Shaquil O'Neill speaks, everyone listens. Shak has made a name for himself — a name associated with achievement and excellence, good sportsmanship, and drive. When Oprah Winfrey speaks, everyone listens. Oprah has made a name for herself — a name known for talent, caring, courage, going where no woman of color has gone before. The world is populated with people who have made names for themselves. Some of their names have become household words. Some of their names are best known in their households, their work places, their communities, their churches. Have you made a name for yourself? When you speak, do people listen? What kinds of feelings and images does your name invoke in the people whose lives interact with yours? Are you known for your honesty and fairness? Your wisdom, courage, sensitivity, kindness, trustworthiness? Is yours a name people respect? Is your name associated with a winning can do attitude? What you make of your name is up to you.

What's in a name? Everything, if the name is mine!

Day 359

> "I am not fighting just for myself and my people . . . I fight for the moral and political health of Americans as a whole."
>
> —Marian Wright Edelman

Everytime you succeed at something you increase the likelihood for success by those who come after. The first black congressman, the first female judge, the first physically-challenged teacher — all made it easier for other minority persons to successfully enter those fields. Whatever you do, do it for yourself and for the glory of God who is in you. Whatever you do, realize that it will have an impact on others. Help others glorify God by helping them to realize the potential He has put in them. If you fight to rise above a can't do environment and succeed, you will show others that success is possible. Guion (Guy) Bluford, the first black astronaut, was not chosen because he is black. Yet because he achieved his dream of going into space, he has become an example to others. There were no press reports of a fight based on gender and race, yet I'll bet that there were some backroom fights and inner-circle arguments.

I'll fight the good fight for myself, for others.

Day 360

"As a child, I could not dare dream that I would even see the Supreme Court, let alone be nominated to it."

—Clarence Thomas

Dreams — that's where success starts! Sometimes our dreams are inspired by an outside source — a parent, teacher, athlete, writer, preacher, etc. Sometimes we have no idea where our dreams come from. It's not the source that's important, it's the fact that we have dreams. But having a dream is the easy part; holding on to the dream is more difficult. That's where the real work begins. Dreams have a way of growing once we begin pursuing them. If Clarence Thomas could not dare dream of even seeing the Supreme Court, what made him strive for good grades in elementary and high school? How did the dream expand to include going to college? What inspired him to go to law school, to become one of the best in his profession, to seek ever higher goals? Clarence Thomas could have stopped at any point along the way and not been considered a failure. Just completing high school in his time and his circumstances — and the circumstances of many today — made him a success. Going to college made him an ultra-success and won for him the admiration of all he knew. But dreams fulfilled give birth to new dreams. Each level achieved opens doors to choices you've never considered, maybe never even heard of. You've made it this far, why stop now? You'll reach many peaks and keep on climbing. That's the thrill of a life spent following your dreams.

I'll reach many peaks as I pursue many dreams.

DAY 361

"The only certainty in life is change. The
only hindrance against change is the lack
of planning."

—Whitney Young

At the far end of the Island of Maui in Hawaii there
is a road called the Road to Hanna. It is over a hundred miles of such constant twists and turns that you
can never hold the steering wheel straight for more
than a few seconds. It's a beautiful road through the
tropic-like land, so densely foliaged that often even
the strong Hawaiian sun has difficulty getting through.
Each year thousands of tourists set out to travel the
Road to Hanna. At first they enjoy the scenery. But
soon it becomes monotonous; around every curve lies
more of the same. It's a two-hour ride from the starting point to the little town of Hanna. Visitors arrive
hot, thirsty, and tired. Then the disappointment sets
in. The town of Hanna is little more than a closed
Catholic church, a closed Protestant church, a soda
machine and a souvenir stand. "Is this it?" they ask
themselves. "Is this what I traveled so far to see?"
Ahead of them lies the two-hour ride back along the
same road, past the same scenery, around the same
curves, and a day of vacation has been lost. Just remember, if you don't check out your new destination
first, you may be wasting a day of travel and be in for
a big disappointment.

*The only certainty in life is change. The only hedge
against change in life is planning.*

> "Of all my possessions, my reputation
> means the most to me."
>
> —Arthur Ashe

Who are you? Who do others think you are? How close does your opinion of yourself come to the opinion others have of you? If the difference is great, who's right and who's wrong? Could you be holding yourself in higher esteem than others hold you? Are you preventing others from getting to know the real you? I ask these questions as a jump-off point for self-evaluation. There's a fine line between caring too much about the opinion of others and caring too little. There has never been a person born whom everyone likes; you won't be the first. On the other hand, when many people dislike a person, there is usually a reason. Your reputation is important; it may well be your most important possession. Handle it carefully. One mistake can crumble a reputation you've spent a lifetime building. If you have a reputation for honesty, integrity, hard work, fairness, everyone may not like you, but it will be difficult for them not to respect you. Self-respect draws respect from others as naturally as the sun draws moisture from the land. The two are interdependent. Don't jeopardize your reputation. It's your most valuable possession.

My word is my name, and my good name counts.

> "When I decided to run for Congress, I
> knew I would encounter both antiblack
> and antifeminist sentiments."
>   —Congresswoman Shirley Chisholm

Success is like chocolate — once you taste it, you can't get enough. That's why it's so important to help our children experience success from birth. When they do well in school, sports, music, whatever, it's easy to praise them. You can actually see this praise inspiring them to greater heights of achievement. But what about when they miss the mark? Do we praise them for their efforts? Trying hard and giving something your whole heart is certainly praiseworthy. Yet I once heard an Olympic athlete say, "You don't 'win' a silver, you just lose the gold." I admit this statement troubles me. I believe every sincere, all-out effort is a success in itself. Growth takes place through trying. Maybe the growth gained through the last try will be enough to make the next attempt a victory. Of course, there will always be forces working against us. We must prepare our children for that. We must teach them the value of trying despite the odds. *P.S. What works for your children just might inspire you, too.*

I'm building my strength through the exercise of effort.

"Integration without preparation leads to frustration."

—Rev. Leon Sullivan

Today you have endless opportunities. Nothing is closed to you. No halls are barred, no offices locked. You can be anything you want to be, go anywhere you want to go, do anything you want to do. Are you prepared to accept this responsibility? For decades, your sisters and brothers fought to bring you to this point and time in history. Are you prepared to accept the gifts of their struggles? If you're not prepared, you're not going anywhere. It's as simple as that! So what to do? Get prepared! Prepare yourself to take your rightful place in today's world. Get the best education possible. Stay in school, return to school, enter a job training program, whatever it takes. It's your responsibility to prepare yourself to live as a financially independent person. Prepare yourself emotionally. You must understand your feelings in order to direct them. Uncontrolled emotions lead to unwise decisions. Prepare yourself physically. The dictionary defines opportunity as an "opening." You must have the physical strength to walk through the opening.

I'm working on a merger. I'm merging the many parts of me.

Day 365

"God calls us to be eagles."
—Rev. Jim Holley

The eagle is called the king of birds. It dwells in high and lofty places. It's freedom, strength, and speed are the epitome of majesty in flight. In the minds of the biblical writers, the eagle was the symbol for greatness in general and for God, the greatest of all, in particular. The eagle is also an appropriate symbol for the latent greatness inherent in all human beings created by God, and that includes you and me. Sometimes, as we strive for greatness against great odds we forget that eagles are not produced overnight. It takes time to produce an eagle. As we strive to find companions worthy of our love we forget that eagles are solitary birds. Eagles do not fly in flocks. As we strive for strength, we forget that while our own strength is in our wings, the source of our strength is in God. As you walk toward greatness, there are those who, out of meanness, jealousy, or lack of vision, would make a chicken out of you. Never forget: No creature God has intended for flying in lofty places is beyond redemption no matter how long it has been in the barnyard. Deep down within, where your environment can't reach, God has placed the heart and soul of an eagle. Fly! Fly! Fly!

Today I'll be an eagle. I won't settle for anything less.

For
additional
information
visit our web site @

http://www.AfricanAmericanImages.com

NOTES

NOTES

NOTES

_____

_____

_____

_____

_____

_____

_____

_____

_____

_____

_____

_____